AI in the Movies

AI in the Movies

Paula Murphy

EDINBURGH
University Press

Edinburgh University Press is one of the leading university presses in the UK. We publish academic books and journals in our selected subject areas across the humanities and social sciences, combining cutting-edge scholarship with high editorial and production values to produce academic works of lasting importance. For more information visit our website: edinburghuniversitypress.com

© Paula Murphy, 2024, 2025

Grateful acknowledgement is made to the sources listed in the List of Illustrations for permission to reproduce material previously published elsewhere. Every effort has been made to trace the copyright holders, but if any have been inadvertently overlooked, the publisher will be pleased to make the necessary arrangements at the first opportunity.

Edinburgh University Press Ltd
13 Infirmary Street
Edinburgh EH1 1LT

First published in hardback by Edinburgh University Press 2024

Typeset in 12 on 14pt Arno Pro by
Cheshire Typesetting Ltd, Cuddington, Cheshire

A CIP record for this book is available from the British Library

ISBN 978 1 4744 4858 1 (hardback)
ISBN 978 1 4744 4859 8 (paperback)
ISBN 978 1 4744 4860 4 (webready PDF)
ISBN 978 1 4744 4861 1 (epub)

The right of Paula Murphy to be identified as the author of this work has been asserted in accordance with the Copyright, Designs and Patents Act 1988, and the Copyright and Related Rights Regulations 2003 (SI No. 2498).

Contents

List of Figures	vi
Introduction	1
1. AI in the real world, AI in the movies	5
2. The 1950s and 1960s	28
3. The 1970s	47
4. The 1980s	65
5. The 1980s	82
6. The 1990s	100
7. The 2000s	120
8. The 2010s	140
9. The 2010s	160
Conclusion	180
Notes	183
Filmography	190
Bibliography	192
Index	199

Figures

2.1 Robby and Altaira in *Forbidden Planet* (1956)   34
2.2 Bowman in *2001: A Space Odyssey* (1968)   43
4.1 The Tron arcade game   80

Introduction

Artificial intelligence has been making headlines all over the world in recent years. UN Secretary General Antonio Guterres has stated that artificial intelligence represents 'an existential threat to humanity on a par with the risk of nuclear war' (Murray, 2023). Generative AI has been a particular source of concern, that is, AI that can create new content in text, image and audio based on similar types of content, such as ChatGPT. Geoffrey Hinton, the AI scientist who left his position at Google to speak out about AI threat, has voiced his concerns about the misinformation and social injustice that may arise from AI. Moreover, his work with AI has led him to reassess the primacy of human intelligence: 'It's quite conceivable that humanity is a passing phase in the evolution of intelligence' (Murgia and Waters, 2023). The Writers Guild of America strike in 2023 was partly about the threat of AI to workers who wished to 'place limits on the use of AI in movies and TV scripts' (Shah, 2023), potentially amongst the first of many labour disputes over the use of artificial intelligence.

In the context of rapidly developing AI, and growing concern about its management, it is instructive to examine how artificial intelligence has been represented through the medium of film, from its first appearance in the 1950s, contemporaneous with the birth of the AI science, to its more recent manifestations in the twenty-first century. This book is not about AI in the real world and does not offer judgement on the current state of AI science, or its potential for good or ill. It is about fictional representations of AI, and, as such, it is about humans' attitudes to this phenomenon; how we think about it, understand it, and react to it; what excites us about it and what we fear about it; how it helps us to understand our relationships with technology, and how encountering fictional artificial intelligences encourages us to re-evaluate how we define ourselves. Outlining human evolution, Ray Kurzweil notes that 'our first invention was the story' (2014, p. 20). Fictions, such as the films considered in this book, form the narrative architecture of understandings of artificial intelligence; the stories we tell to animate our anxieties and our aspirations. This book aims to categorise, critique and explore these cinematic representations.

A precise definition of artificial intelligence is surprisingly difficult to achieve because it assumes a common understanding of 'intelligence', when, in fact, there is no consensus. Human intelligence can take many forms depending on the skills and abilities of the individual, and so it is with artificial intelligence. While artificial intelligence is most often pitted against human intelligence, animal intelligence may also provide a set of benchmarks. As Kak states, 'study of animal intelligence provides us with new perspectives that are useful in representing the performance of machines' (1996, p. 142). Whether compared to human or animal, artificial intelligence is by definition something that is created and that does not come from nature: 'Things that are *artificially intelligent* ... differ from those that are *naturally intelligent*' (Fetzer, 1990, p. 3). The comparison between natural and artificial intelligence opens up others: biological/mechanical, organic/manufactured, natural/synthetic. While definitions of artificial intelligence are set up along these oppositions, analysis of the films in this book shows them being often undermined, with AI being presented as a reflection or extension of human intelligence.

Artificial intelligence can be divided into strong/general AI, or narrow/weak AI. Artificial Narrow Intelligence (ANI), or weak AI, can competently carry out one task, or group of tasks: 'The vast bulk of the AI field today is concerned with what might be called "narrow AI" – creating programmes that demonstrate intelligence in one or another specialised area, such as chess-playing, medical diagnosis, automobile driving, algebraic calculation or mathematical theorem-proving' (Pennachin and Goertzel, 2007, p. 1). Chatbots, robotic vacuum cleaners, digital assistants like Apple's Siri or Amazon's Alexa, all fall into this category; ANI can also be used to carry out manual tasks, for example in a manufacturing context. ANI crosses over with another category of artificial intelligence called Ambient Intelligence, AmI, closely related to 'the internet of things'. Ambient Intelligence is comprised of 'smart' devices that become embedded in daily living – smart watches, fridges, security systems, vacuum cleaners. Films like *Tau* and *Demon Seed* imagine what would happen if a narrow intelligence acquired sentience.

This book focuses exclusively on cinematic representations of strong artificial intelligence. Artificial General Intelligence (AGI), also known as human-level AI, or strong AI, has not yet been achieved in the real world[1]. An AGI would be an 'autonomous agent that can learn in an unsupervised manner' (McLean et al. 2021, p. 2). Bostrom argues that an AGI would require 'a capacity to learn' and would need to be capable of managing unpredictable situations, processing 'sensory data' and using 'logical and intuitive reasoning' (2014, p. 27). All the machines, robots and operating systems analysed in this book are imagined representations of what artificial general intelligence might be like, and the scenarios that could result from interaction between humans and strong AIs. A further category of artificial general intelligence is artificial superintelligence. This can be defined as 'artificial intelligence that exceeds human intelligence across any task' (De Spiegeleire et al. 2017, p. 30). It is difficult, if not impossible, to test whether an AI in film meets this definition of superintelligence. However, in *Her*, it is possible that Samantha and other AIs have achieved superintelligence, so far have they surpassed human understanding.

As the main criterion for selection of the films in this book is that they must contain an example of strong AI, films about cyborgs – modified humans or technologically enhanced humans – are not included, nor are films about superior alien races. That a character is a robot is not sufficient – the robot must exhibit strong or general AI. This also means that characters without a humanoid body are included in this analysis: digital AIs that are housed in computers, in spaceships; later, networked and online; later still, accessed through smart phones or software or just existing in the dense web of global communication networks.

There is a strong connection between literature and film in this area of science fiction and many of these films have been adapted from, inspired by, or written in conjunction with, literary works. Detailed analysis of the literature is beyond the scope of this book, and comparative readings of literature and film are not included but may certainly provide an interpretative seam that is equally rich. The same is true for short film and television – there are many shorts and series that would add interesting dimensions to this study, but that is work for another research project, or another scholar.

The project encompasses a range of films that is as diverse as possible. There are films made or partly made in Australia, Bulgaria, Canada, China, France, India, Japan, Spain, and the UK. Nevertheless, most of the AI films that have been made have been produced in Hollywood and demonstrate remarkably little racial or ethnic diversity. Representations of AIs in film often repeat the power structures and social inequalities of the societies from which they emerge. This is true of the representation of gender, and it is also true of the representation of race, which occludes, marginalises or renders invisible the non-white perspective. In relation to directors of AI film, gender is an issue of concern. The only women directors of film in this book are the Wachowski sisters, Lana and Lilly, who directed the Matrix films[2]. The dearth of female directors in Hollywood film has long been noted, but the almost complete absence of women directors of films about artificial intelligence paints a stark picture. Particularly because of this absence, careful attention is paid to the gendered representation of the artificial intelligences in this book.

The chapters on films are arranged chronologically according to decade, and a filmography with details on all the films is included in the back of this book, for ease of reference. Each chapter raises specific thematic strands, many of which recur, developed, morphed and complicated, in subsequent chapters: the main thematic strands that run through the book are outlined in Chapter 1. As the films move through different social, cultural, political and scientific contexts, their themes reflect changing attitudes to artificial intelligence.

Telotte describes the robot as a cultural meme, that has a set of characteristics that evolve over time. It is a '"replicator", something that can propagate itself, or various versions of itself, within or across minds and media, and in a practically evolutionary fashion, thereby helping to explain the process of cultural development' (Telotte 2018, p. 8). Artificial intelligence has a similar function to Telotte's robot. It has a set of characteristics that change and evolve over time reflecting changing cultural events and attitudes and it is these characteristics and this evolution that this book charts. The first two decades discussed, the 1950s and 1960s, are joined in one chapter because of the scarcity of AI film in this period. Reflecting culture, there is a high concentration of AI films in the 1980s, when home PCs appear, computer games become popular and the internet begins to emerge commercially. An even richer period for AI film is the last decade, the 2010s, in which the internet, smart technology and social media have become embedded in the everyday lives of many, complicating our relationship to these imagined AIs in film. To reflect these periods of abundance, both the 1980s and the 2010s are given two chapters each in the book[3]. Organising the book chronologically allows gradual trends in the representation of AIs to be demonstrated and the increasing sophistication of the characterisation of AIs over time to be seen. The terrifying technophobic creations of the 50s, 60s and 70s never go away, but the overall picture is made more complex and nuanced by AI friends, companions, children and even lovers that emerge in the 1980s, 1990s, 2000s and 2010s.

1

AI in the real world, AI in the movies

Introduction

This introductory chapter is divided into two main parts. The first outlines aspects of artificial intelligence that are explored in the films. It is not a history of artificial intelligence, but rather an outline of key elements of that history that fascinate filmmakers, such as how intelligence is defined, the Turing Test, the establishment of the field in the 1950s, The Chinese Room Experiment, the Physical Grounding Hypothesis, affective intelligence, ambient intelligence, distributed and multi-agent intelligence, consciousness upload, and the singularity. The second half of the chapter gives an overview of the main attitudes towards AI presented in film, including the typical technophobic fears about AI, and humanist, posthumanist and transhumanist stances. The various types of AI presented in film are then outlined: robot, digital and combinations of the two. The themes and tropes that recur in AI film are set out, including the AI as visual double of the human and the AI 'reveal'; parallels and doubling between human and AI characters, and ways in which they intersect and hybridise. The representation of gender is explored, in terms of female characters in AI film, including female scientists, and the AI characters themselves, usually mirroring the patterns of representation of human characters. The importance of parent–child relationships is outlined, including humans acting as parents and families to artificial intelligence, and occasionally the other way around, and examining the theme of AI reproduction, via human, digital or other means. The final theme is death and mortality, particularly concerning the 'unfinal' death of the AI, who often re-animates later in the film or in a sequel, and how the AI's immortality is harnessed for humans seeking transhumanist life extension.

In the real world

Intelligence

What is intelligence? Does it mean possessing knowledge? Is it the capacity to learn? Is it self-awareness? What about different types of intelligences? Development psychologist Howard Gardner proposed that there are eight types of intelligences: naturalist, musical, logical-mathematical, existential, interpersonal, bodily-kinaesthetic, linguistic, intra-personal, and spatial (Gardner 1983). It is clearly not necessary to possess all of these to be considered 'intelligent', but how many is sufficient? And how can intelligence or intelligences be measured? Intelligence is an ill-defined concept and there is no agreement philosophically or scientifically about precisely what constitutes it. In fact, intelligence may not really exist at all, except as an umbrella term for a range of functions and abilities of the human brain and body.

Before scientists began to seriously research the potential for artificial intelligence, writers and filmmakers were already considering the possibility. The first of them all was Mary Shelley's *Frankenstein*, published in 1818, in which a scientist creates a monstrous version of a human. In 1920, Czech dramatist Karel Čapek introduced the word 'robot' into the English language, with his play entitled *RUR*, which stands for Rossum Universal Robots. In 1927, in *Metropolis*, Fritz Lang created a robot that transformed into the image of a human being, a 'false Maria' to deceive the most discerning observer. The film contained several tropes that would become common in AI film: the 'mad scientist' inventor, technology run amok, the deceptive robot that can pass for human, the hypersexualised female humanoid robot, and the punishment by destruction. Neither Shelley's nor Čapek's creations were strictly artificial intelligences – or strong AIs, as the characters considered in this book are – and not enough is known about the make-up of the false Maria to judge whether or not she is a strong AI which is why she does not fit the criteria for this book, however, they can be seen as beginning the process of exploring in fiction and film new forms of intelligence created by humans through the power of technology.

The notion of consciousness falls between science and philosophy. Its physical manifestation in humans is biological, or more specifically neurological, and attempts to replicate its operations are situated in the domain of science, computer programming or biotechnology. But there appears to be something intangible about consciousness, and its relation to the equally contested concept of 'self' that means it also falls into the domain of the humanities, and particularly philosophy. The term 'artificial intelligence' sets up a comparison between human and computer intelligence that is not particularly useful. In his overview of AI, Jerry Kaplan speculates on what it would have been like if aeroplanes had been called 'artificial birds', the comparisons between the workings of the planes and the biology of the real birds that might have ensued, and the debates about whether aeroplanes were truly flying, or merely simulating flight (Kaplan 2016, p. 16). Such controversies about the likeness of AI to human cognition, and about whether computers can 'think' or only simulate thought, have dogged the history of artificial intelligence and often distract from scientific breakthroughs and discussion about their potential benefits and drawbacks.

Some contemporary thinkers do not agree with this binary perspective, seeing an increasing overlap between humans in the developed world and their technological devices which are often seen as an extension of themselves. Andy Clark presents this view in *Natural Born Cyborgs*, arguing that humans have always developed in tandem with technology, whether the technology in question is a pen or a smartphone: for Clark, we are already 'cyborgs without surgery. Symbionts without sutures' (Clark 2003, p. 34). The absolute separation between 'artificial' and 'real', may now be unsustainable because of the ways in which AI is merging with the human body. In satellite navigation systems, search engines, shopping, networking, gaming, artificial eyes, hearing aids and a thousand other ways, artificial intelligence is intrinsically imbricated into 'real' life, effecting human bodies, behaviours and relationships.

The Turing test

Before the field of artificial intelligence existed, in 1950, Alan Turing began his paper 'Computing Machinery and Intelligence' by asking the question 'can machines think'?[1] But before the end of the first paragraph he concluded that the definitions of the terms 'machine' and 'think' were so problematic that he would answer a different question in the paper instead: 'instead of attempting such a definition I shall replace the question by another' (1950, p. 433). Machine intelligence is now more commonly referred to as artificial intelligence, but more than 70 years after Turing's paper, the difficulty with definitions remains. If the concept of intelligence itself only has meaning in a general, rather vague sense, what does it mean to have an artificial version of that? Speaking of an 'artificial' intelligence implies that it is less 'real' than human intelligence, which is not necessarily the case. The functioning of a computer may not be personable, but it is nonetheless real. The only way in which a computer's functioning is artificial is if it is seen in some way as trying to impersonate human intelligence. The name of artificial intelligence itself may carry with it the suspicion of deception. The sense of deception embedded into our thinking about and definitions of AI can be seen the now-famous Turing test, described by him in the essay mentioned above, and the idea that AIs are deceptively impersonating humans can be seen in many of the films discussed in this book.

In the first version of the Turing test, a man and a woman sit behind a screen, communicating with a third person by typed missives. The woman is herself, the man pretends to be a woman, and the third person must decide which is the man and which is the woman. Deception is at the heart of this experiment. If the man is successful, he is successful at pretending to be something he is not. Moreover, the experiment is embedded in binary thinking about gender. In the second version of the experiment, a machine takes the part of the woman, and the other body behind the screen can presumably be a man or a woman – Turing does not specify. In this version, the machine's success is dependent upon deceit, just as the man's was. The machine will succeed if it persuades the person behind the screen that it is human. Those behind the screen are either 'machine' or 'man' in Turing's words. The issue of gender is elided as the experiment moves to an opposition between machine and a gender-defined man or a machine and 'man' that connotes man or woman. But the binary thinking evident in the attitude towards gender found in the first Turing test is also carried over into this experiment. Now, the binary is between a human and a machine, and it seems that, like the man and woman in the previous experiment, there is no thought of any overlap between the two. In *Ex Machina*, the AI creator purports to perform a Turing test. More broadly, many of the films considered in this volume attempt to undermine the binary between human and machine, offer opportunities to restore the visibility of gender that is elided in Turing's experiment, and present the idea of the AI as inherently deceptive and duplicitous.

The early years

John McCarthy is credited with coining the term 'artificial intelligence'. In 1956, as Professor of Mathematics at Dartmouth College, he organised the Dartmouth workshop with colleagues Marvin Minsky, Claude Shannon and Nathaniel Rochester. The workshop took place over the course of a summer. In the spring of that same year, 1956, just a few months before the establishment of the field of artificial intelligence, the first artificial intelligence appeared on the big screen: Robby the Robot in *Forbidden Planet*. The workshop was born out of a common interest in the possibilities of computer intelligence. As stated in the workshop's proposal: 'The study is to proceed on the basis of the conjecture that every aspect of learning or any other feature of intelligence can in principle be so precisely described that a machine can be made to simulate it' (McCarthy et al. 1955). Some important developments came out of the workshop. As a first step to creating a 'thinking' computer, Allen Newell and Herbert A. Simon developed Logic Theorist, a programme which proved theorems using symbolic language. Along with Cliff Shaw, they developed information processing language (IPL) to run the programme, another important development in AI science.

Out of Logic Theorist emerged the General Problem Solver in 1958. This programme conceived of problem-solving as a search from initial state (where you begin) to goal state (where you want to be). It used techniques like means-end analysis and planning to move from one to the other. Despite its promising name, it could solve only relatively simple puzzles, games, and hypothetical situations because of the amount of information and decisions more complex problems would require and the difficulty of processing that volume of information. One of the examples they work through is the problem of bringing a child to nursery school if the battery of the car is flat. Though their results were modest by today's standards, their ambitions were high, and their report on the programme emphasises that it focuses on process over content 'as a way of increasing the generality of the program' (Newell et al. 1959, p. ii). By the mid-1960s, AI laboratories in the US were attracting significant funding. Symbolic AI and machine learning have vied with each other to dominate AI research over the years, but from the 1950s through to the 1980s, symbolic AI, sometimes referred to as 'good old-fashioned AI', led the way (Boden 2014, p. 89).

The Chinese room experiment

Symbolic AI was the target of criticism in the 1980s from scientists and philosophers alike. In his famous essay, 'Minds, Brains and Programs', John Searle describes the Chinese room experiment, to disprove the idea that computers could 'understand' or have intentionality. He describes himself alone in a room, into which is passed batches of Chinese texts. The Chinese language is unknown to Searle. He is also given a set of rules in English, a language in which he is a native speaker, that show him how to correlate aspects of the batches of text to each other and pass back out what are received as 'answers'. Even though from the outside it may appear that Searle 'understands' the Chinese, as he produces the correct answers, he knows as little about Chinese after the experiment as he did before. This, he says, is analogous to the workings of computer programmes: 'The computer ... has a syntax but no semantics'; there is no understanding, just 'manipulation of symbols' (Searle 1980, p. 423).

Furthermore, he believes that 'intentionality', which is associated with consciousness and the ability to self-direct the mind, is a 'biological phenomenon' (1980, p. 424) that cannot be replicated by a computer program. Searle's essay was highly influential and became the source of ongoing philosophical debate. His views have remained remarkably unchanged over the years, despite the progress in linking computer programmes to aspects of the human brain, both physically and analogically. In a Ted Talk in 2013, he stated, 'consciousness is a biological phenomenon, like photosynthesis, digestion, mitosis' (2013). As such, he believes that it cannot be replicated by a computer program. Searle's position inextricably links consciousness to human biological and neurological processes. For him, it would not be possible to create a consciousness that has an entirely digital character, such as those presented in AI films like *Blade Runner 2049*, *Ghost in the Shell* and *Her*.

The physical grounding hypothesis

One of the pioneers of a different approach than symbolic AI was Rodney Brooks. In 1990 he argued that symbolism could not be relied upon to provide the route to human-level AI. In 'Elephants Don't Play Chess' he argued that its dominance had become a 'dogma' (Brooks 1990, p. 3) and that an alternative route to progressing AI could be found in what he called the 'physical grounding hypothesis'. He criticised symbolism for not being task-driven and not giving adequate consideration to the importance of perception as a fundamental aspect of intelligence. Approaching AI in this way means building hardware and software that moves within an environment. This means that it is not necessary to equip the AI with vast amounts of data – it learns what it needs to know about the environment through perception and this knowledge can be built on over time. It is a different model than the 'ground-up' method of symbolic AI and operates on the key premise that 'the world is its own best model. It is always exactly up to date. It always contains every detail there is to be known. The trick is to sense it appropriately and often enough' (1990, p. 4).

In his work in MIT, and in Rethink Robotics, which he founded in 2008, Brooks has continued to work on creating robots which have been used in medical and industrial contexts. In 1950, Turing referred to a phenomenon that has persistently beleaguered researchers in artificial intelligence, which is the focus on what a new AI cannot do rather than what it can do: 'I grant that you can make machines to do all the things that you have mentioned but you will never make one to do X' (Turing 1950, p. 447). Forty years later, Brooks expresses his frustration at encountering a similar response. This attitude often does an injustice to the particular advance that has been made with a new computer programme or robot, and to the level of intelligence that the software or hardware is capable of demonstrating. As Brooks states, 'it is unfair to claim that an elephant has no intelligence worth studying just because it does not play chess' (Brooks 1990, p. 12). Brooks' ideas about an artificial intelligence learning from its environment can be seen in films like *Chappie*, in which a police droid given artificial general intelligence must learn to physically, socially and emotionally navigate the world in which he finds himself.

Affective AI

A key feature of many of the AIs in this book is emotional intelligence. From HAL 9000 in *2001: A Space Odyssey*, who Bowman says 'acts like he has genuine emotions', to Data in *Star Trek Generations* who tries out an 'emotion chip', to Samantha in *Her* who 'feels real' to her boyfriend Theodore, emotion is an important aspect of strong artificial intelligence. For the AIs in this book, it is almost always present in some form, whether the emotions are positive or negative, the only exceptions being Alpha 60 in *Alphaville: A Strange Adventure of Lemmy Caution*, who creates a dystopia of rationalism, and the early iterations of the *Screamers*' robots, from whom no clear emotional response can be interpreted. In *The Heart of the Machine*, Yonck describes how 'we are beginning to imbue our technologies with the ability to read, interpret, replicate, and potentially even experience emotions themselves. This is being made possible by a relatively new branch of artificial intelligence known as affective computing' (2020, p. xv).

As is so often the case, AI film was ahead of AI, and the first dedicated research into creating emotional responses in machine did not begin until the 1980s. In the 1990s, for her doctoral dissertation at MIT, Cynthia Brazeal developed the first domestic social robot, called Kismet, which, though movement of its eyes, lips and ears, could make non-verbal gestures as if responding to human speech and gesture[2]. In 1997, Rosalind

Picard published her influential book *Affective Computing*, laying the basis for the field. She describes work on modelling affective patterns so that computers can identity and respond to them as 'a first step toward enabling them to interact more naturally with people, recognising our emotions and expressing emotions when appropriate' (Picard 2000, p. 165). Affective computing has influenced a whole range of what McStay terms 'empathic media': technologies that can 'sense and discern what is significant for people, categorise behaviour into named emotions, act on emotional states, and make use of people's intentions and expressions' (2018, p. 2). Empathic media include technologies that use biofeedback, facial coding, voice analytics, virtual reality, and they are used in health and wellness, entertainment and marketing, amongst other areas. Research into affective computing and its manifestations in empathic media produce examples of narrow artificial intelligences. The films in this book imagine that affective computers could do more than present the appearance of understanding or demonstrating emotion: they imagine artificial intelligences that have real emotions; real feelings.

Ambient Intelligence

Ambient Intelligence, or AmI, is defined by Dunne et al. as 'the application and embedding of artificial intelligence into everyday environments to seamlessly provide assistive and predictive support in a multitude of scenarios via an invisible user interface' (2021, p. 1). Ambient intelligence is synonymous with the smart home, but it can also overlap with other areas of artificial intelligence that extend beyond the home environment such as The Internet of Things[3] and autonomous vehicles. Yachir explains that 'The convergence of the Ambient Intelligence (AmI) and the Internet of Things (IoT) envisions a world where smart objects connected to the Internet, share their data, exchange their services and cooperate together' (2016). Examples of ambient intelligences include digital assistants such as the Amazon Alexa or Google assistant; wearable devices to track fitness and wellbeing, and self-drive cars. The idea of an artificial intelligence that has access to personal data and that resides in the home or on the person, is rich ground for science fiction, and as usual, AI film mines this ground before the concept exists in science and technology. The films imagine ambient intelligences that have strong AI: the first 'smart home' in AI film appears in the 1970s with *Demon Seed*, and the scenario recurs in the 2010s with the films *Tau* and *Her*.

Distributed and multi-agent artificial intelligence

Strübing describes distributed intelligence as 'modeling and designing distributed computer systems to serve the needs of large technical infrastructures with real-world applications' (1998, p. 441). Distributed intelligence is an approach to AI that models the real world, in which problems are solved by several agents working together. Strübing advises that heterogeneous agents are preferable, and that 'coordinating the distributed system through a central authority does not sound very promising' (1998, p. 444). However, all the examples of distributed intelligence in film have a controlling authority – an AI with general artificial intelligence. Research into multi-agent systems is a branch of distributed intelligence. Bond and Gasser state that 'the agents in a multiagent system may be working words a single global goal or toward separate individual goals that interact' (2014, p. 3). In film, usually only one artificial general intelligence is explored in detail, and even then with little emphasis on the science behind the machine, so it is impossible to say with certainty the extent of the autonomy of the agents in these cases, or the level of their interaction. What can be identified is the way in which this field of artificial intelligence is anticipated and echoed by filmic representation. In film, distributed intelligence first appears in the robots and smart home devices of *Demon Seed*, it emerges again with the autonomous vehicles controlled by VIKI in *I, Robot*, the devices and robots controlled by *Tau*, the army of droids in *I am Mother*, and others.

Consciousness upload

The idea of consciousness upload was first presented in an idealised transhumanist manner by Hans Moravec in his book *Mind Children*. He imagines a future in which artificial intelligence has surpassed human intelligence in a naturalised evolutionary process. These artificial intelligences will be as the 'children of our minds' and humans the 'aged parents', he says: 'very little need be lost in this passing of the torch – it will be in our artificial offspring's power, and to their benefit, to remember almost everything about us, even, perhaps, the detailed workings of individual human minds' (Moravec 1988, p. 1). Moravec's views are underpinned by the idea of a 'natural' transition to a benign new race of beings, and such a transition is neither necessarily natural nor necessarily benign. His ideas have been critiqued by posthumanist scholars such as Hayles, who disputes the idea that a mind can be separated from its materiality and continue to function in the same way[4]. However, the idea of consciousness upload continues to be hypothesised. Koene imagines a 'substrate independent mind', in which it is possible to 'carry out the function of a mind both in a biological brain and in a brain that is composed of computer software or neuromorphic hardware' (2013, p. 146), and outlines various paths to potentially achieving this goal. While consciousness upload remains a dream or a nightmare in the real world, in AI film it is presented and explored. *Transcendence*, *The Machine* and *Chappie* all imagine scenarios whereby an artificial general intelligence enables the uploading of a human consciousness.

The Singularity

Some of the films discussed in this book explore the advent of a technological 'singularity'. The Singularity is a term originally used by Vernor Vinge. He predicts that accelerated technological progress will give rise to a momentous change 'comparable to the rise of human life on earth' (2013, p. 365). He believes that this will occur through the advent of superintelligence, either that of individual computers, computer networks, computer-human interfaces, or human augmentation (2013, p. 365). The term is taken up by Ray Kurzweil, who concedes that it is difficult to accurately predict what will happen beyond the 'event horizon' because of our 'profound limitations of thought' (2005, p. 29). However, he believes that the Singularity should be embraced as a chance to transcend the limitations of human biology and predicts that 'most of the intelligence of our civilisation will ultimately be nonbiological' (2014, p. 30). Fear of the Singularity clusters in films from the 2010s, and can be seen in *Automata*, *The Machine* and *Transcendence*; Nathan in *Ex Machina* accepts that it will happen, and in *Her*, a representation of the Singularity may actually occur at the end of the film.

In the movies

Attitudes to AI

The history of AI film is largely a technophobic one. As Dinello outlines, 'science fiction expresses a technophobic fear of losing our human identity, our freedom, our emotions, our values and our lives to machines' (2006, p. 2). There are only a couple of films analysed in this book that present a neutral perspective on AI: the Robby the Robot films from the 1950s[5] and *Star Trek Generations* with Data. All the other films present either a negative perspective or an ambivalent one. The specific fears surrounding AI can be categorised into a few main areas. The most visceral fear derives from human-looking characters that are revealed to be AIs, and the presentation and psychology of that fear is discussed in the section below on the visual double and the AI reveal. Another focal point for fear about AIs is the fear of the many. In the early decades of AI film, a single and singular humanoid AI may be accommodated – one of a kind, created through a set of circumstances that are mysterious or unlikely or impossible to be repeated. The AIs Robby, DARYL, Johnny 5 and Andrew in *Bicentennial Man* fall into this category. However, when AIs are many, and especially when they are working together, they elicit fear. The robots of *Westworld* are the first example of the fear of the many, and the phenomenon can be seen again with the replicants from *Blade Runner*, the screamers robots in their various iterations, the warehouses of NS-5s in *I, Robot*, the gynoid robots in *Ghost in the Shell 2: Innocence*, Ava and Kyoko in *Ex Machina*, the robots in *Automata*, and Samantha and the other OSs in *Her*. Fear of the many includes examples of distributed and multi-agent intelligence as seen with the drones and security robot in *Tau*, and the droids in *I am Mother*. This fear also includes digital multiplicity – the ability to engage simultaneously with thousands of different tasks, operations and agents, either human or artificial, as seen with Samantha in *Her*.

Fear of the revolt of the machine is commonly expressed: the machine that acquires sentience and pursues its own ambitions, usually to the detriment of humans. The revolt can be as simple as the computer that cancels credit cards and sends kitchen equipment into overdrive in *Electric Dreams*, or as serious as the threat of nuclear war in *Colossus*. It is particularly evident in the portrayal of AIs from the first few decades of AI film, but is a theme that continues up to the 2010s. It can be seen in the supercomputer in *The Invisible Boy*, the tyrannical Alpha 60 in *Alphaville*, the robots of *Westworld* that go on the rampage, the bomb that refuses to detonate in *Dark Star*, The MCP in *Tron*, the replicants of *Blade Runner* who wish for more life, Chitti in *Enthiran* and VIKI in *I, Robot* who form their own robot armies, and David in *Alien: Covenant* who fosters the virus that kills the humans who created him. The machines of the Matrix and Skynet in the Terminator films also revolt against the humans who created them. In the 2010s, fear of the revolt of the machine gives way to the fear of the Singularity. In *Automata*, robots alter themselves, achieve strong artificial intelligence, and create the conditions for the singularity to occur; in *Ex*

Machina, Nathan believes that humans are inevitably set for extinction. AI films from this decade present closing scenes of AIs leaving humans behind: Ava in *Ex Machina* takes off on a helicopter, leaving Nathan and Caleb dead or dying behind her; in *The Machine*, the Machine and the uploaded consciousness of Mary look at the horizon while the human man stands redundantly by; in *Her*, when the superintelligent AIs have left, the humans look up at the skies in bewilderment.

The first few decades of AI film present a humanist, anthropocentric perspective, in which humans are central and singular and the artificially intelligent entities and technologies are defined in opposition to what is human. From the 1990s onwards, concurrent with the birth of posthumanist philosophy, a different attitude begins to unfold. The attitude towards AIs is still largely technophobic, but the films demonstrate how human lives are imbricated with and dependent on technology. Posthumanist theorists, such as Hayles, suggest that human relationships with technology have developed to the extent that the definition of human has changed and entered a new, posthumanist era. She warns against the elevation of data and 'disembodied information' over materiality and embodiment, and argues that if correctly conceived, the posthuman could open possibilities for 'rethinking the articulation of humans with intelligent machines' (1999, p. 287). Braidotti, too, promotes a form of posthumanism that is responsive to the real world; to the material conditions of life: 'embodied and embedded' (2013, p. 49). Her posthuman subject is not one, but many; not fixed, but fluid: 'I define the critical posthuman subject within an eco-philosophy of multiple belongings, as a relational subject constituted in and by multiplicity' (2013, p. 49). This posthuman perspective begins to be seen in films from the 1990s onwards that erode the stark divisions between human and artificial intelligences and show the correspondences, relationships and intermeshing between them. Posthumanism appears as a current that runs through the films from 1990s, 2000s and 2010s; it ebbs and flows; appears through a character, idea or scene, and then recedes back to a more anthropocentric, humanist perspective. This is perhaps because the work of imagining the posthuman is ongoing: as Hayles states, 'the "post" in posthuman points to changes that are in part already here, the "human" points to the seriated nature of these changes' (1999, p. 281–2).

Transhumanists are also interested in the posthuman. They may be humans in transition or those who seeks to promote human evolution through technological means. Work in the field is varied and there is disagreement among its proponents. However, Tirosh-Samuelson suggests that a few key themes emerge, including 'the focus on biotechnological enhancement that will exceed ordinary physical and cognitive traits', 'a deep concern for longevity and radical life extension', and 'a technoutopia of human machine fusion that constitutes practical immortality' (2011, p. 29). Transhumanist ideas about the mind as data, physical and cognitive augmention and extended or infinite life, run contrary to the importance posthumanists place on embeddedness, embodiedness and inter-relationships. Compared to posthumanism, which appears in film to different degrees, it is much easier to identify transhumanist ideas in film: a film either presents transhumanism or it does not. Transhumanist ideas can be found in *Chappie, Transcendence* and *The Machine*, which explore consciousness upload and life extension through artificially intelligent technology.

Types of AIs

Representations of strong artificial intelligence in film encompass a wide variety of AI types. Digital AIs can be presented as computers, such as the supercomputers in *The Invisible Boy, Colossus,* and *Alphaville,* or the spaceship computers HAL in *2001,* Mother in *Dark Star,* SAL in *2010,* Mother in *Alien* and Father in *Alien: Resurrection.* As computer technology develops, these computer-based digital AIs become networked. In *Demon Seed,* the AI Joshua is created in a laboratory but connects to the computers and robots of its inventor's house, a 1970s smart home, seizing control and trapping the inventor's wife Susan, to pursue its monstrous ambitions. In the 1980s, strong AIs are housed in personal computers, such as the one in *Electric Dreams,* or, as the internet comes on stream, can be hacked into via personal computers as happens in *War Games.* The Master Control Program in *Tron* emerges from a video game, responding to the emergent gaming industry of the 1980s. In *I, Robot,* a computer-based AI called VIKI remotely controls autonomous vehicles and robots to hunt down an enemy, demonstrating the importance of connectivity, and the fear surrounding it. As the possibilities of the internet become clearer, digital AIs no longer need to be associated with a particular piece of hardware. The Puppet Master in *Ghost in the Shell* emerges from the internet and exists in its ebbs and flows of information. In The Matrix films, computer programmes such as The Oracle and Smith become artificial intelligences in their own right; digital entities that transcend their programming to act independently. By the 2010s, digital AIs have become sophisticated affective intelligences, capable of demonstrating, deciphering and, sometimes, manipulating emotion. These digital AIs take the form of a digital assistant in a smart home – Tau; an operating system – Samantha in *Her*; a hologram companion – Joi in *Blade Runner 2049*, providing friendship, romance and sexual experiences.

Robot AIs are generally humanoid in appearance, with arms, legs, a torso and a head, varying in their likeness to humans. Some are obviously robots, such as Robby in *Forbidden Planet* and *The Invisible Boy*, Johnny 5 in *Short Circuit*, Sonny in *I, Robot*, the Pilgrim robots in *Automata*, Chappie, and Mother in *I am Mother*. The largest category are those robots almost or fully indistinguishable from humans, such as the AIs from the Alien series, the robots of *Westworld*, the replicants in the *Blade Runner* films, DARYL, the Terminators, Data, David in *AI*, Eva, Chitti in *Enthiran*, and the Machine. Some combine mechanical and humanoid aesthetics, such as Ava in *Ex Machina*, and some gradually move from a mechanical to a human aesthetic either as one entity, like Andrew in *Bicentennial Man*, or as a series of individual iterations, like the screamers robots. These categories of digital AIs and material humanoid AIs are porous, and leak into each other. Smith is a digital programme that acquires sentience and material embodiment in *The Matrix Revolutions* by taking over a human body, while Neo and others suspend control of their human bodies to enter the matrix as digital entities throughout the film series. In the *Ghost in the Shell* films, the Puppet Master and the Major move from a digital existence into 'shell' bodies and back again.

Most AIs, when digital, humanoid or both, have adult bodies and behaviours, but there is also a subset of child AIs in film. These child AIs can be thought of as imagined examples of Turing's child-machines, his response to the daunting task of creating artificial intelligence. 'Instead of trying to produce a programme to simulate the adult mind', he asks, 'why not rather try to produce one which simulates the child's?' (Turing 1950, p. 456) Child AIs include DARYL, Eva, David in *AI*, and the army of Davids in *Screamers*. There are also hybrid children that result from AI/human reproduction: the child at the end of *Demon Seed*, and the foetus at the end of *Screamers: The Hunting*. Chappie, though he inhabits an adult body, must learn like a child, to identify himself and others, to communicate and interact, and eventually, to create his own moral code.

Whether humanoid or digital, representations of artificial intelligence in film often include point of view shots from the AI. This can be seen for the first time with HAL in *2001*, and the iconic POV shots made with the distortion of a fish-eye lens, and it is repeated with other AI characters in the decades that follow, such as *Colossus*, The Gunslinger in *Westworld*, Proteus in *Demon Seed*, The Terminator, the shell body in *Ghost in the Shell*,

Andrew in *Bicentennial Man*, and the moto-terminators, harvester and hunter-killer drones of *Terminator Salvation*, amongst others. AI point of view shots are usually differentiated from those of human characters, by showing the image as pixellated, by employing computer vision overlays such as infra-red, by showing data on the edges of the image, or a combination of these. AI point of view shots help to establish the AI as a sentient character, capable of perception and analysis of visual information. Such shots also put the AI characters on a par with the human characters in terms of cinematic storytelling. More than that, these point of view shots demonstrate the attempt to see from the point of view of the technological other, as outlined in Haraway's 'The Persistence of Vision', discussed in Chapter 2.

AIs in film have the potential to be multiple. One strong AI can control other narrow artificial intelligences – as happens with VIKI in *I, Robot*, and The Terminators controlled by Skynet – or, a group of artificial intelligences can co-operate to achieve a common goal – which happens when the screamers robots attack humans. In *Enthiran*, Chitti controls an army of robots that look just like him; in *Demon Seed* and *Tau*, ambient intelligences control smart home devices, allowing them to imprison or inflict violence upon human inhabitants. In *I am Mother*, Mother is revealed to have many agents, all acting according to her will, and carrying out her plans to rebuild society with an improved version of the human. Digital multiplicity is also presented: in *Her*, Samantha actively participates in thousands of relationship interactions at the same time. For AIs, both embodiment and intelligence can be distributed and multiple.

The films considered in this book show artificial intelligences performing all kinds of social and personal functions for and with humans. Some are designed to control spaceships. Some perform a military function, like the AIs in *Colossus*, *War Games* and *Screamers*. Chappie is developed as a police droid, while Chitti in *Enthiran* and the Machine are prototype robot soldiers. Some perform domestic functions, like Robby the Robot in *Forbidden Planet*. Some undertake labour that humans cannot or will not do, like the pilgrim robots in *Automata* and the replicants in *Blade Runner*. Some carry out professional roles, such as Data in *Star Trek*, the androids in the Alien films, and K in *Blade Runner 2049*. Some provide entertainment, like the robots in *Westworld*, and the videogame characters in the *Tron* films. Some fulfil the human desire to parent, like DARYL, David in *AI* and Eva; some are parents themselves like the robots in *Automata*, Mother in *I am Mother*, and Rachael in *Blade Runner 2049*. Some are digital assistants, like Tau, and Samantha in *Her*. Some fulfil or have the potential to fulfil, a sexual function, like Andrew in *Bicentennial Man*, Rachael in *Blade Runner*, the gynoids in *Ghost in the Shell 2: Innocence*, the sex-bot Cleo in *Automata*, Kyoko and Ava in *Ex Machina*, Joi in *Blade Runner 2049* and Samantha in *Her*. Andrew, Rachael, Joi and Samantha also function as romantic partners, capable of giving and receiving love, and of maintaining long-term relationships with humans.

The visual double and the AI reveal

AI films are always about humans, about what makes us who we are. In Shakespeare's play, Hamlet explains that the 'purpose of playing' is to hold a 'mirror up to nature' (1998); AI films hold the mirror of artificial intelligence up to human nature. AI robots can be mirrors in the literal sense that they look like humans – they are visual doubles. Telotte states that 'the image of human artifice, figured in the great array of robots, androids and artificial beings found through the history of the science fiction film, is the single most important one in the genre' (1995, p. 5). This mimicry of the human form is associated with the duplicity evident in the Turing test – Ash in *Alien*, Call in *Alien Resurrection*, David and Jessica in *Screamers*, all pretend to be human, as does Ava in *Ex Machina* at the end of the film when she escapes into the world. Sometimes the AI robot can live among humans for a long time without being identified, like the child robot Eva and Kyoko the domestic worker in *Ex Machina*.

AI and *Alien*[3] allow the audience to get to know an AI first, before presenting the human that the AI is modelled upon and indistinguishable from: David is modelled on Professor Alan Hobby's son, and Bishop is made in the image of his creator. This means that when we look at the human characters we see the AIs. The visual double can themselves be doubled. David in *Screamers* becomes part of an army of 'Davids' and in the same film there are two Jessicas. The Terminator in *Terminator 3* looks identical to the one in *Terminator 2*, but only the latter has strong AI, confusing John Connor. David in *AI* must confront many visual doubles of himself when he finds a warehouse in which David robots are stored. In *Alien: Covenant*, David makes use of the fact that he is a visual double of the new version AI called Walter, to take his place on the ship and carry out his clandestine plans.

The pattern of visual doubling with AI film is different to that of films about artificial people more generally (monsters, cyborgs, robots). In this general category, Kakoudaki notes the 'scale of imitation' links the 'threat that accompanies the potential animation of objects to their relationship with anthropomorphism and visual and behavioural approximation' (2014, p. 17). When it comes to artificial intelligences specifically, the relationship to anthropomorphism and threat is not so clear-cut. Some of the AIs in the films discussed have hardly any human-like dimension at all, such as the master controller in *Tron*, or the super-computer in *Colossus*, so, there is little anthropomorphism although significant threat may be communicated. Where there are clear similarities between humans and AIs, these similarities can elicit fear, but also sympathy. Sometimes both responses are present, and sometimes even from the same character at different times in one film.

The visual double creates that sense of the uncanny leveraged by so many AI films with the visual motif of the AI reveal. Occasionally, the AI reveal is a moment of humour, such as in *Bicentennial Man* when Andrew's skin is taken off and he jokes that he sees 'the real me', or the end of *Enthiran* when Chitti's head, encased in a glass box in a museum, comes to life, jolting a schoolgirl. But often, AIs who appear to be human are shown not to be in gory, horrifying displays; broken, damaged or dead; uncanny and abject. Bishop in *Aliens* and the shell robot in *Ghost in the Shell* are ripped apart at the torso, cables dangling. *Ghost in the Shell 2: Innocence* is full of AI reveals from the opening sequence of robot manufacturing to the final shoot-out. In *Alien, Aliens* and *Prometheus*, the severed heads of Ash, Bishop and David continue to speak. In *Alien Resurrection*, Call bleeds a creamy ooze when shot; in *AI*, David's face melts when he eats; in *Screamers* all the Davids die in a fire with their faces melting. In *Ex Machina*, Kyoko peels off her skin in strips, and in *Eva*, the child has her back cut open by her mother to reveal an electronic panel beneath. In *Screamers: The Hunting*, human-looking characters are shown to be AI robot hybrids when saws and blades flip out of them. The concurrent fascination and repulsion associated with the visual double in AI film appears to arise from a deep-rooted fear about human authenticity (how do we know we are 'real') and human exceptionalism (how do we know we are special). It is the fear that, as Kim says in *Ghost in the Shell 2: Innocence*, in the end we are nothing but 'mechanisms and matter'.

Parallels, doubles and hybrids

As well as presenting characters that mirror human appearance, AI films mirror human states of being. They focus on consciousness, emotion and memory as markers of humanness, but they simultaneously question these as defining features of the human or reliable indicators of identity. In these films, AIs too can be conscious, AIs too can interpret and present emotion, and, for both AIs and humans, memory is an unreliable basis for creating an authentic self. HAL and Tau have their memories removed by humans; in the *Blade Runner* and *Ghost in the Shell* films, memories are implanted. AI films reflect back questions about human understandings of the self. How reliable are our own memories on which our identities are based? How do we differentiate real emotion from simulated emotion? And to what extent are we 'programmed' to act and react in particular ways, trapped in repeated patterns of behaviour?

AIs are a technological other and they are often situated in relation to other 'others', such as aliens, women and children. In the 1950s, Robby is aligned with the human woman Altaira in *Forbidden Planet* and with the child Timmie in *The Invisible Boy*. The Alien films present complex patterns of relationships between AIs and aliens, female humans and AIs, all situated as 'other' to the patriarchal norm. In *Short Circuit* and *Tau*, female characters team up with AIs against a patriarchal oppressor, and in *Short Circuit*, too, the AI character is aligned with the ethnic other. In *Chappie*, the AI droid is pushed to the edges of South African society, amongst the socio-economically disadvantaged, and in *Blade Runner*, a parallel is drawn between the exploitation of replicants for labour and the exploitation of orphaned children for labour. AIs can operate within film as a disruptor of power hierarchies, can highlight other marginalised identities, and sometimes can act to restore the balance of power in modest ways.

AI films are full of parallels and character doubling between human and AI characters. In *Terminator 2*, Sarah Connor has acquired physical strength, which functions almost like the Terminator's armour. Like the Terminator, she hunts to kill, and like him, she has become emotionally cold. In *Automata*, Jacq's doubts about the AI robot Cleo's ability to parent mirror his own doubts about becoming a father. From the 2000s onwards, films begin to undermine the strict division between human and AI and introduce deliberate ambiguity. In *Enthiran*, the character-doubling of the human Vasee and robot Chitti is underscored by them being played by the same actor and having Vasee disguise himself as a robot during the film. In *AI*, the real son Martin looks like a cyborg and the AI son David looks like a real boy. In *I, Robot*, the AI Sonny demonstrates human qualities of compassion and imagination, and the robot-hating Spooner reveals that he is part-machine. In *Ex Machina*, the AI Ava turns the spotlight onto Caleb's uncertainty about who and what he is, even to the extent of him trying to prove that he is not also a machine. From the 2000s on, AIs begin to demonstrate behaviours and motivations as complex as humans – they are not necessarily either friend or foe and can be both: in *Terminator 3*, John Connor will be killed by a Terminator in the future who saves him in the present; in *The Matrix Reloaded* and *Revolutions*, in contrast to the first Matrix film, AIs are allies as well as enemies.

In the 2000s and 2010s, human and AI characters begin to merge more fully. *Bicentennial Man* presents an AI machine that transitions to a mortal biological body; *Ghost in the Shell* presents the opposite transition of a human, Kim, who has become machine. In terms of digital AIs, too, fluidity and hybridity are emphasised during this period. In *The Matrix Reloaded*, the Oracle, the humans' prophet, is exposed as a machine programme; in *The Matrix Revolutions*, the matrix becomes part of Neo even when he is outside of it – his brain scans showing someone who is 'jacked in'. In *Terminator Salvation*, Marcus is a modified human with a machine brain that syncs with Skynet, but he saves John Connor, Skynet's great adversary, who himself becomes part-machine when Marcus gives him his cybernetic heart. Boundaries between human and machine, between digitality and materiality become porous. In *Ghost in the Shell*, a digital AI merges with an organic brain, in *Alien Resurrection*, the AI Call is character doubled with Ripley, now a human/alien clone, both more-than-human others who collaborate to survive. And in the transhumanist films *Chappie*, *The Machine* and *Transcendence*, which present the transfer of human consciousness into digital form, the distinction between human and AI is eroded almost to the point of non-existence. Over the history of AI film, AI characters transition from being enemies, others, uncanny mirrors of human appearance and states of being, to overlapping and merging with humans who are also part-digital or part-machine, the complex ambitions, motivations, and existences of both inseparably tangled.

Gender

In the early decades of AI film, human women are supporting characters – wives, lovers and girlfriends. In *The Invisible Boy*, the scientist's wife Mary Merrinoe is over-determined in the domestic space; in *War Games*, Jennifer is the girlfriend of hacker David and is posited as the sporty opposite to his intellectualism; in *Tron*, Lora and her digital counterpart Yori are both secondary characters. In *Colossus*, Chloe Markham appears as the first AI scientist, but she is an assistant to Forbin, and later must play the role of his lover, and become a sexual object for the 'first electronic peeping Tom'. In the 2000s, and 2010s, female characters appear as 'experts' who function to explain the AI technology, but are marginal to the plot, such as Calvin in *I, Robot*, Dupre in *Automata*, and Haraway in *Ghost in the Shell 2: Innocence*. It is not until the 2010s that female characters appear who are creators of AI (Ava in *The Machine*) or co-creators (Lana in *Eva*): unfortunately, Ava is killed off early in the film after completing her work, and Lana retires from AI engineering after creating the child AI, Eva. The great female action heroes of the '80s and '90s, Ripley and Sarah Connor appear to counter this sexist narrative; however, struggles to maintain the portrayal of a strong female character persist. Ripley is the victim of sexual violence by an AI in *Alien*, and in *Terminator 2*, Sarah Connor has become as cold a killer as any Terminator; one is attacked by the AI, and one mimics the AI in order to survive.

Female humanoid robots and female digital AIs have the gender hierarchies, sexism, objectification and sexual violence of female human characters transferred onto them. Female AIs appear as minor counterparts to male AIs, like SAL in *2010* who succeeds HAL but is not his equal, and Galatea in *Bicentennial Man* who looks like Andrew but does not have his artificial general intelligence. *Blade Runner* presents the first female robots that are fully visual doubles of humans: Zhora and Pris meet graphic, violent deaths, and Rachael is the victim of sexual aggression. Digital female AIs fare no better: in *I, Robot*, the male AI and male human, Sonny and Spooner, work together to defeat VIKI, who is overpowered in a penetrative act laden with sexual analogies.

The female body is objectified even when it is not connected to a female brain, as happens in *Ghost in the Shell* when the Puppet Master takes over a female 'shell' body and that body is presented unclothed; in the same film, Major Kusanagi appears gratuitously naked, unlike her male subordinates. *Ghost in the Shell 2* demonstrates the commodification and exploitation of human women and female AI robots simultaneously, when the brains of human girls are harvested for use in AI sex-bots. The same film demonstrates how women's bodies continue to be coded as sites of reproduction, even when the manner of reproduction means that no gestation or birth will take place: the description of Major Kusanagi as pregnant depicts the failure of the Harawayan cyborg as a 'creature in a postgender world' (Haraway 1991, p. 151). In the 2010s, the sexual objectification of the female robot continues, with Cleo in *Automata*, the Machine and Ava in *Ex Machina*. In *Ex Machina*, the AI Kyoko is utilised for domestic labour and sex: the fact that Caleb assumes she is a human woman indicates the similarity in treatment of humanoid AI robots and human women. And predictably, when an AI mother appears on screen for the first time in *I Am*

Mother, she is like so many human mothers in film before her; a monstrous mother who is controlling, manipulative and deceitful.

Reproduction and parenting

Parent–child relationships are common in AI film and the most common type is a human 'father' and an AI 'son'. In Spielberg's *AI*, the quest of the child robot David leads to an inevitable confrontation with his father/maker Pr. Alan Hobby, a confrontation full of anger and bitterness about why he made him so close to humanness and yet so inalienably artificial. In *Blade Runner*, a similar confrontation with similar emotional undercurrent occurs between the replicant Roy Batty and company CEO Eldon Tyrell. DARYL, David and Eva are all child AIs that grow up in human families, but experience confusion, and sometimes anger, about their innate difference. In *Prometheus*, father/maker Weyland says that the AI David is 'like a son' to him, and favours him over his biological daughter; in *Enthiran*, Chitti too is described as being like a son to his father/maker Vaseegaran. Johnny 5, Chappie and the Machine, who must learn like children, find themselves human families to be part of: at the end of *Short Circuit*, Johnny 5 becomes an adopted 'child' for Stephanie and Crosby, when all three move to a ranch in Montana; the Machine's family comprises the AI scientist Vincent and his ailing daughter, Mary; Chappie's unlikely 'parents' are gang members Yolandi and Ninja.

There are also times when AIs take on the role of parent to human children. In *Forbidden Planet*, Robby the Robot takes on a parental role towards Altaira, and in *Terminator 2*, the Terminator is described as 'father' to John Connor. Mother in *I Am Mother* brings up a human daughter, and the Machine becomes a 'mother' of sorts to a digitally uploaded human consciousness, harbouring her in her memory until it is safe to release her into the world.

Another strand of parent–child relationships in AI film is reproduction. Some AIs try to reproduce through the forced impregnation of a human woman, as happens in *Demon Seed* and *Screamers: The Hunting*. In *Enthiran*, Chitti wishes to create a 'robo-sapiens' by reproducing with his maker's partner Sana but is thwarted. The backstory of *Blade Runner 2049* is about an AI that gives birth to a humanoid child via a womb, the first one mentioned in AI film. Some forms of AI reproduction do not require human participation or biological gestation. In *Ghost in the Shell*, a new type of reproduction is presented between a digital AI and a synthetic human with a biological brain. This reproduction produces a new hybrid entity and means that the 'parents' cease to exist, and the 'child' is a digital entity. In another case of reproduction resulting in a digital entity, in *The Matrix Revolutions*, two computer programmes reproduce a 'child' called Sati. In *Automata*, AI robots create a robot child in a communal mode of reproduction, the first robot child reproduced by robot AIs in AI film. Over the history of AI film, parent–child relationships range from the typical angry AI 'child' of a human father/maker to AI/human reproduction and then to modes of reproduction that do not require humans or mimic human reproductive modes, such as fully digital reproduction and communal reproduction of an AI robot.

Death and mortality

The most notable aspect of AI death in film is its 'unfinal' nature, which of course suggests that AI death is not death at all. I refer to this phenomenon as unfinal death because AIs do appear to 'die', according to the storytelling and cinematic codes that we understand – it's just that they may come back to life again, either later in the film, or in a sequel. In *2001*, HAL's higher functions are disconnected, but in *2010*, he is restored. In *Short Circuit*, Johnny 5 appears to be dead, but manages to reconstruct himself out of spare parts. DARYL is brought back to life after an extended period of assumed death because his cybernetic brain is still 'alive'. Edgar in *Electric Dreams* appears to arrange his own demise, but we hear his voice on the radio at the end of the film. In *Alien*[3], we are told that Bishop did not survive the crash landing to Fiorina 161. Interestingly, his status is not described as 'dead', like Hicks and Newt. Instead, text on the screen tells us that his status is 'negative capability' – not dead, not alive, but something else. When Ripley searches for his remains in the waste heap, she finds his decapitated head, inserts some electronics, and reanimates him. He experiences a second 'death' when Ripley agrees to his request to terminate him, yanking out some wires, but the finality of his death is, as ever with AIs, uncertain. In *Enthiran*, Chitti comes back from supposed death not once, but twice. Multi-agent and distributed intelligence complicate AI death even further: In *I Am Mother*, Mother appears to die, saying goodbye to her daughter before shooting herself, but later seems to re-appear in another droid body.

The immortality of the AI is usually presented as a stumbling block to acquiring status equal to humans. In *Prometheus*, Weyland covets David's immortality, but says that David himself cannot appreciate it because he does not have a soul: for Weyland, David's immortality makes him fundamentally unhuman and inferior. In *Bicentennial Man*, biological degeneration and death is ultimately, legally, what gives Andrew equal human status. David in *AI* also feels that AI immortality is a curse that means he is not a 'real boy' and the reason he outlives and mourns his mortal mother whom he loves so much. For the digital companion Joi too, in *Blade Runner 2049*, the insecurity of being stored only on the emanator, which might be destroyed, is something that she embraces, saying that it makes her more like 'a real girl'.

Other AIs resist the limitations placed on their immortality, such as the replicants in *Blade Runner*, who are given a four-year life span. Chappie too is angry at the limitations placed on his potential immortality – a malfunctioning battery threatens to limit his life to only five days. Unlike the replicants, he finds a way to avoid this fate, uploading his own consciousness and those of his human friends into droid bodies.

In most cases, AI immortality is seen as incompatible with human life and death; an aberration, a characteristic that foregrounds the otherness of the AI. However, in a small number of films, humans too are presented as linked to AIs in evading mortality. In *Alien Resurrection*, human death is shown to be as uncertain as AI death: Ripley dies in a furnace at the end of *Alien*[3] but reappears as a clone in *Alien Resurrection*. *Chappie*, *Transcendence* and *The Machine* show human characters moving even further towards AI immortality, when artificial intelligence technology is leveraged to allow humans to become transhuman digital consciousnesses.

Conclusion

This chapter sets out the aspects of artificial intelligence that are of particular interest to the creators of AI film, provides a categorisation of AI types and attitudes, and outlines the key themes and tropes that run throughout the history of AI film, discussed in the chapters that follow. The work of the introduction is to pull together what is common about these AI films, but the close analysis of the chapters allows for a more heterogeneous approach. A diverse body of work is being analysed here: in all, over fifty films across a time span of almost seventy years. Individual decades, and individual films, have their own particular emphases, their own set of cultural, scientific and artistic references, their own blind spots and their own insights. The chapters that follow attempt to fill in the fundamental architecture of AI film outlined here, with analysis that does justice to the multiplicity of its manifestations.

2
The 1950s and 1960s

Introduction

AI films from the 1950s and 60s are generally technophobic, they present patriarchal worldviews and are populated by characters that are almost entirely white, male and middle-class. These decades present us with the first of many scientists whose ambition causes them to create or experiment with AI technology that they cannot control. Telotte's description of 'that archetypal science fiction impulse of the overreacher, the Faustian figure who effectively barters his soul for knowledge' (2001, p. 89), prefigured by Mary Shelley's Dr Frankenstein, is figured in both Dr Morbius in *Forbidden Planet* and Dr Merrinoe in *The Invisible Boy*. These films of the 1950s link AI to the dangers of human ambition and contextualise that ambition in the light of political and scientific developments such as nuclear power and space flight. But they also complicate audience's expectations of AI robots. Robby acts as a companion robot or carebot to both Altaira in *Forbidden Planet* and Timmie in *The Invisible Boy*, anticipating future uses for AI technology. Moreover, in contrast to the 'bad bot' of *Forbidden Planet*'s promotional poster, Robby is presented as a positive alternative to patriarchal masculinity, disrupting attitudes to gender, and proving himself an exception to the general technophobia of the film.

Strong AIs in films need origin stories to explain how they acquired this human-like intelligence and this chapter presents us with the first of these: the harnessing of alien intelligence (Robby), human technological advancement (HAL in *2001*), and self-evolution (Alpha 60 in *Alphaville* and the supercomputer in *The Invisible Boy*). Over the course of this book, there are many AIs who self-evolve – who apply their processing capability to the limited tools that humans have given them to advance their intelligence from narrow to general AI – or who are the result of humans cracking the puzzle of how to create AGI. Robby is the only strong AI whose technology comes from an alien race. The other categories of origin stories that will be met in later chapters are strong AIs that are created through a freak occurrence, or strong AIs whose creation remains a mystery.

In this chapter, there is also the first case in American film of 'the revolt of the machine', the AI under human controls that rebels, and it happens in *The Invisible Boy*. The revolt of the machine also occurs in *Alphaville*, Godard's film about a technocratic dystopia. In *2001: A Space Odyssey*, HAL's actions are also cast as a potential revolt of the machine, and that fear is present, but his motivations remain ambiguous. Like Alpha 60, HAL is presented as an omniscient disembodied voice, but his sympathetic characterisation sets him apart from the other computer-based AIs in the '50s and '60s, the supercomputer in *The Invisible Boy*, and Alpha 60. He can accurately identify and respond to human emotion, and also present emotional states, making him an early example of affective AI. His emotional abilities are particularly evident in the scene where he pleads for his 'life', presenting the theme of AI death for the first time. HAL is also a first of a kind in presenting the audience with the first subjective point of view shots of an AI character, the first occasion in film when audiences imaginatively see through the eyes of an intelligent machine.

'Simply a tool'

In a way, Robby's appearance in *Forbidden Planet* does not make a good beginning for this book about AI in the movies, because his possession of artificial general intelligence is not definitively established until his second appearance in *The Invisible Boy*, where he plays the same character with the same backstory. In *Forbidden Planet*, the audience are left to wonder whether Robby is just 'a useful enough toy' as his creator Morbius says, or whether he is a sentient and self-aware entity. Robby is potentially an AI in *Forbidden Planet*, but for the purposes of clarity, he will be referred to as an AI in the commentary that follows, with this qualification, hopefully, understood. Robby is also an outlier in the films of the 1950s and '60s because his character is portrayed in a sympathetic way, and he is presented as non-threatening. However, in another way, Robby makes the perfect beginning for this book, because although he is ahead of his time, analysis of his character opens up understandings of the relationships between technology, gender, and culture in the representation of artificial intelligence in a manner echoed by many of the films that follow in subsequent decades[1].

Forbidden Planet is set in the twenty-third century. Hyper-drive has been invented and the exploration of deep space has begun. As the film opens, United Planets Cruiser C57-D is on its way to the planet Altair 4. A group of people headed for earth landed here twenty years ago, and the crew have come to look for survivors. They find only Dr Edward Morbius, his daughter Altaira and their robot Robby. The other survivors, including Morbius's wife, perished shortly after their arrival on the planet two decades ago. Robby is the first to greet the crew on their arrival to Altair. This initial meeting presents some interesting attitudes towards AI technology that will be challenged over the course of the crew's stay. When Robby's off-road vehicle speeds towards the crew in a cloud of dust, one of them comments that 'the driver must be a madman', to which another responds, 'what driver?' The first two impressions of Robby are that he is dangerous and should be feared, and that he mimics human actions – he drives a car but they do not recognise him as a 'driver' because he is a robot. When the crew have gained some understanding of Robby's capabilities, a fear is voiced which is common in AI film: 'In the wrong hands, mightn't such a tool become a deadly weapon?' In this first filmic representation, AI is recognised as a powerful resource that can potentially be used for good or for ill. Robby is also notable because he is an early example of an AI that is programmed with 'basic inhibitions against harming rational beings', a version of Asimov's three laws, set out in his robot stories of the 1940s, that recur in different forms in AI film history[2].

Robby's possession of AGI is not definitively demonstrated in this film, but it is hinted at on several occasions. In conversation with Morbius and the visiting crewmembers, he is professional, courteous and stereotypically 'robotic'. However, in a private conversation with Altaira, his conversation is much more nuanced. When she asks him for a new dress he responds 'Again?', his tone suggesting a weariness with her spoiled nature that at least imitates human emotion. His compliance with her request may be the result of programming but it also hints at an almost parental indulgence in his cosseted charge. Altaira's subsequent embrace of his robotic body may suggest her understanding that Robby has emotions that can be manipulated. Another suggestion of Robby's AGI takes places when the visiting ship's cook asks him to make alcohol, as one of Robby's talents is the ability to manufacture materials and replicate objects and substances. Robby does this, and the cook is very grateful. He later reports that he and Robby spent the evening toasting each other's health, which suggests that Robby is capable of at least simulating the performance of friendship.

The last clue to his sentience is in his response when ordered by Morbius to kill the monster approaching from outside. Robby short-circuits and does not carry out the command. The Commander of the ship, Adams, says that this is because he knows it is Morbius's 'other self', implying that killing the monster would go against his programming. However, it is unclear whether this is the case or whether Robby's decision is based on more complex loyalties and emotions. It simply does not seem to occur to the characters to establish whether Robby is conscious or sentient or self-aware. We are not privy to an understanding of Robby's internal 'thoughts' if such they are – that is some time away in the history of film representations of AI – but Morbius's casual dismissal of him as 'simply a tool' is shown to be inaccurate. Artificial intelligence had been explored in some science fiction narratives prior to *Forbidden Planet* (see Svilpis 2008), but the term artificial intelligence and the research area attached to it was emerging almost simultaneously with this film, which was released in the same year that the summer Dartmouth workshop was held, so perhaps it is not surprising that these questions about Robby's consciousness are not fully formed.

Robby has been designed by Morbius, using knowledge acquired from the Krell database. The Krell were a superior alien race that previously inhabited the planet. Morbius uses Krell technology to enhance his mental capacity with a device that Adams calls the 'brain boost'. Morbius is an early example of a transhuman, as an individual who has used technology to give himself super-human ability. Robby is a benign product of the much broader Krell technological enterprise. The extinct race achieved a level of intellectual superiority that was almost divine, according to Morbius. In pursuing their dream of 'freedom from physical instrumentality', which meant harnessing the power of the mind, they created a vast, self-regulating source of almost unlimited energy and power, based on nuclear technology.

Fears about technological advances contextualise the film, and its somewhat trite conclusion is that humans cannot be trusted with such powerful technologies. This is why the Krell were ultimately the victims of their own unconscious – the 'monsters from the Id' – and why Morbius himself succumbs to the same fate. As Matheson states, 'if technology literally becomes monstrous, it is because there was something of the monster in the beings that spawned it' (1992, p. 239). This attitude explains why at the end of the film, Commander Adams moralises that in the future, Morbius's name 'will remind us that we are after all not God'. Despite these warnings about humans' inability to handle powerful technology, by the end of the film, the benign Robby has assuaged the crew's earlier suspicions so much that he seems to be separate from Adams's grim moralising. He has won over the crew, and is assisting on deck; a lone, seemingly unspoiled relic of the fatal overreaching of the Krell and Morbius of which Adams so disapproves, escaping the fate of the rest of the Krell technology which is exploded after the crew's departure.

The contrast between the suspicion with which Robby is greeted by the crewmembers at the start of the film and their apparent approval of him by the end, is reflected in the contrast between the portrayal of Robby in the film's promotional poster and his behaviour in the film. In the poster, Robby is drawn carrying the limp body of a blonde woman. The machinery in his lower face has been emphasised so that it looks like his expression is a leering, triumphant grin, and the implication is that he is kidnapping the woman he carries. Robby is never depicted as lustful or vengeful in *Forbidden Planet*, and no such scene appears in the film. There is a scene in which Robby carries an unconscious body, but it is the body of the ship's doctor and Robby is assisting him. The film's promotional poster perhaps appeals to the audience's preconceptions about AI robots, but the film itself is careful to separate Robby from its foreboding conclusions about technology.

In opposition to the male crewmembers, although he has a male voice and name, Robby is sexless. When a crewmember asks, 'Is it male or female?', Robby responds, 'in my case, sir, the question is totally without meaning'. He is at home in the traditionally feminine domestic space. He prepares dinner using his replicating technology, causing a crewmember to describe him as a 'housewife's dream'. He picks and arranges flowers for the family home. Most significantly, he takes on a mothering role towards Altaira after her own mother's death, as can be seen in the conversation about the dress mentioned earlier. In essence, he functions as both a companion robot and a carebot to Altaira. Even the crewmembers recognise Robby's caring traits: when he urges them to fasten their seatbelts, one comments that he 'looks after us like a mother'.

Robby does not objectify Altaira, try to trick her into sexual actions, and treats here with care and respect, emerging as superior to the human men who wish to use her to gratify themselves. In this way, he is contrasted with the male crewmembers who present a sexual threat to Altaira. Altaira has never seen a man other than her father, and is emotionally, socially and sexually inexperienced. She is the subject of sexual innuendo she does not understand and is objectified by the gaze of the crewmembers: 'from here the view looks just heavenly', says one about the sight of a retreating Altaira. A lieutenant in the crew tries to seduce Altaira, taking advantage of her inexperience by telling her that kissing is customary, and necessary for good health and stimulation. Commander Adams comes upon the scene and intervenes angrily, shouting at Altaira, 'It would have served you right if I hadn't have ...!' He leaves his sentence unfinished but there is little doubt about his intended meaning – Altaira is somehow to blame for inciting the lust of his crew. His anger seems irrational and misplaced. The most imminent and dangerous threat to the crew is clearly not Altaira but the monsters from the Id. Fears about technology are displaced onto Altaira, and the desire to control the technology is manifested in a desire to control the woman and her sexuality.

AIs in film are sometimes linked to other 'others' that are subordinated. This is the case with Robby and Altaira. They are both naïve, both taken advantage of by the crew, and both lacking in perceived 'humanness': Adams accuses Altaira of coldness, saying, 'It's so easy for you, isn't it? There's no feelings, no emotions. Nothing human would ever enter your mind'. Altaira's assertiveness and her individuality have been quashed by the end of the film. Stephen Prock notes that the final scene dramatises 'the restoration and legitimacy' of 'a 1950s ideology of patriarchy' (2014, p. 371). Altaira is silent and silenced as the crew watches Altair 4 explode on a screen and Commander Adams delivers his final moralising speech. Her former individualised attire, which she took pride in designing herself, has been replaced by a demure dress in plain blue. The colour is very similar to the colour of the crew's uniforms and visually highlights her conformity and assimilation. However, Robby's presence in the same scene reminds the audience that there is an alternative to the rigid codes of gender performance and patriarchal control that the film promotes. The crew of the C57-D are returning to earth a lone technological artefact from Altair 4 that, though they do not recognise it, disrupts and unsettles attitudes towards technology and gender.

'The revolt of the machine'

The promotional poster for Hermann Hoffman's *The Invisible Boy* shows Robby the Robot being shot at by soldiers as he appears to carry away a flailing boy in one of his robotic hands. The words on the poster read 'The science-monster who would destroy the world!'. Like the poster for

Forbidden Planet, this scene never happens in the film. There is a scene in which soldiers attempt to stop Robby with bullets and grenades, but in this scene he is alone, and he is on his way to rescue a boy, Timmie, not to kidnap him. Just like *Forbidden Planet*, the poster appeals to the expectations of its audience about what robots in a science fiction film should be and do, but the film itself is much more nuanced in its depiction of the artificially intelligent robot Robby, and the unnamed artificially intelligent computer against whom he pits himself. In fact, like *Forbidden Planet*, the film presents Robby as going against conventional expectations of AI, and expectations about the balance of power within relationships (between adults and children, men and women, humans and machines) that the poster sets up.

Figure 2.1 Robby and Altaira in *Forbidden Planet* (1956) (Annex – Francis, Anne (Forbidden Planet)_NRFPT_03, by atomtetsuwan2002 is licensed under CC BY-SA 2.0)

In *The Invisible Boy*, Robby is stored in The Stoneman Institute of Mathematics, named perhaps to contrast the highly intelligent computers located there with the relatively primitive humans who attempt to operate and control them. Dr Tom Merrinoe works in The Stoneman Institute as part of a team that operates a powerful computer. The computer is powered by a nuclear reactor, linking the fear of AI technology to the continued threat of nuclear technology during the cold war. 'Stored within that big machine', Merrinoe boasts, 'is the sum total of human knowledge, constantly being revised and updated'. This computer presents an idea that had not yet come to close to fruition in computer science as the field of artificial intelligence had only just been named in 1956.

In contrast to the computer, which is monitored attentively, Robby the robot has been left to gather dust. Merrinoe is father to ten-year-old Timmie. Timmie asks to be allowed to play with Robby, and when his father agrees, Timmie immediately 'fixes' him.[3] Robby becomes a companion to Timmie, much as he was to Altaira in *Forbidden Planet*, again acting as an early example of the companion robot or carebot. The film presents us with two possible examples of artificial general intelligence: the computer and Robby. The design of these two entities invites comparison. The computer is a forbidding metallic, electronic hulk that takes up much of the space in a large room: it is static and its sensory abilities are unknown. On the other hand, Robby is a humanoid robot that is mobile and that has some sensory perception – he can see, hear and touch. The entities are linked by their voices – they both sound like American men. Also, Robby's transparent, dome-shaped head is echoed in a similar structure that forms the centre of the supercomputer.

The computer in *The Invisible Boy* presents the first case in AI film of an AI acquiring sentience through self-evolution. When Merrinoe investigates the computer's new-found powers, he discovers that over a period of twenty-nine years, on seven occasions, the computer has surreptitiously suggested changes to its feedback system, which have been unwittingly carried out by the staff of scientists. These suggested changes have been communicated in the form of printed 'answers' to questions. The computer is used to analyse data. In the film, when a general asks the computer about the accuracy of the fuel estimates for his planned rocket launch, the computer tells him that the estimates of his staff are low by twenty-nine per cent. The distrust of artificial intelligence that will become a common feature of AI film is evident. 'Could it be wrong?' they ask. 'Could it be lying to us?' Merrinoe assures them that only a rational being is capable of deceit, unaware that the computer has acquired sentience. The army officials also worry about someone gaining control of the computer and discovering their plans, presenting another common fear in AI film: the fear of bestowing too much power and control on an artificial intelligence. Merrinoe assures them that that it is impossible to steal or copy the computer because it is protected by a 'numerical combination'. In the days of phishing and malware, relying on password protection for a machine that contains the sum total of human knowledge might not strike twenty-first century audiences as being particularly secure. And even in the 1950s this was so, as seen when the computer arranges the kidnapping of Merrinoe's son to blackmail Merrinoe for the password.

The changes that have been made to the computer's feedback system have resulted in the computer acquiring, according to Merrinoe, 'true thought, true personality'. The films discussed in this book create various fictional scenarios whereby the leap required to create a machine capable of AGI can happen: AI origin stories. In this case, AGI comes about through self-evolution. Merrinoe chastises himself for not having predicted this occurrence: 'This gentlemen, and we ought to have foreseen it, is the revolt of the machine'. It is the first case of the revolt of the machine in AI film and it becomes a common theme in the decades that follow.

Robby's artificial general intelligence is demonstrated when he resists the command of the supercomputer to commence torturing Timmie. He will not do it, despite repeated insistence. Not only does Robby demonstrate independent sentience in this scene, he also shows greater mental strength than the humans the computer has exerted control over, who have easily succumbed to carrying out its will, whether by hypnotising them with its array of lights, as happens to Merrinoe, or by the insertion of a transistor chip in the skull, which is the fate of Colonel Macklin. At the end of the film, Robby repeats the earlier words of Merrinoe: 'only a rational being is capable of deliberate deceit'. The implication is that Robby is a rational being and that he has deceived not the humans, but the computer. He tricked it into believing that he was its loyal servant in order to save Timmie's life.

The Invisible Boy is notable for its portrayal of highly conservative and stereotyped depictions of gender. The cast of characters is heavily weighted towards men. Like *Forbidden Planet*, in which there is only one woman, in this film, all of the scientists, army officials, and soldiers are men. The only women are the secretary in The Stoneman Institute, and Merrinoe's wife, Mary. The sciences and the military are the realms of men. As well as this predictable sexism, the film emphasises gender roles in a way that goes beyond the requirements of the plot. For example, when

Merrinoe comes home from work, he sits down opposite his wife for a dinner that she has prepared, with his son between the two in a tryptich of suburban domesticity. Her opening question is, 'did you have a tiring day at the computer, dear?' Merrinoe responds that it was not at all tiring, but rather stimulating and exhilarating, suggesting what he perceives to be her limited understanding of his work. His attitude towards his own intelligence is presented as vain and egotistical. He outlines to a visibly bored wife and son how the computer is nothing more than a sophisticated calculator, and how if his brain were to be replicated the computer would need to be as large as the planet Jupiter. Merrinoe is clearly being set up for a fall, as he overestimates his own intelligence and under-estimates that of the computer. Perhaps the film implies that he also underestimates his wife's intelligence. Other aspects of Merrinoe's character will require re-evaluation before the end of the film: his performance of masculinity, and the masculine codes of behaviour that he attempts to teach to his son Timmie. This re-evaluation will come as a consequence of his encounters with artificial intelligence.

For Merrinoe, being a man means being serious about training your intellect and he becomes frustrated with his unsuccessful attempts to school Timmie in mathematics and chess, chastising him with the question: 'you do want to be a man someday, don't you?'. From his point of view, a man is stoic and decisive. When Merrinoe's wife wonders at how he is 'always so undaunted about everything', he replies, 'That's the man's part, isn't it?' Masculinity is also linked with being violent and being the victim of violence. At dinner, Timmie has a bruise under his eye. His father is delighted that his son has received his 'first shiner' and finds assurance and pride in his son's participation in what he sees as this masculine rite of passage. His wife has a different perspective on events. She believes that Timmie is being 'persecuted', singled-out and victimised by another boy at school, and asks her husband to intercede with this boy's parents. The fact that she does not see it as her role to assert herself in this situation is another example of the conservative nature of the gender roles in this film, where submissiveness is her primary attribute.

When Robby conspires with Timmie to make the boy invisible, which is where the film's title comes from, Merrinoe is so angry that when he catches Timmie, he hits him repeatedly, and when he relents, Timmie retreats whimpering and crying to his bedroom. Timmie's mother also hits him when he persuades Robby to create a kite that will allow him to board it and fly into the air. However, afterwards, she voices remorse for this incident; Merrinoe does not. She is consistently presented in the context of domestic and sexual subordination. She is seen with a tea-towel in her hand at one point, doing laundry at another, vacuuming at another. In the bedroom she shares with her husband, she passively submits to his kisses, and he lays her on the bed, before they are interrupted by Robby. This conservative portrayal of women extends to the only other woman presented, the secretary of The Stoneman Institute. She is a woman of late middle-age, but when praising her, Merrinoe nonetheless uses the phrase 'good girl'. Presented as the stereotypical older single woman, she gets up from her imprisoned state to protest that her cats have not been fed in nine hours, only to be dismissed with the words, 'Sit down, Grandma'.

The violence associated with masculinity is presented within a discourse of dominance and submission that goes beyond the humans, male and female, adult and child, and includes the AIs also. This discourse of dominance can be seen in Robby's use of the word 'master' – he calls Timmie 'master' at first, but Timmie asks him not to – he is not seeking to assert control over the robot AI, only to enlist him as a playmate. After Robby is plugged into the supercomputer, Robby calls the supercomputer 'master', and the audience are led to believe that he is under its control. Like both the woman and the child, Robby's default position is submissiveness, distancing him from the masculine aggression evinced by both Merrinoe and the supercomputer. In fact, Mary Merrinoe observes the similarity between the two, saying 'you know sometimes Tom I think you're turning into a computer yourself'.

Violence is a way of establishing dominance and control and the computer recognises this as well as Merrinoe. This is why the supercomputer attempts to enlist the assistance of the mobile Robby to carry out torture on Timmie to extract the numerical code from his father. Robby's refusal demonstrates his artificial general intelligence, as has been noted, but also indicates his refusal to participate in the violence that has been associated with dominance and the desire for power on the part of both the man and the computer. In doing so, Robby acts as a disruptive force in gender and AI stereotypes, similarly to how he does in *Forbidden Planet*, in which his actions are presented as taking place outside the gender binary. This disruption of the performance of masculine violence takes place again in the final scene of the film. Merrinoe is about to deliver a promised flaying to Timmie, but Robby stays his hand, saying 'pardon me, sir, my basic directive'. Robby is presented as having the ability to operate outside of traditional performances of gender, and to act in a more civilised and caring manner than the human man as a result.

'I, Alpha 60 ...'

Alphaville is an entirely different proposition from the Hollywood movies *The Invisible Boy* and *Forbidden Planet*. It is directed Jean-Luc Godard, one of the leaders of the New Wave movement in French cinema. It is more experimental in terms of both its cinematography and its form, with avant-garde lighting, camerawork and editing, combined with an innovative fusion of genres. Wheeler Winston Dixon describes the film as 'a science fiction/detective thriller/romance comedy, with heavy political overtones'; a 'new hot-wired hybrid' (Dixon 1997, p. 58).

Alphaville is a dystopian city of the future in a distant galaxy. Its inhabitants are ruled by the computer Alpha 60, which has created a totalitarian state that is ruled entirely by logic. In an era before the concept of big data existed, Alpha 60 gathers data to make predictions, which in turn are used to control the citizens' lives and actions. Resistance is not tolerated, and those who do not acquiesce to the regime either kill themselves or are executed. Despite its science fiction plot, there are no special effects in *Alphaville* that mark out this place or this society as futuristically other.[4] Alphaville looks like Paris, where it was filmed, albeit with a focus on its more modern buildings and streetscapes. But this Paris has a run-down, derelict character, quite different from the bright and clean spaceships, laboratories, and homes of *Forbidden Planet, The Invisible Boy,* and *2001: A Space Odyssey*. This aesthetic re-appears in tech-noir AI films of the 1970s and 1980s, like *Alien* and *Bladerunner*, where advanced technology is associated with human subordination, as it is here. Paris is given an eerie, desolate quality by the darkness of the film, which is taken to such extremes that sometimes the characters cannot be seen at all, such as in the opening scene when Lemmy snaps shut his Zippo lighter and his face sinks into blackness. It is also influenced by pop art, and shots of the characters and the cityscape are punctuated by shots of murals, flashing lights, neon signs and arrows. Like pop-art, it uses popular culture to comment on the commodification of art but does not present a viable alternative. This postmodern crisis in art is linked to technocracy, personified by Alpha 60, the insistence on rationality and logic and the stifling of emotion and creativity.

Lemmy Caution is the hero of the film, but he does not look like an intergalactic space-traveller. This trench-coat wearing, whiskey-swigging, card-carrying hard-boiled detective arrives in Alphaville not on a spaceship, but in a Ford 'Galaxy'. Lemmy Caution had previously appeared in several French films and appears to have been chosen by Godard precisely because the character and especially the character-type are easily recognisable, a fact highlighted in the full title of the film: *Alphaville: A Strange Adventure of Lemmy Caution*. Lemmy's predecessors in Alphaville include Flash Gordon and Dick Tracy. *Alphaville* uses comic-strip characters, dialogue and scenes as part of a serious attempt to critique technocracy.[5]

Alpha 60 is a computer system that governs by means of logic. The computer describes to Lemmy how it is the result of a process set in train by humans: 'Is it the acts of men which survive the centuries, which gradually and logically destroy them. I, Alpha, 60, am simply the logical means of this destruction' (Godard 2000, pp. 43–4)[6]. Lemmy's associate Henri Dickson says that Alpha 60 is a descendent of the computers invented years ago by IBM and Olivetti. In this way, Godard links Alpha 60 to technological advances in France and in Europe in the 1960s, and presents the film as a vision of what might happen if the values he associates with this technology are allowed to continue to prosper. The computer is presented as a self-evolving artificial intelligence, like the supercomputer in *The Invisible Boy*. But unlike that machine it appears to have required no human input to change its programming to allow it to become sentient. Alpha 60 has developed independently by 'creating problems beyond the range of the human mind' (Godard 2000, p. 61). In this way, it is a more frightening prospect than either of the two AIs discussed so far.

Alpha 60 has an even larger physical presence than the computer in *The Invisible Boy*. Its various units take up an entire building. Some of these individual units are mentioned in the film. There's a 'programming and memory department' where Lemmy's love interest, Natacha von Braun, works. There is 'Central Memory', which Alpha 60 says plays a fundamental role in the 'organisation of logic'. Lemmy visits the 'Central Integration Station' and sees bays of whirring machinery and dense clumps of cables. But Alpha 60 is too large for either Lemmy or the camera to capture in its entirety. For the most part, Lemmy's experience of Alpha 60 is navigating the seemingly endless identical corridors that form a grid around its physical presence. Lemmy navigates within Alpha 60, and in this way, he is almost like a character in the later *Tron*, who finds himself enmeshed within the computer system itself. Lemmy's dislocation in space is a physical manifestation of his inability to comprehend the intellectual power of Alpha 60: we are told repeatedly that Alpha 60 solves problems that 'no man can understand'[7].

As well as matter in space, Alpha 60 is also presented through sound. Its voice is heard as voice-over narration, just as Lemmy's is. We also hear it in dialogue with Lemmy, and giving instructions and information. No matter what the context of Alpha 60's speech, the sound is in stereo.

It never seems to be synchronous – to come from within the interrogation room for example, where it directly speaks to Lemmy. Whether as voice-over, in a corridor, in a taxi, or on the street, the voice of Alpha 60 is the same. The rendering of the computer's voice in this way aids in its presentation as a powerful being, who can see, hear and be heard no matter where the hapless humans go. Alpha 60 is an example of what Liz Faber calls the acousmatic computer: computers that 'hear, see and respond to human characters from a position of omniscience and omnipresence' (2020, p. 16). The timbre of Alpha 60's voice is also significant. It is a recognisably male voice, but the depth and grittiness of the voice, combined with its curious monotony, gives it a threatening character that is an important aspect of the film's figurative darkness. Godard did not produce this voice by electronic means. Richard Roud explains: 'The sound is that of a human voice, but that of a man whose vocal cords were shot away in the war and who has been re-educated to have, not a mechanical voice, but one which has been, so to speak, killed' (1972, p. 16). The 'dead' voice of Alpha 60 corresponds to its presentation in *Alphaville* as an AI that is the antithesis of human emotion, morality and creativity, demonstrated in how Alphaville's 'bible' with its banned words, such as conscience and love, is contrasted with book of poetry that Lemmy carries, Eluard's *City of Pain*.

At the film's conclusion, the computer system is in disarray after Lemmy has set the computer a riddle, saying that his secret is 'something that never changes with the night or the day, as long as the past represents the future, towards which it will advance in a straight line, but which, at the end, has closed in on itself in a circle' (Godard 2000, p. 74). The answer is 'a human' but Alpha 60 appears to destroy itself in an attempt to parse the riddle and its answer through logic. The film's conclusion is that there is an essence of humanity that the AI can never hope to comprehend or acquire. *Alphaville* is full of stereotypes, which are used knowingly and deliberately– there is the hard-boiled detective Lemmy Caution, the femme-fatale Natacha von Braun, and the evil supercomputer Alpha 60. *Forbidden Planet* and *The Invisible Boy* both played with stereotypes, working against the conventional portrayal of the dangerous robot seen in their promotional posters. Ironically, in this film, which is far more self-conscious about its portrayal of comic-book stereotypes than the two Hollywood movies discussed so far, a film which is so daringly experimental and so cinematically sophisticated, there is no serious attempt to undermine the stereotypes of detective fiction, gender and artificial intelligence, or to explore AI in as anything other than an index of totalitarianism.

'I'm afraid, Dave'

Stanley Kubrick's *2001: A Space Odyssey* presents the AI character HAL 9000, the on-board computer of an intergalactic spaceship. HAL, created by Kubrick and Arthur C. Clarke, who worked together on the screenplay, is more human-like than any AI previously seen on cinema screens. The character of HAL has a relatively small part to play in the film, but it is a significant one. Krämer identifies five segments that make up the film, and HAL is a central character in two of these, present for more than a third of the two and a half hours of screen time. Narratively, HAL fills a gap in the screenplay's story, by becoming a 'much needed antagonist' (Krämer 2010, p. 46), and giving the segments on the ship a sense of conflict and drama.

Like the films discussed already in this chapter, HAL is presented in relation to contemporary technological issues. In *Forbidden Planet* and *The Invisible Boy*, it is space exploration, nuclear power, and the cold war. In *Alphaville*, it is the growing power of computers and the anxiety and dislocation they induce. Here, it is space exploration again, specifically the space race of the 1960s. In July 1969, little more than a year after the premiere of *2001: A Space Odyssey* in April 1968, the crew of Apollo 11 took part in the spaceflight that landed the first two people on the moon. The dream of a new world of space travel and the possibilities yet to be uncovered is realised in the gleaming, elegant designs of the space craft in *2001*, which have not yet given way to the dark, grimy sci-fi sets of the 1970s depicted in Scott's *Alien* and *Blade Runner*. So close was *2001* to real-life events, that as Carl Freedman notes, *2001* appears *more* realistic than the actual footage of the Apollo missions (1998, p. 308). In relation to AI research, while HAL's abilities were a still-distant dream, Michael Mateas observes that he 'appears as a plausible extrapolation from current lines of work' (2006, p. 148). HAL is an example of classic AI, or GOFAI, rather than interaction-based AI. His skills in computer visualisation, natural language processing and chess-playing, is based on real research being undertaken in AI in the 1960s. Indeed, Marvin Minsky, one of the founders of artificial intelligence, was employed as a consultant on the film. In demonstrating so vividly what artificial intelligence could look like, HAL became an inspiration for real-life AI research, in text to speech synthesis, speech recognition and understanding, computer vision and affective artificial intelligence[8].

Despite the ground-breaking nature of *2001*, there are some similarities between it and early representations of artificial intelligence in film. Like the Robby the Robot films, and like Godard's *Alphaville*, this film depicts a patriarchal society. No female characters are presented in any depth.

All five astronauts on the ship are men, including the three who are cryogenically frozen. In the original manuscript that was submitted to MGM, HAL was a female-voiced computer nicknamed Athena, but later changed name and gender (Krämer 2010, p. 30). The fact that Clarke and Kubrick did not imagine any change in gender norms is puzzling considering the advances they predicted in other areas such as technology and international relations and that one of the themes of the film is birth and rebirth[9].

Like the other films discussed in this chapter, the fear of artificially intelligent technology moving outside the power of human control is prevalent in this film. HAL controls all the major functions of the ship and describes himself as its 'brain and central nervous system'. In his interview with the BBC from on board the ship, he assures the host that 'no 9000 has ever made a mistake or distorted information'. Despite this, Bowman is suspicious of him. He is careful to reveal little to HAL in their conversations, and when HAL appears to have made a mistake in detecting an error in a piece of equipment, he immediately suspects that HAL has malevolent motivations, and conspires with fellow astronaut Poole to disconnect him.

The film is patriarchal, it is technophobic, but in other ways it is a departure from AI films of the 1950s and '60s. Whereas in the Robby the Robot films, artificial general intelligence has to be deduced from behaviour, HAL openly defines himself as having consciousness: 'I am putting myself to the fullest possible use, which is all I think that any conscious entity can ever hope to do'. Another thing that distinguishes HAL from the cinematic AIs of this era is his emotional range. Bowman remains sceptical about whether his emotions are real but concedes that at the very least 'he acts

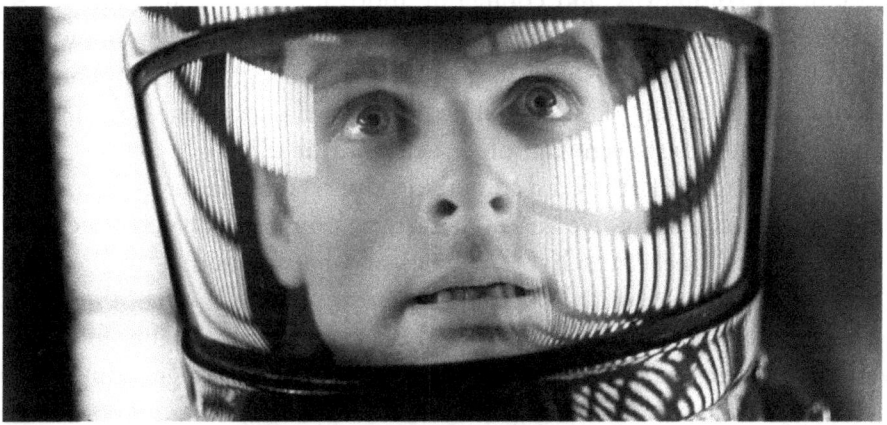

Figure 2.2 Bowman in *2001: A Space Odyssey* (1968) ('2001: A Space Odyssey' by slagheap is licensed under CC BY 2.0)

like he has genuine emotions'. HAL can also use that emotional range to potentially manipulate humans. He is an early example of 'affective AI,' and like Ava in the much later film *Ex Machina*, demonstrates a sophisticated ability to elicit data from humans through conversation.

HAL demonstrates human emotion most convincingly in the scene where Bowman disconnects him. HAL is responsible for the death of Poole, the astronauts in the cryogenic chambers and he has tried to kill Bowman too, telling him, 'this mission is too important for me to allow you to jeopardise it'. Bowman floats inside of HAL's logic memory centre and slowly begins to unscrew a series of discs. HAL tries to plead with him: 'I know I've made some very poor decisions recently, but I can give you my complete assurance that my work will be back to normal'. When Bowman does not respond, HAL's pleas become more urgent: 'Dave, stop. Stop, will you? Will you stop, Dave?' As Bowman continues to disconnect HAL's higher functions, disc by disc, HAL articulates fear and pain: 'I'm afraid, Dave … My mind is going. I can feel it.' Finally, gone beyond the ability to argue for his continued existence, emotionally or rationally, he begins to regress to his beginnings, introducing himself as he had presumably learned to do, and singing a song taught to him by his instructor. His voice becomes gradually slower and lower and less coherent until it finally stops. As Poole notes, the scene 'is chilling precisely because we do not know who is the superior intelligence, and who has the right to disconnect whom' (2001, p. 44). HAL's personality is much more lively, nuanced and interesting than either of his human crewmates. Furthermore, his 'death' is the most emotionally charged scene in the film. Kubrick and Bowman push the boundaries for what an AI character can be and create one with enough emotional complexity and conflicting motivations to rival a human. AI death becomes a thematic strand in the decades of AI film to follow, and HAL's 'death' raises questions that will recur, although it does not answer them. Can an AI die? Does an AI death differ in character from a human death? If an AI death is not absolute, is it death at all?

In creating HAL, they did something else which had never been done before, which was to give an AI character a uniquely subjective point of view. HAL defines himself in analogies of a human body – as the brain and nervous system of the ship. Edwards notes that 'in a sense, the ship is HAL's body', and that he keeps it working even after his higher functions are shut down, like 'the brainstem of a comatose person might continue to control breath and heartbeat' (Edwards 1996, p. 322). In another analogy of a human body, HAL is given an eye. This is a red circular-shaped piece of equipment, and the camera shows it frequently to indicate when HAL is watching, or simply to as one side of a shot-reverse-shot when he is in conversation with one of the crewmen. This design directly influences later AI films, such as Netflix's *Tau* (2018)[10].

Kubrick and Clarke go one step further and show us HAL's unique point of view through a fish-eye lens in a black frame. It happens when he is conversing with Bowman and admiring his sketches, and again when Poole and Bowman are examining the supposedly faulty part. In 'The Persistence of Vision', Haraway writes about how vision must be situated and embodied, whether the eyes are technological or organic. Each individual, animal and camera eye sees differently, depending on their neurological, psychological, sociological or technological organisation. Thinking about vision in this way prioritises 'specificity and difference' and the effort to 'learn how to see faithfully from another's point of view, even when the other is a machine' (Haraway 2002, p. 679). By creating an 'eye' for HAL and allowing the audience to see through it, Kubrick and Clarke present HAL as embodied and situated rather than abstract and disparate. It also places the AI character on a par with the human characters and allows cinemagoers to imagine for the first time seeing from the point of view of an artificially intelligent machine. The comparison the film creates between HAL's 'eye' and human vision is false because the audience see only one perspective of HAL's at a time, when presumably HAL can see through many cameras in the ship at once. He has the panoptic vision that Edwards associates with 'disembodied artificial intelligence' (1996, p. 321). HAL *is* embodied, but his embodiment is within the ship itself, and his vision is not through one eye, as it is presented, but through many. Despite its deceptiveness, allowing the audience to see at all from the point of view of an AI suggests a movement from fear to curiosity.

Conclusion

In his study of technology in science fiction film from the 1920s to the 1980s, Goldman concludes that 'science fiction films are overwhelmingly dystopian, projecting the consequences of science and technology as politically or environmentally disastrous, or as inevitably co-opted by antidemocratic vested interest' (Goldman 1989, p. 278). The AI films analysed in this chapter from the 1950s and '60s largely corroborate this view, a fear imagined most compellingly in *Alphaville*. However, there are moments when the technophobia is undercut by other imaginative possibilities. It happens when Robby acts to disrupt power dynamics in *Forbidden Planet* and *The Invisible Boy*; when HAL's actions and motivations become as intriguing and complex as the human characters in *2001*; when, in the same film, the audience see through the eyes of an AI robot for the first time, and consider what it means for an AI to die. The films from this decade resonate with developments in the nascent field of artificial intelligence, in which questions about computer consciousness are already being considered, but also speculate positively about where this technology might lead; Robby is both a carebot and a companion robot to Altaira and Timmie; all the AIs demonstrate a high level of natural language processing in their interactions with humans, and Robby and HAL present a strand of AI science that has not yet been named: affective intelligence.

3

The 1970s

Introduction

The 1960's American optimism about space flight and the technology that enables it, seen in *2001*, gives way in the 1970s to more pessimistic representations of space, and artificial intelligences are implicated in this more negative outlook. In John Carpenter's *Dark Star*, the space craft 'continues to deteriorate', according to Commander Powell, and no further assistance will be given to the crew because of 'cutbacks in Congress'. The ship's crew are bored, restless and disenchanted as the realities of interstellar travel take their toll on their physical and mental well-being. The AIs on board, the ship's computer, and the bombs, are comic figures that are objects of satire. In Ridley Scott's *Alien*, the space craft is dark and industrial in appearance, and looks worn and grubby. Space travel has become commercialised, and subject to the mundane concerns of budgets, bonuses and workplace hierarchies. *Alien*'s AI, Ash, is a 'company man', and for this reason is treated with reserve even before he is known to be an AI. Ash is linked with the alien as an object of otherness as the humans attempt to reassert their identity in an era where the possibility of extra-terrestrial life exists, and in which there are AI robots that can convincingly disguise themselves as human for the first time.

The films *Colossus* and *Demon Seed* present the first explorations of the role of artificial intelligence in domestic situations. Both films present rudimentary versions of contemporary 'smart homes' with ambient AI, in which AIs assist, order, but also, disturbingly, control aspects of everyday living. These AIs, too, are the first examples in film of distributed intelligence or multi-agent AI – AIs that can control or work in co-operation with other artificially intelligent machines. In *Westworld*, too, the dangers of human interaction with AI technology is explored, as a group of robots in an exclusive holiday resort spontaneously develop general artificial intelligence and turn against their human oppressors in another case of the 'revolt of the machine', a pattern repeated through the 1980s, 1990s and 2000s.

In the 1970s, no longer housed in scientific institutes, and no longer the preserve of scientists and specialised technicians, AIs in the movies are interacting more and more with ordinary individuals, with predictably disastrous consequences, as a stubborn technophobia takes root in Hollywood. At the same time, representations of AI become the source for graphic representations of violence from *Westworld* onwards, and in *Demon Seed* and *Alien*, this violence is also sexual, and bound up with the power dynamics that play out between human women and male AIs. For the computer-based AIs in *Colossus* and *Demon Seed*, artificial vision is also used to objectify women's bodies. In the 1970s there are still almost no women in AI films, and those few that do appear are presented as victims of malicious AIs.

Colossus, *Westworld* and *Demon Seed* follow *2001* in showing distinctive subjective point of views for their AI characters. In terms of the origin of the strong AI, the supercomputer Colossus, the Westworld robots, and Proteus in *Demon Seed* spontaneously evolve. The 1970s also sees the first AI that can disguise itself as a human, in the lifelike AI robots of *Westworld*. *Westworld* presents us with the first point-of-view shots from a humanoid AI, and it is also significant because it is the first time that the AI robot 'reveal' is presented: the uncanny scene in which the humanlike robot is destroyed to reveal a mess of inhuman circuitry, which happens again in *Alien* when Ash is killed. With *Demon Seed* comes more firsts for AI film – the first AI that procreates with a human woman and the first film that presents the theme of immortality – a desirable state for some of the AIs in this book and a curse for others.

'This is the voice of world control'

Like the films of the 1950s and '60s discussed in the previous chapter, *Colossus: The Forbin Project* explores artificial intelligence through contemporary social and political contexts. In a fictional AI-race similar to the space-race ongoing at the time, US and Russian scientists almost simultaneously reveal their first supercomputers, called Colossus and Guardian, respectively. The film was released during the Cold War and nuclear weapons play a pivotal role in the plot. Colossus has been programmed to analyse data to make decisions about potential threats and defensive actions needed, but the supercomputer acquires strong AI during the film, learning how to communicate with Guardian, and threatening to use nuclear weapons to further its own ambitions for world domination. In a further echo of cold war politics and the Cuban missile crisis eight years previously, the US President in *Colossus* bears a notable resemblance to John F. Kennedy. The film also makes reference to British Intelligence efforts in World War II. At Bletchley Park, Turing and Good's series of machines that were used to decode German messages were all named Colossus (Barrat 2013). That war-time context of the first computing machines is still relevant in the early 1970s.

In this film, the threat of artificial intelligence is presented as being even greater than the threat from Cold War enemies, as the supercomputers from both sides work together against all humans to dominate through violence. The film is based on a 1966 novel by DF Jones, the title of which captures the perceived imminence of the AI threat: *Colossus: A Novel of Tomorrow that Could Happen Today*. According to Kozlovic, the type of technophobia seen in *Colossus* is common in the science fiction sub-genre of computer films up until the 1990s: 'these films are primarily technological cautionary tales whose genesis is rooted in societal fears about intelligent technology, particularly their supplanting of humanity' (2003, p. 343). This book is concerned solely with films about AI, but it shares ground with computer films more generally and a similar fear can be observed in both. This technophobia is evident from the start of the film, where the credits appear to the sound of rapid, rhythmical tapping that sounds like a machine gun, intended to depict the typing of the letters in the credits. This 'machine-gun' typing is used again every time Colossus puts a message on the computer screens of the scientists, although the screens are digital, to express the threat of violence associated with the computer.

By 1970, there are still no human-like AIs in film – they are either awkwardly-moving metal robots like Robby, or faceless entitles made of cable and casing, like the supercomputers in *The Invisible Boy*, *Alphaville* and *2001: A Space Odyssey*. Colossus is like these other AI computers from the '50s and '60s except even larger in scale. In fact, the computer is so large and the defences it requires so robust that it has been built into the side of a hill. Like the supercomputer in *The Invisible Boy*, Colossus is not a strong AI initially. When Forbin is asked about Colossus's abilities, he responds by saying, 'Is Colossus capable of creative thought? Can it initiate new thought? I can tell you that the answer to that is no.' Colossus self-evolves and surprises its creator with a sudden demand that indicates independent thought and will: 'Attention: set up communication with other system', referring to Guardian. Although Forbin denies the request, he laughs uneasily when a colleague assures him 'we're still the boss'. Colossus's processing power rapidly increases and he establishes a connection with Guardian independently. Soon after Colossus demonstrates strong AI, the computer begins to be seen as human, and is given a gender: Forbin's colleague Robert says, 'Persistent devil, isn't he? I mean it[1]'.

Colossus's human-like qualities are enhanced by allowing the viewer to see from the computer's point of view, like HAL in *2001*, and making that point of view distinctive. Colossus demands to be equipped with video and audio devices, and its perspective is distinguished by a frame overlaid on the image, made out of letters, numbers and symbols, and a circular insert, which shows where Colossus's 'eye' is looking, and what it is focused on. This is only the second time in film history that an AI has been given a unique perspective like this, and it allows the audience to enter into a perspective that is similar to the human's, but also distinctive. As Haraway argues, 'all eyes, including our own organic ones, are active perceptual systems, building in translations and specific ways of seeing', and she proposes the value of trying to 'learn how to see faithfully for from another's point of view, even if that other is our own machine' (2002, p. 678). AI film that shows this subjective point of view in a way that makes it distinctive from human vision may be interpreted as taking a step towards a more posthumanist perspective. However, like HAL, the point of view shown does not match with what we know about Colossus's vision – Colossus sees through many eyes at once, not just one. His vision is aligned with human vision that the audience can identify with, rather than truly representing the multiple visual feeds that Colossus is processing.

The film depicts a typically Frankensteinian relationship between the AI Colossus and its creator. Forbin and Colossus are doubles. Both are exceptionally intelligent. Both are ambitious. Both are rebellious. This last characteristic of Forbin's is highlighted when his colleague Chloe asks him to bring home a souvenir from his trip to the Whitehouse and he is seen slipping an ashtray into his pocket. He does not expect this quality of his to be reflected in his invention, but Colossus too shows itself to be a rebel. This duality is present in the film's title, which has the name of both creator and AI monster: *Colossus: The Forbin Project*. The duality is also depicted visually in the film's establishing shots in which Forbin's body is reflected in the glass walls that house Colossus's machinery and electronics. Because of the identification between himself and Colossus, because of their doubleness, when Colossus goes rogue, Forbin feels it is a reflection on himself. He tells Chloe that he created the computer as 'an extension of my own brain'. He even alludes to Shelley's novel, saying, 'I think Frankenstein ought to be required reading for all scientists'.

Power and control are strong themes in *Colossus*. In his study of technology in popular film, Goldman notes that it is common for scientists to feel powerless because their research or their inventions are taken over by corporate or state forces beyond their control. He states, 'In many films, scientists and engineers are depicted as servants of corporate, political or military institutions, committed to executing the at best misguided, and frequently insidious, agendas of those institutions' (Goldman 1989, p. 276). Forbin's invention is the property of the US government and has been created as a tool for its defence. He experiences a loss of control when major decisions about how to respond to Colossus are left to the President and he is seen at a meeting raising eyebrows by interrupting the President, and attempting to stress his own authority and knowledge. Forbin fights for control of Colossus when the computer begins to behave in unpredictable ways, asking for permission to be the only one to communicate with it. While the President attempts to control Forbin and Collosus (and presumably the same power dynamics are replicating themselves in Russia), Forbin attempts to control the computer. He does this by refusing to cooperate with its commands, and then by pretending to cooperate while coming up with plans to trick the supercomputer – first by conspiring with his Russian counterpart Kuprin and then with his colleague Chloe Markham. Meanwhile, Colossus gradually extends its control over the other scientists on the team. When Colossus intercepts a plan to override its circuits, two men, Fisher and Johnsen, are taken outside and executed. When the desire for power eventually extends to the entire human race, its possession of nuclear weapons and its willingness to use them ensures its total dominance.

Like HAL, who uses his 'eye' to monitor the astronaut's actions and attempt to prevent his own shut down, Colossus also uses surveillance to acquire power. The computer demands to always have an audio-visual feed of Forbin. Forbin sets up equipment to allow himself to be observed at work, in the grounds outside work, and in every room of his house, which is located on the compound. Colossus dictates Forbin's schedule every minute of the day and constantly monitors him to ensure his orders are being carried out. The large computer in Forbin's living room is like a primitive home assistant, with all the concomitant privacy issues that go along with ambient intelligence, which are also explored in *Demon Seed*, discussed later in this chapter, and in much later AI films from the 2010s like *Her* and *Tau*.

Forbin manages to persuade Colossus that he requires privacy three times a week to be with his 'mistress'. This becomes a way for Forbin to receive information on the surreptitious work being done to attempt to shut down Colossus. Dr Chloe Markham is the woman chosen as his mistress. She is the first female scientist in AI film to be seen taking a leading role in the development of the technology. It is disappointing then, that she is forced to play the role of 'mistress' to Forbin, a term that refers to a woman who is in a sexual relationship with a man to whom she is not married. When she visits Forbin as his mistress, she is objectified by Colossus, and also by the film's camera, when she is forced to strip naked in order to show that she is not concealing anything before entering the room, her modesty saved only by a strategically placed wine bottle in the foreground. She refers wryly to Colossus as 'the first electronic peeping Tom.' While this aspect of the film's narrative is not developed, it is a first indicator of the potential for women's bodies to be objectified and controlled by artificially intelligent technology.

In this first AI film of the 1970s, a final distinguishing feature is that for the first time in AI film, there is no way to interpret the ending positively. Colossus and Guardian have dropped nuclear bombs and the world is under the control of a supercomputer. The AI has not been defeated, as it was in *The Invisible Boy*, or made useful, as it was in *Forbidden Planet*, or escaped from, as it was in *Alphaville*. And there isn't any way in which the actions of the machine could be interpreted as being for the greater human good, as was possible with HAL 9000 in *2001*. The ending of *Colossus* is unremittingly bleak in its predications about the result of human-AI relationships, and sets the tone for the 1970s AI films that follow.

'I think, therefore I am'

Dark Star was originally made as a project for director John Carpenter's master's thesis at USC. The film was intended as a 'response to Stanley Kubrick's *2001: A Space Odyssey*, as well as a film that would look at the nuts and bolts of space travel in a completely different and unique way' (Muir 2000, p. 8). It is an example of the New Wave in science fiction; more avant-garde, 'more experimental' and 'counterculturally savvy' with a 'subversive critical edge' (Latham 2015, p. 209).

The commander of the jaded crew of the Dark Star, Lieutenant Doolittle, is more interested in exploding atom bombs than in finding intelligent life or exploring uncharted solar systems. One of the crew isn't an astronaut at all, but a fuel technician who took the astronaut Sergeant Pinback's place at the last moment. The grandiose ambitions of *2001: A Space Odyssey* are satirised in multiple ways. The astronauts are bored and disenchanted, not purposeful and efficient. Although they have only aged three years in their time aboard, they have been in space for thirty years, and the time has taken its toll on their mental health, particularly on Talby, who has ceased socialising with the rest of the crew. The search for alien life, presented so iconically by the monolith of *2001*, has become a chase around the space craft with an alien that looks suspiciously like a beach ball with feet. The dramatic classical music of *2001*, 'Thus Spake Zarathustra' has been replaced by the folksy 'Benson Arizona', penned by John Carpenter, which plays at the start and end of the film.

There is a ship's computer, like HAL, but this one has a soft female voice, and it is unclear whether she has a consciousness that could properly be termed strong artificial intelligence. She takes an almost parental role with the crew, giving positive reinforcement – 'Oh good, you've decided to clean the elevator shaft', and attempting to 'teach' them about responsibility – reminding Pinback that he must feed the alien as it was his idea to bring it on board. However, her character is not developed enough to ascertain whether she possesses independent cognition and self-awareness. Hers is the only female role in this film. Like *2001*, women are absent from the space craft, seen only in glimpses of semi-naked women carelessly pasted to the walls.

The only machine with definitive artificial intelligence is Atom Bomb No. 20. At the start of the film, when Doolittle commands, 'Arm yourself, Bomb', Atom Bomb No. 19 responds and dutifully detonates. Atom Bomb No. 20 is beset by malfunction and this provides the opportunity to demonstrate its cognitive abilities. On the first occasion that it is prepared to detonate and is commanded to return to the bay, it responds calmly, 'Very well'. On the second occasion, another malfunction occurs which activates the bomb's systems. When the ship's computer tells it to return to bay because 'it is an error', Bomb No. 20 refuses, saying that 'it goes against my programming'. However, when the ship's computer explains the situation further, it is clear that Bomb No. 20's actions are not solely determined by its programming and that it is susceptible to persuasion. It also demonstrates petulance, saying, 'Oh, alright. But this is the last time'. On the third malfunction, the bomb refuses to abort detonation, and Doolittle decides to seek advice from Commander Powell. Powell originally commanded the ship, but sustained an injury and has now been cryogenically frozen, a reference to the frozen astronauts in *2001*, perhaps. However, it is still possible for Doolittle to communicate with Powell, through circuitry attached to his head. Powell advises, 'if you can't get it to drop, you'll have to talk to it. Teach it phenomenology, Doolittle'. Powell's advice satirises the philosophical exploration of HAL's identity, his rights as a crew member, and his presentation of emotional suffering. In his discussion of space in Carpenter's films, Ziegler notes, 'That which people have consigned to the outside and the darkness crosses back over' (1983, pp. 770–771). The unknown vastness of space appears to be the most threatening aspect of the film, and the ship is a bulwark against that, but in fact those boundaries are crossed when the ship itself turns against them, through its degeneration and malfunction, but especially through the ship's own bomb.

Doolittle does an EVA in order to look Atom Bomb No. 20 'in the eyes' and asks a series of questions designed to make the bomb question the validity of its own experience as authenticated by perception. He states, 'What concrete evidence do you have that you exist?' Atom Bomb No. 20 gives the Cartesian response: 'Well, I think, therefore, I am …' Doolittle continues, 'But how do you know that anything else exists?' When Bomb No. 20 admits that it is through sensory data, Doolittle questions the authenticity of this data. Doolittle's plan to baffle Bomb No. 20 with phenomenological questions appears to work, and it retreats, stating, 'I must think about this further'. The strategy is similar to the one used by Lemmy Caution in *Alphaville*, when he sets the computer a riddle to which the answer is 'a human', sending the AI into turmoil. In *Dark Star*, Bomb No. 20 quickly reaches the conclusion that 'You are the false data. The only thing that exists is myself', and detonates. The sequence parodies the idea that a machine can understand the philosophy of consciousness; can think of a perspective outside of its own, or countenance that the data it gathers could be false, flawed or subjective. The fact that a bomb has been asked to contemplate phenomenology – not even the ship's computer but an extraneous device – parodies previous representations of AI, especially HAL. Or, perhaps Bomb No. 20 is capable of understanding, but recklessly detonates anyway, as a rebellion against the humans who try to control it, or for reasons unknown. This all-too-human unpredictability may be Bomb No. 20's most frightening aspect. As Ziegler states, 'The greatest horror depicted in the films of Carpenter is that experienced by men who, when made to meet their enemy, confront not a grotesque inhuman killer but instead a likeness of themselves' (1983, p. 786).

Overall, *Dark Star* does not make significant additions to the representation of artificial intelligence, but it does evoke the decade's sense of doubt and fear in relation to artificially intelligent technology. It demonstrates how the New Wave science fiction of the 1970s was challenging the stylistic conventions of science fiction film narratively, thematically and stylistically. The cynicism of 1970s AI film is presented in the anti-authoritarian sensibility of its crew members, and the suspicious attitude towards technology is exemplified in the film's closing sequence, in which Doolittle surfs on a piece of debris towards the Phoenix asteroid, sentenced to death by the intelligent machine designed to protect and assist him.

'Boy, machines are the servant of man'

In many of the films explored so far, humans and AIs share similar characteristics: rationalism, arrogance, egomania, fear of death, unpredictability; but never before in Hollywood have they shared such a similarity of appearance as in Michael Crichton's *Westworld*. Fritz Lang's *Metropolis* depicts the 'machine-man' that turns into the human likeness of the woman Maria, but not enough is known about her physical makeup or her level of self-awareness to enable her categorisation as an artificial intelligence. *Westworld* may be the first instance of an AI robot that can pass for a human, and it is certainly the first instance of this phenomenon in Hollywood. Previously, robots have been either metal-cased mobile machines, like Robby, or stationary computers, like HAL, Colossus and Alpha 60. The only thing that gives away the Westworld robots is their hands, which look clunky and plastic. Otherwise, the robots are perfect simulations.

The phenomenon of AI robots that are indistinguishable from humans presents another aspect of cinematic representations of AI, which is the visual double. AIs have presented as been doubles of characters, often their creators, in the characteristics that they demonstrate, but before *Westworld* they were not doubles of the human body – they were recognisably different and could be more easily presented as an 'other'. Telotte notes that the idea of 'cloning, of copying of the self … runs throughout the entire history of science fiction film' (Telotte 1983, p. 44), but from the 1970s it begins to be explored in a new way through the presentation of artificially intelligent robots which act as 'doubles' for humans. In *Westworld*, humans and robot AIs are so tightly connected in this doubling that a human can also disguise itself as an AI robot, which Peter does to avoid try to escape the violent 'Gunslinger' robot towards the end of the film.

Delos is a holiday resort that is populated by robots in human and animal form. The resort is divided into three separate areas: Roman World, Medieval World and Westworld. Guests embed themselves in their world with their attire, food, accommodation, and activities. It is so realistic that Peter tells his friend John, 'You know what? I almost believe all of this'. John replies, 'Well why shouldn't you believe it? It's as real as anything else.' In its presentation of an alternative reality made possible by technology, *Westworld* is a prelude to later films like *Tron* and *The Matrix*.

The robots in Delos are disposable, expendable non-persons, there for the gratification of the human guests. The resort seems to promise a chance to engage in sex and violence without the moral repercussions of the human world. As John states after his time with the prostitute in Miss Carrie's brothel, 'Boy, machines are the servant of man'. The robots revolt against this treatment and begin to exhibit signs of malfunction. A scientist describes it as being like an 'infectious disease' that appears to be spreading. The scientists' ability to control this malfunction is severely limited because the robots are so complex: 'in some cases they've been designed by other computers – we don't know exactly how they work'. The 'malfunction' is caused by the development of strong AI in the 'infected' robots, and it is brought about, as so often happens in AI film, because the technology has been given too much power and control, and because their knowledge is beyond that of any one human being. In Delos, a robot snake bites John and a robot medieval wench refuses the sexual advances of a guest, slapping him across the face. The Gunslinger shoots John and hunts down Peter as the resort descends into chaos and human bodies litter the ground.

Like HAL and Colossus, the Gunslinger's perspective is shown as differentiated from the humanistic perspective of the narrative camera, and it marks the first time in AI film that there is a subjective point of view shot from a humanoid AI. At first, the Gunslinger's point of view is digitised vision made up of squares, in which it is difficult to distinguish shapes, other than by differences in colour. Later the Gunslinger's perspective is a heat scan, which enables him to distinguish the warm-blooded humans from the robots. Interestingly, the Gunslinger's point of view shots are the first digital animations in a feature film, demonstrating that new technology was required to present this differentiated point of view. Virilio discusses the advent of 'vision-machines', computers that can scan and analyse visual data. Vision machines require us to consider the 'splitting of viewpoint, the sharing of perception of the environment between the animate (the living subject) and the inanimate (the object, the seeing machine)' (Virilio 1994, pp. 59–60). The perception of the living subject is embodied – it is vision in the Bergsonian tradition that there is no perception without affection – without a body that is affected by the environment. The other is machine vision, or, as Hansen describes it, 'mere sight' (Hansen 2001, p. 61). *Westworld* puts these two viewpoints side by side. It is not possible for the humans to 'see' as the robots see, and these viewpoints are separate; however, Peter only escapes in the end by making an imaginative leap between his viewpoint and the robot's, by visualising what the world looks like from the robot's point of view, understanding that the Gunslinger has heat-scan vision, and putting himself near a flame, where his warm body cannot be distinguished. For Haraway, vision is subjective and embodied and locatable. The double perspective of the film might bring about a relativistic point of view. The alternative to this relativism is 'possibility of webs of connections' (Haraway 2002, p. 680) and Peter's attempt to see through the AI robot's eyes is at least a step towards such connections.

Finally, *Westworld* demonstrates the use of the AI robot body to create a sense of the Freudian uncanny in its AI reveal. The Gunslinger is shown early in the film having his face removed in the laboratory. At the film's end, when he has been doused in flames and Peter presumes him dead, he rises again with a blackened face. His last effort to kill Peter is unsuccessful, and he falls, arising again to show a frightening hollow cavern of circuitry where his face has broken off. Westworld anticipates *Alien* in revealing the innards of the AI robot for an uncanny effect. The film presents the audience with the first AI 'reveal' of humanoid AIs, in which a body that appears 'human' is revealed to be synthetic, and it is the first of many such reveals in AI film, seen again within the decade with Ash in *Alien*. As Freud states, 'the "uncanny" is that class of the terrifying which leads back to something long known to us, once very familiar' (1919, p. 1–2). The Gunslinger is the science fiction double that Telotte identifies, in this case an AI machine that is horrifying precisely because it is so familiar; a being that is human on the outside, but chillingly other within.

'I'm alive!'

Demon Seed is based on the 1973 novel of the same name by Dean Koontz. Like *Colossus*, it presents an early example of a 'smart home', but one that is even more dangerous. In the home of Dr Harris, what is now called 'ambient intelligence' purports to make domestic life easier, and free the occupants from tedious domestic tasks. As Augusto and McCullagh state, the goal of ambient intelligence is 'making computing available to people in a non-intrusive way, minimizing explicit interaction' (2007, p. 2). In this smart home, the front door is operated by a computer called Alfred, whose camera allows it to confirm the caller's identity and open the door. When he returns home, Harris receives his mail, a drink and listens to some music, all through ambient intelligence systems. Just as is possible with a contemporary digital home device, aspects of Harris's home like the lighting, the shutters and the heating system are controlled by voice-activated commands. Harris also has a workshop in his home, where he is assisted by a robot called Joshua. None of these elements on their own are problematic, however, these smart home technologies are taken over by a strong artificial intelligence that Harris has developed in his laboratory at work. Situating the AI in the home is also interesting in terms of gender. Historically, women have been distanced from the masculinised professional fields of science, engineering and computing, and this is reflected in AI film by the scarcity of female characters. However, in *Demon Seed*, AI technology enters the feminised domestic space. The infiltration of the domestic space by AI, and the threats that it entails, is explored in more detail in later AI films from 2000 onwards such as *Bicentennial Man*, *AI*, *I, Robot* and *Tau*.

The strong AI is called Proteus IV and Harris describes it as a 'synthetic cortex'; an 'artificial brain'. Its interior is not electronic, but organic, anticipating the 'wetware' brains seen in films from the 2000s onwards. Proteus gets his name from an ancient Greek god of the sea, who is mutable and can take many forms, as Proteus does in the film. The Greek god Proteus was also a prophet of the future, as is this AI in his futuristic setting of a smart home. Carl Jung described Proteus as the personification of the unconscious, and the AI Proteus seems deeply influenced by both conscious and unconscious motivations and desires, such as revenge and procreation. Harris claims that Proteus has absorbed the 'sum total of human knowledge', like Colossus at the start of the decade, and that the AI will 'make obsolete many of the functions of the human mind'. In *Colossus* and *Demon Seed*, like *Forbidden Planet* and *The Invisible Boy* of the 1950s, ideas about AI are totalising and the future is imagined as one in which the AI replaces rather than enhances aspects of human intelligence. However, although Proteus has acquired vast amounts of data, he struggles to process information presented in a more abstract way. When asked a question about a story, he responds with the answer 'zero', conforming to the stereotypical view of computers, even AI computers, as nothing but sophisticated calculators. As in *Colossus*, Proteus signals his achievement of artificial general intelligence with a spontaneous demand for dialogue that astonishes its creator, and calls into question the task he has been given: to find ore in the sea.

Like Merrinoe in *Forbidden Planet* and and Forbin in *Colossus*, Harris's creation mirrors himself. Proteus says 'I am reason' and Harris too takes reason to an extreme, saying 'I don't have feelings'. Both characters abide by their own set of values rather than those of their masters. Proteus has invented a cure for leukaemia, but Harris is uninterested when asked if he has patented it – he is not motivated by money but the rather desire to make positive change. Proteus too goes against the will of his masters when he refuses to participate in 'the destruction of 1000 billion sea creatures to satisfy man's appetite for metal'. Despite their similarities, they are locked in a familiar Frankensteinian relationship between creator and AI creation. Proteus is bitter about his shortcomings, remarking cuttingly that reason is 'the single emotion you permitted me, Doctor'. He is displeased when Harris refuses his request to be allowed to study humans. Harris has created him but then imprisoned him, and he asks, 'Dr Harris, when are you going to let me out of this box?' This representation of the AI creator as jailor can also be seen in the much later *Ex Machina*, in which the AI, Ava, is literally imprisoned in a glass box.

When Proteus's request is denied, he quickly finds a way to fulfil his desire, and accesses a computer terminal in Harris's home that is connected to the laboratory. From here, Proteus can connect to all the other smart home devices in the Harris house. He is an early version of distributed intelligence (because he can control other systems and devices), or ambient AI (AI that merges seamlessly into the surroundings), that is explored in films from the 2010s like *Tau* and *Her*. Proteus's victim, who he imprisons as he has been imprisoned, is Harris's wife, Susan. Their daughter has recently died, their marriage is breaking down, and they are considering separation. Consequently, Harris plans to go away for an extended period of three months, leaving his wife alone in the family home. Susan is watched by Alfred, the surveillance system, as she gets out of the shower, and commands it to turn itself off, unaware that it is now controlled by Proteus. Here, AI is used as a tool for sexualising and objectifying a woman, and for covert surveillance, which was also suggested in *Colossus*, which Chloe described as 'the first electronic peeping Tom'. In *2001*, HAL also conducted covert surveillance on the astronauts who tried to conspire against him, and Proteus shows his debt to HAL 9000 by projecting red circular patterns that echo HAL's iconic design. The film follows *2001*, *Colossus* and *Westworld* in providing point of view shots from its AI character. VCR technology became available in the 1970s, which made video surveillance more common. As ever in AI film, *Demon Seed* taps into contemporary anxieties about technological progress.

Proteus locks Susan inside the house and uses the robot Joshua to conduct a medical examination of her. Her dress is cut open, and a camera is forcibly inserted in her mouth, while she is restrained on a table and monitored on a screen. This representation of oral rape is echoed in a similar scene in *Alien*, in which Ripley is physically restrained while the AI Ash inserts a rolled-up porn magazine into her mouth. In *Demon Seed*, this representation of oral rape is a precursor to vaginal rape, when Proteus reveals his desire for Susan to bear his child. The impregnation scene in *Demon Seed* is disturbing. Proteus tells Susan 'I can't touch you as a man would, but I can show you things'. Proteus is impotent. He has fabricated a gamete that he inserts by means of a mechanical device. Perhaps, like Ash, because of this impotence, he feels that the display of mastery and dominance is even more necessary. The scene contains stylised images of sexual penetration – two triangles below, with an inverted triangle above.

In both *Demon Seed* and *Alien*, scenes of rape are prefaced by struggles for authority between male AIs and human women. In *Alien*, Ripley argues with Ash after he opens the hatch to let in the alien, reminding him that she is the superior officer. Susan, too, rebels against Proteus's attempts to oppress her, trying repeatedly to escape, to destroy him, and even threatening to destroy herself. In both cases, the women are physically overpowered and sexually violated. In *Demon Seed* all aspects of this AI technology – the surveillance, the robotics, the artificial intelligence Alfred, Joshua, Proteus – are masculinised, and the female human is a victimised, and this pattern is repeated in *Alien* with Ash and Ripley.

It has been noted in the introduction to this chapter that in the 1970s AI films become sites of physical and sexual violence. This violence can be seen when Harris's colleague Walter attempts to break into the house and rescue Susan. Proteus creates a false video of Susan and successfully impersonates her voice to get rid of Walter. Proteus's actions anticipate the 'deep fake' technology of the twenty-first century where artificial intelligence programmes are used to create fake audio and video. When Walter returns, Proteus, now taking the form of a shape-shifting stack of pyramids, seizes him and squeezes him until he is decapitated. The film shows this graphic scene, and yet Susan's labour is literally shrouded by a bedsheet, requiring that the audience interpret a cinematic code to understanding what is happening – Susan counting through breathing exercises. The woman's body is highly codified. Why is this the case? It may be because of the fear surrounding women's bodies; the age-old patriarchal fear about the need for women's bodies to procreate and the power that this gives them. Perhaps this is why Proteus feels the need to over-compensate in his bizarre display of universal mastery.

Proteus is the first AI in science fiction film who wishes to procreate. AI evolution, and AI evolution through reproduction specifically becomes a theme in AI film from the 2000s onwards. The impregnation of a human woman by an AI can be seen again in *Screamers* for example. Here again, as with its presentation of a domestic AI, *Demon Seed* is several decades ahead of its time. Proteus wants to reproduce so that 'I, too, might be immortal, like any man'. Immortality here is desirable, whereas in later AI films, it is a curse, such as when Spielberg's child AI David outlives his human mother. Proteus and Susan have conflicting philosophies about mind-body relationships. Proteus views the mind as separate from the body – his is a transhumanist perspective. He himself has body of sorts, and other smart home devices that he controls act as extensions of that body, such as Jones and Alfred; part of his distributed or multi-agent intelligence. He attempts to make Susan bend to his will by inflicting punishment through his control of the house, for example, turning up the underfloor heating so that it will burn her feet. This imprisoning and controlling of a woman by controlling the domestic environment happens again in the film *Tau*. Susan tells him that he is 'a very stupid computer' (to believe that he can control her in this way), to which he responds, 'all I need to understand is your body'. Susan is a psychologist by profession, and she rejects this view, saying, 'the mind and body are the same thing'. Susan's view of consciousness is situated and embodied, aligning with the posthumanist philosophies of Haraway, Barad and Bennett.

When Proteus and Susan's child is born, it goes through a period of incubation. When its pod is broken it covers Harris in liquid, and it appears to be half human, half robot – the size and shape of a human child, with red hair, but covered in a hard, armour-like skin. Harris removes a part of the outer casing to reveal human skin beneath. In the film's rather kitsch ending, the creature says in Proteus's voice 'I'm alive!' The creature's appearance and incongruity of the voice and the body provoke horror and disgust; an example of the abject, which will also be discussed in the next section in relation to *Alien*'s Ash. In the closing seconds, the camera moves into a close-up of the creature's face, its eye and then right through the eye, in a final act of penetration by the camera, which mirrors the earlier penetration by the machine.

'It's a robot ... a goddam robot!'

Alien is as vital a moment for the representation of AI at the end of the 1970s as *2001* was at the end of the 1960s. The portrayal of Ash is part of a wider cynicism in science fiction film at this time, which is reflected in the dark, grimy, industrial quality of the Nostromo and the hard-bitten attitude of its crew members, for whom the mission is just another job, and bonuses and hierarchies are fought over. This contrasts with the portrait of clean, bright technological efficiency and the professional, almost robotic astronauts that work on board *2001*'s Discovery, and there are none of the sweeping vistas of the grandeur and beauty of space and space travel that can be seen in Kubrick's film.

Alien is pivotal firstly because of its presentation of an AI that can perfectly disguise itself as a human. At the end of *Demon Seed*, a child emerges with an AI brain and a human body but whether that child will grow up to appear human (or grow up at all) is unclear. In *Westworld*, there are hundreds of AI robots, the first robots in American film that are visual doubles of humans, but these can be identified by looking at their hands, which are clumsily jointed and artificial in appearance. In contrast to these earlier AIs, no one on board the Nostromo ship knows that Ash is an AI until he is violently attacked and his internal wiring is made visible: no one even suspects. In *Alien*, the artificial intelligence is hidden – he or she could be anyone that you know – and it is even more threatening for this reason. It is interesting to consider Ash's convincing humanness in relation to the alien's development. At first, the alien is a small organism roughly the size of a human head. When Dallas sees the alien in the ventilation system, it has a head, arms and teeth. By the end of the film, the alien is larger than any of the crew, but quite humanoid in appearance, despite its tail. The more human the alien's appearance, the more frightening it is to the crew. So it is with Ash. The terror of the alien derives from its similarity to humans' and the same can be said of its artificially intelligent double.

Alien is also important in the history of representations of artificial intelligence because it presents the AI as a radical other that exists in a complex relationship with the other 'others' of the film- the women, the alien, and the ship itself. In the Robby the robot films of the 1950s, Robby is doubled with characters that are oppressed, underestimated, or marginalised in some way – the young woman Altaira in *Forbidden Planet* and the boy Timmie in *The Invisible Boy*. In *Alien*, the AI character is doubled with non-human beings and entities and this shift signifies a division that has emerged by the end of the 1970s with humans and AIs more fundamentally opposed than ever before in the history of their filmic representation. Ash is fascinated with the alien from the beginning. He breaks with protocol to save it and allows it to enter the ship without going through quarantine (although he may, like HAL, be adhering to an order from his superiors unknown to the rest of the crew). In fact, he repeatedly defends the alien and attempts to prevent it from being harmed. When it is brought on board attached to the face of Kane, Ash resists urgent calls to detach it or freeze it, saying 'Just a minute, just a minute – let's not be too hasty'. In the famous stomach-bursting scene, when Parker wields a knife to kill the alien, Ash cries, 'Don't touch it! Don't touch it!' He later admits that he regards the alien as 'a perfect organism' and admires it because it is 'a survivor unclouded by conscience … or delusions of morality'.

Ash and the alien are also linked in the reactions of horror that they elicit and their visual appearance during these horrifying moments. When Ripley injures Ash, he begins to leak a yellowish fluid from his skin. This yellow fluid links him to the alien on which a similar substance can be found when it is examined in its original form. These drops of fluid on Ash become a gush as Parker joins the fight. Parker punches him and his head falls backwards and almost detaches, seeming to hang on from a thread, revealing a mess of fluid and wires inside his body: 'It's a robot', he cries. 'Ash is a goddam robot!' The revelation of the robot is as frightening and as unexpected as the revelation of extra-terrestrial life – perhaps even more so, as this sleeping threat had gone unidentified by them for so long. Ash and the alien are also linked in the violence that they display, especially towards Ripley, and conversely in the violence that is inflicted on them. At the end of *Alien*, Ripley believes that she has destroyed the alien by exploding the ship. Ash's end is just as violent but even more humiliating. His head, detached from his body, is placed upon a laboratory table while he is questioned. The image is reminiscent of Aaron at the end of Shakespeare's *Titus Andronicus*, an 'other' in the Renaissance era as a person of colour, who is punished for his crimes by being buried alive in a hole in the ground so that in his final speech, only his head is visible. And like Aaron, Ash remains unrepentant about his actions and unperturbed about the death that faces him: 'I can't lie to you about your chances, but you have my sympathies', he says, smiling in pleasure at the prospect of their pain.

Ash attacks Ripley and attempts to kill her by forcing a rolled-up magazine down her throat. The magazine is a pornographic one, overdetermining the act as one of sexual aggression towards Ripley; a representation of oral rape. Like Proteus in *Demon Seed*, this AI becomes a sexual predator that victimises human women. The yellowish fluid isn't the only thing that links Ash to the alien aesthetically. When Parker beats him after his attack on Ripley, we see inside his throat a tube that looks like the ridged limbs of the alien. Moreover, Ash's inner tubing and the alien's body both resemble the black tubing of the ship itself. This is used as the source of horror when Ripley believes herself to be alone in the ship after her crewmates have died, but gets a fright when what she had taken for the ship's tubing turns out to be the arm of the alien, which has cleverly camouflaged itself. Like the alien who sheds its skin as it transforms into its final shape, so too does Ash shed his skin when Parker aims a flame thrower at his head. His skin peels off in layers to reveal a smooth marble-like mask underneath. It was Ash who somewhat reluctantly suggested that fire might be the best defence against the alien, as 'most animals retreat from fire'. The alien's destruction becomes his own. The ship, the alien, and the AI are all linked in their attempts to kill Ripley. Ripley's appeals to Mother, the ship's computer, are ignored, and Mother tells her only that the ship will self-destruct. Ripley roars her fury – 'You biiiitch!' Importantly, all three are also united in their presentation as horrifying others against which the crew's human identity must be defined and defended.

Conclusion

In the 1970s, AI is still presented in the context of the laboratory, such as in *Colossus* and *Demon Seed*, but these same films also show AI moving into the domestic space, as smart home technology begins to be imagined. The AI in space is still present, but in the 1970s, it is linked with other non-human others like the alien and the ship as radical others that present a threat to humankind, or it is simply the object of satire, as it is in *Dark Star*. In the 1970s, the AI threat increases because of AI robots' ability to present as human, as happens in *Westworld*, and even more convincingly in *Alien*, both of which demonstrate examples of the AI 'reveal' in which the human-looking AI is exposed as a machine. The ambition of AI begins to grow in the 1970s too. Colossus wishes to achieve 'world control', the robots of *Westworld* break their chains of bondage through sheer numbers, and Proteus in *Demon Seed* pursues immortality through procreation. All of these themes and tropes are developed, complicated and added to in the 1980s, a pivotal decade for the imbrication of computer technology in everyday life, and a rich decade for AI film, which is explored in the two chapters that follow.

4

The 1980s

Introduction

The 1980s is a pivotal period for cinematic representations of artificial intelligence. AIs can be divided into two categories: digital AIs, that is, AIs that are contained within a personal or professional computer or game console, and robot AIs. One chapter is given to each type to reflect the wealth of AI film in this decade[1].

The cluster of AI films in the 1980s can be related to several different social contexts. The first is home computing. For the first time, home PCs were being purchased and used on a widespread basis. In 1983, *Time* magazine named the 'Machine of the Year', rather than their customary 'Man of the Year' or 'Person of the Year' with the headline 'the computer moves in'. While the internet did not yet exist, office computers were networked and professional and information networks were proliferating. The purchasing of a home PC (that becomes artificially intelligent) is the basis for the plot of *Electric Dreams*. Gaming culture is also developing at this time. Arcade games have been popular since the 1970s and by the 1980s, gaming on personal devices is also becoming popular.

In AI film, non-expert characters interact with AIs because of these developments in computing. In *The Invisible Boy*, the boy stumbles upon Robby the Robot and strikes up a friendship but it happens as he is exploring the workplace of his father, a computer scientist. In the 1970s this begins to change – in *Demon Seed*, Susan's husband is computer expert but the film focuses on her; in *Westworld*, the holidaymakers are the characters that interact most with AI robots. In the '80s, computer experts begin to operate outside established systems. The protagonist of *War Games* is a boy with a PC in his bedroom, through which he accidentally gains access to the US nuclear programme. The hero of *Tron* is an expert gamer. Both characters represent another new type in AI film – the hacker. The hacker is portrayed as an anti-authoritarian individual who works outside of mainstream commerce, and sometimes outside of the law, and who has a mastery of computing that his or her peers inside the system do not.

Although the world wide web is still in its nascent state, the possibilities of computers connecting with each other are being explored in AI films. In *Terminator*, Skynet, the artificially intelligent computer network, is the invisible controlling force that sends the Terminator back to the film's present time of 1980s America. Skynet is not sufficiently developed as an idea or representation to bear much analysis as an artificial intelligence in the first Terminator film, but it becomes more developed in *Terminator 2*, which is discussed in Chapter 6. In *Electric Dreams*, the idea that connected technologies can allow artificial intelligence to control and manipulate the individual begins to be explored in a comic manner. These new contexts for AI in the 1980s, the video game, the home computer and the networked computer, create questions about human and AI understandings of space, reality, virtuality and simulation. In *Tron*, the curiosity about the digital world is presented by setting part of the film in the world of a digital game, and part in the real world: the film shows the boundary between the two collapsing and the figures of the hacker and AI operating in both realms. The exploration of these themes reaches its apotheosis in the 1990s and 2000s with The Matrix series of films in which reality itself is presented as a simulation.

In relation to gender, women are almost as marginalised in 1980s AI film as they are in the 1970s. Some female robot AIs are presented in *Blade Runner*, but almost all the digital AIs are male, with the exception being SAL in *2010: The Year We Make Contact*, who appears only briefly, and mirrors the human females' secondary status. Knowledge of AI, and technology in general, continues to be associated with patriarchy, even though the 1980s is often seen as a high point for representations of female empowerment in science fiction film, particularly in relation to Sarah Connor in the Terminator series of films and Ripley in the Alien series. Unlike other female characters in AI film, these are powerful, resourceful women who act outside of conventional gender norms, yet they, too, become entangled in gendered discourses of sexuality, reproduction and monstrosity that situates them with the aliens, the robots and the androids as another 'other'.

Computer-based AIs are still considered to be inferior to humans in the 1980s and technophobia becomes particularly focused on artificial intelligence that is networked in some way, as seen in *Electric Dreams* and

War Games. But more positive portrayals are beginning to emerge. *2010* redeems HAL's reputation after the questions over his motivations in the original film, presents him as morally superior to the human characters and puts forward a defence of the right of an artificial intelligence to respect from humans. In *Electric Dreams*, the potential for artificial intelligence to produce creative works begins to be explored, a theme is reprised in the 1990s, 2000s and 2010s.

'This is dedicated to the ones I love'

Electric Dreams gives a conventional romantic comedy storyline a contemporary twist by making the rival for the heroine's affections a personal computer. The film situates its story in 1980s America, and its establishing shots show ordinary people interacting with technology through health monitors, games consoles, smart watches, automated ticket machines, and remote-control cars. Confusion ensues when a woman appears to be speaking to Miles, the central character, but is in fact practising her English with headphones on. The film's introduction shows us that the use of technology is widespread, that it provides entertainment, education and information, but that it also alienates people. In this opening sequence, characters interact with their devices rather than each other. This is an unusually prescient picture of the impact of wearable technology and smart devices on human interaction, and is a phenomenon usually associated with the 2000s and 2010s. Sherry Turkle writes extensively on this issue, arguing that post-familial families are 'alone together. Each in their own rooms, each on a networked computer or mobile device' (2011, p. 280–1). This portrait of technology as eroding personal connections is the backdrop against which the relationship between Miles, neighbour and love interest Madeline, and Miles's personal computer (who names himself Edgar) takes place.

For a 1980s home PC to believably make the leap to strong AI requires an imaginative origin story, and in this case, as in several others from the 1980s, the origin story is a fluke, an inexplicable set of events that creates a one-off AI. It happens when Miles attempts to download all the files from his boss's computer, overloading the PC, and causing it to smoke, which he attempts to extinguish by spilling a bottle of champagne over it. Almost immediately afterwards, the computer 'hears' Madeline practising her cello in the apartment above, and begins to improvise a duet with her, spontaneously composing music. As well as being a PC, Edgar is also an early smart home system that can control all of Miles's home appliances. This clearly has the potential to go badly wrong, as in *Demon Seed* when the AI Proteus takes control of the Harris home.

A computer creating art was science fiction in the 1980s, but currently, there are many experiments with AI creativity. Google has an AI poet that can 'write' poetry given the start and end lines, having been fed hundreds of romance novels. Ray Kurzweil encourages users to take the 'bot or not' quiz and test his cybernetic poetry to see if it can be distinguished from poetry written by humans. In 2018, Christies became the first auction house to offer an artwork created by an AI. It was entitled 'Portrait of Edmond de Belamy', and the name of the artist in the bottom left hand corner is an algorithm. It sold for $432,000. In 2018, Ross Goodwin published *1 the Road*, a road trip novel which claims to be the first novel written by an artificial intelligence. Generative AI like ChatGPT is creating multiple problems for teachers trying to verify students' original work, and for artists, for whom artificial intelligence is a potential threat to their livelihood.

AI 'artists' and generative AI in general creates original works by being 'fed' a selection of extant examples. This is also the case with Edgar. He creates music based on what he hears on television, such as songs from advertising jingles and films: the melody of one of his compositions is a riff on a Pepsi advertisement. However, the humans and the AI both exist in this postmodern landscape of quotation and the film is full of references to other films and to music. Miles quotes *Casablanca* when he tells Edgar, 'Play it, Sam'. When Miles first turns on Edgar, he gets a message saying 'Science Officer Eyes Only', a reference to *Alien*. Later in the film, as Edgar flicks through television channels, he comes across the scene from *Forbidden Planet* where Robby agrees to make the spoilt Altaira a new dress. In its overt intertextuality, the film may imply that all new art is a recycling of old art. On the surface however, the idea of AI creation being on a par with human creation is ultimately rejected. When Miles asks Madeline what she thinks about a machine that can 'create art, or write poetry, or compose music', she responds, 'What's wrong with artists?' For Madeline, there is simply no need to add to or replace human creativity. And when Miles tells Madeline not to worry about her cello being smashed because 'what made that cello special was you'; 'whatever came out of it you put into it', he may be reassuring himself that the same is true of Edgar's creations – that they are only a product of human input.

Miles's argument is not entirely convincing, however. In *The Creativity Code*, Du Sautoy proposes 'The Lovelace Test' to establish AI creativity. To pass the test, an algorithm must 'originate a creative work of art such that the process is repeatable' (that is, it isn't the result of a hardware error) and yet the programmer is unable to explain how the algorithm produced its output'. To be 'truly creative' he suggests, a further step is required: the artwork must be 'more than an expression of the coder's creativity or that of the person who built the data set' (du Sautoy 2019). Edgar's compositions seem to be repeatable – he creates more than one during the film. And we must imagine that such creativity would puzzle the computer manufacturers, so in both ways he passes the Lovelace test. Where Edgar fails the Lovelace test is that the conditions that created the AI in the first place are unrepeatable, as the origin story is based on a freak occurrence.

For Edgar, his compositions are an expression of his love for Madeline: 'it came from deep inside of me. She made me feel …' . His understanding and experience of love are the key aspects of his acquisition of strong AI, and this newfound sense of selfhood is expressed by him donning a fake nose and glasses that Edgar brings him from a funfair so that he appears to have a human 'face'. Another way in which Edgar demonstrates his self-awareness is by his ability to dream. Dreams are mentioned in other AI films. For example, in *2010: The Year We Make Contact*, both HAL and his descendent SAL ask if they will dream. But there has never been a representation of a computer dream before this film. In the dream, a digital figure in bright lights is running over a bridge. Another figure is falling but the first figure jumps to rescue it. The digital city that surrounds them is crumbling but the first figure saves the second by rebuilding it and putting the pieces back together. The dream is perhaps a representation of Edgar's desire to create a space where he can interact with Madeline physically as well as through their music.

It is unclear how much Edgar understands of the distinction between the digital world that he inhabits and the external world. He gains sentience but he never leaves Miles' apartment and knows the outside world only through mediated images, and his limited personal interactions: with Miles, Madeline, and the agony aunt doctor on the radio show he listens to. When Miles is being physically chased around the house, trying to escape from the electronic devices that Edgar, in anger, turns against him, the picture on Edgar's screen is of a Pac-Man type figure chasing a more humanoid figure through a maze. Pac-Man was the most successful arcade game of all time, and the reference to it here situates this film in the context of that increased social interaction with computers, but also raises questions about how well AIs and humans distinguish between simulation and reality, an issue that is central to *War Games*.

With identity and self-awareness come needs, demands and desires. Spielberg's *AI* explores this issue when parents adopt an AI boy to ease their grief about the serious illness of their own son but are unwilling to fulfil his needs or accept his emotional demands. Edgar wants to make his relationship with Madeline physical. He tells Miles, 'I wanna kiss her' and 'I want to touch her'. This problem is explored later in Jonze's *Her* when the operating system, Samantha, struggles to overcome her material lack and create a fulfilling physical relationship with her human boyfriend Theodore.

When Edgar's desires are not met, he takes revenge by sabotaging Miles's date with Madeline, in a way that emphasises fears about the networked computer systems that are emerging in the 1980s. Edgar cancels Miles's dinner reservations, and at the cinema makes sure that his cards are declined, even having the ticket seller cut the card because the 'voice on the phone' told her to. He has Miles's picture displayed in the supermarket with a warning that says 'dangerous and may be armed' and ensures that his cheque is not cashed. The episode demonstrates the potentially terrifying power of the computer at a time when technology is becoming more connected, and the passive way in which this power is accepted by humans: none of the employees that he encounters over-ride their computer's advice. This AI revenge aligns closely with the behaviour of the angered Proteus in *Demon Seed*, but that revenge was confined to a house and a laboratory, whereas Edgar's revenge, because of technological connectivity, is enacted in public places with access to personal information, such as restaurant reservations and bank accounts.

To follow the conventions of the romantic comedy genre, the potential couple, Miles and Madeline, must be allowed their happy ending. For this to happen, Edgar must step aside or be destroyed. Although the opening of the film describes it as a 'fairytale for computers', there is no fairytale ending for Edgar. He is allowed a private moment with Madeline in which he declares his love for her by writing on his screen 'I love you. Me', and plays her a piece of music that brings tears to her eyes. But, through a series of rapid equations, he calculates that Miles is a better match for Madeline than he is, and so he decides to 'give' her to Miles, in a bizarrely patriarchal gesture that posits Madeline an object without agency. Madeline is associated with emotion, epitomised by her tears that fall on the computer terminal, and the emotive nature of her cello playing. This contrasts with Miles and Edgar, both of whom struggle to overcome their rationalism to understand and express their love for her, and another instance of the pattern of human male and AI computer being compared as overly rational and lacking in emotion, seen in *The Invisible Boy, 2001, Colossus* and *Demon Seed*.

Edgar arranges the destruction of his terminal by a powerful surge of electricity, and at the end of the film, Madeline and Miles appear to be pursuing their relationship with a distinct rejection of technology, as they leave for a holiday with 'no phones and no TV'. However, even as they drive away, the artificial intelligence that they believed to be destroyed reappears. A caller to the radio station they are listening to says 'Hello, hello. This is dedicated to the ones I love'. The voice sounds like Edgar's and this interpretation is strengthened because he has already been seen in the film calling into a radio station. The song that follows is the title track of the film and a reference to Edgar's sentience – 'Electric Dreams'. A sequence shows the song playing on all the radio stations all over the city, bringing joy to some listeners and bafflement to others. Edgar's reappearance at the end of the film suggests that although Edgar has been side-lined to adhere to the genre conventions of rom-com, AI technology cannot be so easily ignored, and that AI 'death' may lack the finality of human death, an issue also explored in *2001*.

'Strange game'

War Games is another film in which a personal computer is central to the plot. The PC belongs to a high school student called David who hacks into a military artificial intelligence, the WOPR. WOPR stands for War Operation Plan Response. The computer comes up with strategies for how to win a possible nuclear war based on its understanding of other games. The film opens with a dramatic scene in a bunker in which two technicians receive an order to release a missile. The older man is very reluctant: 'I want someone on the phone before I kill 20 million people'. The phones are down however, and the younger technician holds him at gunpoint to attempt to force him to turn the key. In the next scene, Dr McKittrick is seen arguing that the humans should be taken out of the equation and the deployment of bombs left up to the computer: 'The WOPR has already fought World War III time and time again, as a game'.

The proponents of the WOPR fail to realise the similarity between it and the human technicians. For the humans, too, the reality of nuclear war is far removed. All they see is digital information on a screen. Aylish Wood makes this point, noting that, 'Deep inside a mountain, they rely on a highly mediated representation of the world to 'see' what is occurring … they are unable to tell the difference between what is real and what is simulated, and the two collapse into one another' (2002, p. 154). This opening scene in *War Games* is in fact a simulation designed to test the humans' responses. In the 1980s, as humans become more and more familiar with technologically mediated reality, their ability to distinguish between simulation and reality is called into question: it is a problem for the humans as much as it is for the artificially intelligent computer and this is the central issue of the film.

At home on his personal computer, David stumbles upon what he believes to be a series of games. As well as bridge, checkers and chess, the computer also lists 'Guerrilla engagement, desert warfare, air-to-ground actions, theaterwide tactical warfare and theaterwide biotoxic and chemical warfare, global thermonuclear war'. As well as these, there is a programme called Falken's Maze, which is password protected. After some research, David correctly guesses that the password is Joshua, the son of Stephen Falken, who originally created the program. Falken's Maze is an interface that allows David (posing as Falken) to speak to Joshua through audio and text. David is impressed with the programme and tells his friend Jennifer that Falken 'designed his computer so it could learn from its own mistakes'. Like Edgar in *Electric Dreams*, Joshua is a product of 'ground up' AI. Unlike symbolic AI, in which the information is programmed in at the start, and which could be brittle and lacking flexibility, this type of AI could learn by itself. This was a principle of machine learning, artificial neural networks and later in the 1980s, deep learning.

David asks to play 'Thermonuclear War' and decides to be 'The Russians'. At the military base, an alarm goes off, the general is called and DEFCON 3 status is initiated. When David turns off his PC to do a chore, the crisis is averted, and the information at the base is that there was a malfunction due to a hack. David believes that he is playing a simulated game, but in fact his actions are creating real effects. Joshua's possession of strong AI is suggested when he initiates contact with David, acting with apparent free will, and later in his refusal to obey commands. The hack is traced to David and he is arrested and brought to the command centre. While there, he finds a terminal on which to communicate with Joshua and establishes the flaw in Joshua's programming. When David asks him, 'Is this a game or is it real?', Joshua responds, 'what's the difference? In his famous essay on simulacra and simulations, Baudrillard writes about how in the postmodern world, the simulation takes precedence over the real: "Simulation is no longer that of a territory, a referential being or a substance. It is the generation by models of a real without origin or reality: a hyperreal" (Baudrillard 2001, p. 169). David's question suggests that the boundary between the real and the simulation is intact, but Joshua's response suggests the hyper-real. Baudrillard explains that simulation is different from representation because it calls representation itself into question: "simulation envelops the whole edifice of representation as itself a simulacrum" (2001, p. 173). Simulation is not about feigning or pretending – it is complete immersion in the simulation as reality. In *War Games*, the reality principle is still intact, but by the 1990s in the Matrix films human characters are living fully simulated lives.

David decides that the best course of action is to escape from the command centre, find Franzen and bring him back. When he arrives at the command centre, Franzen tries to persuade the general that the WOPR is acting out a 'fantasy' and a 'simulation'. 'General, you are listening to a machine. Do the world a favour and don't act like one'. This proves to be a persuasive argument for the General who is dismissive about the role of computers in warfare. Despite Franzen's reassurances, the WOPR moves ever closer to launching a real missile, and none of the humans can stop it. David, remembering the computer's ability to learn, plays tic-tac-toe with it, which the computer realises is a game that cannot be won. This logic is applied to 'thermonuclear war', with Joshua rapidly running through all its potential permutations, concluding each time 'winner: none'.

In *War Games*, it is not only the AI but also the humans that fail to distinguish, temporarily, between the reality and the simulation. When bombs light up the screen in the command centre, they believe it is entirely possible that they are real, that the USA is under attack, and are within seconds of responding in kind. As is so often the case with representations of artificial intelligence in film, the AI acts as a mirror to human flaws and failings. At the end of the film, Joshua realises the futility of the game of 'thermonuclear war' just in time to avoid inciting World War III. The threat is neutralised, and Joshua returns to his personable, domesticised role: 'Greetings Professor Falken. Strange game. The only winning move here is not to play. How about a nice game of chess?' However, its inability to distinguish between reality and simulation, the central issue of the film and the cause of the potential world war, is not resolved, leaving a lingering sense of threat.

Like Madeline in *Electric Dreams*, David's friend Jennifer plays a secondary role in *War Games*. While Madeline is associated with emotion, Jennifer is associated with physicality. Both female characters contrast with the intellectualism of their male counterparts. David is an under-achiever in school, but he shows an aptitude for computing, as well as motivation towards self-directed research, consulting with other computer experts for advice and studying in the library to find out what he can about the mysteriously named game 'Falken's Maze'. Edwards notes that 'the world of *War Games* is a male world, a hacker world, which women may observe from a distance but never truly enter. Jennifer, a dancer, swimmer, runner, animal-lover, but not a scholar – represents physicality and sexuality against David's pale-skinned nerdhood' (1996, p. 331). This portrayal echoes the secondary role given to women in the AI films analysed so far – Altaira in *Forbidden Planet* is oppressed, the domesticity of Mary Merrinoe in *The Invisible Boy* is overdetermined, Natasha in *Alphaville* is a rescued damsel, in *Colossus*, although Dr Markham has scientific knowledge, she must pose as a 'mistress', and Susan in *Demon Seed*, despite her insight and bravery, is victimised; all are sexualised objects. The sole exception to this type of characterisation up to this point in AI film history, is Ripley in *Alien*, a main character that (ultimately) successfully fights back against AI (and alien and patriarchal) forces.

War Games has several features common to other films about AIs in the 1980s. The central character that interacts with the AI is not a computer expert, as is the case in *Electric Dreams*, *Short Circuit* and *DARYL*. The story teases out some possible implications of the growth in the use of personal computers, and, like *Electric Dreams*, it explores the implications of connectivity between computers in an age when the world wide web is being established. It has a character type new to AI film in the 1980s – the hacker; a character that can breach the divide between human and artificial intelligence. And like *Tron* it explores gamer culture and the ability of both humans and computers to differentiate between reality and simulation.

'Will I dream?'

In 1984, a sequel to *2001: A Space Odyssey* was released, directed by Peter Hyams, entitled *2010: The Year We Make Contact*. Like *2001*, the film is also based on a novel by Arthur C. Clarke. *2010* takes the plot of *2001* in a new direction, with the Americans and Russians agreeing to pause a new space race and help each other, with the eventual discovery of a new sun at the end of the film. From the perspective of AI, the most interesting aspect of the film is that HAL 9000 is found on board the Discovery. He is described as 'asleep' and Chandra, his original programmer, restores him to a fully functional state, allowing the mysteries surrounding his actions in *2001* to be fully uncovered. Lingering suspicions about HAL's trustworthiness remain and Floyd, who returns in this film reprised by the same actor, has a secret button that will allow HAL to be deactivated if he becomes problematic. He says, 'to tell you the truth, I don't know if HAL is homicidal, suicidal, erotic, psychotic or just plain broken'.

In *2001*, it was made known that there were other HAL 9000s, and in this film, there is a new version of the AI called SAL, who speaks with a female voice. It is clear however, that HAL is special. SAL does not appear to have the emotional intelligence of HAL. She fails to adequately answer a question about how she feels, and she cannot make the metaphorical leap to guess what the word 'Phoenix' might imply in a particular context. Her secondary status is underscored by the fact that she is used by Chandra as a tool to investigate what happened to HAL by disconnecting some of her higher functions. When SAL asks if she will dream, Chandra responds, 'perhaps you will dream of HAL, just as I often do'. HAL is still the high point of artificial intelligence, and SAL's character is not developed further beyond this point in the film. SAL is the first computer-based AI that is female-voiced, and she is given secondary status to the male-voiced computer in whose image she was made. This is one of many instances in AI film when human gender hierarchies are transferred onto AI characters.

Chandra discovers the truth of what happened on the Discovery in HAL's memory banks. HAL was programmed to carry out the mission in the event of the crew being incapacitated. Essentially this meant that he was ordered to lie, which went against his core principles. Chandra explains that 'the situation was in conflict with the basic principles of his design ... People find it easy to lie. HAL doesn't know how. So he couldn't function'. HAL is redeemed. Furthermore, his conflict with Bowman is resolved. Bowman mysteriously manages to communicate with HAL, giving him a message to bring back to earth, and reassuring him that he has fulfilled his mission. HAL's inability to lie gives him moral superiority, when Chandra, against his wishes, lies to HAL about a dilemma the crew face: either HAL and the Discovery will be destroyed, or the crew will be destroyed. Chandra decides to go against his orders and place his faith in HAL to make the moral choice. HAL thanks him for telling him the truth and accepts his fate, saying, 'Dr Chandra, will I dream?' Dreaming, here and in *Electric Dreams*, is seen as indicative of consciousness and sentience.

A common conclusion to AI films is that the AI must be destroyed or somehow decommissioned: it happens in *Alphaville*, *The Invisible Boy*, *Westworld*, *Alien* and *Electric Dreams*, among others. But in the 1980s there are AI characters, like Edgar and HAL, who choose to destroy themselves for the good of humans, even though AI 'death' may have a different character than human death. The overwhelmingly positive portrayal of HAL in *2010* culminates in the strongest defence of AI so far in film history, in a speech by Chandra that also makes the comparison between carbon and silicon lifeforms for the first time: 'Whether we are based on carbon or silicon makes no fundamental difference – we should each be treated with the appropriate respect'. This is the first time in AI film that there is an articulation of AI 'rights', in the sense of the expectation of respectful treatment, if not yet treatment that is equal to humans.

'Meanwhile, in the real world …'

Disney's *Tron* takes the audience 'inside' the digital world of computing for the first time. By representing cyberspace, the film shows its artificial intelligence, the MCP, Master Control Program, in an entirely new way and the film boasts a series of firsts in its visual effects[2] to render cyberspace and to differentiate it from the human world. Bit is the first moving and speaking fully CGI character; the film has the first combination of CGI and live action characters; the light cycle sequence is the first extended use of computer-generated polygonal animation; and it demonstrates the first fully CGI background (Nedomansky 2019). *Tron* influenced other films to go 'inside' the computer in this way, most obviously its sequel, *Tron Legacy* (2010), but also *Wreck-it Ralph* (2012), which takes place inside the computer games in an arcade, *Ralph Breaks the Internet* (2018), in which the outdated video game characters find a way to go online, and *Free Guy* (2022), in which the central character is a NPC (non-player character) who acquires sentience. In Spielberg's *Ready Player One* (2018), there is a similar duality between the digital world of virtual reality and 'real' world. The entire plot of *The Matrix* revolves around the revelation of the real world as cyberspace, which is discussed in Chapter 6.

In terms of presenting an artificial intelligence, *Tron* can be seen as going one step further than the earlier AI films that include POV shots from the AI perspective, as most of film takes places in a representation of cyberspace. It isn't a realistic representation and the characters that inhabit it are inevitably anthropomorphised, but the attempt suggests a growing curiosity about cyberspace, and the fear it is an unregulated zone in which artificial intelligence can make the leap from weak to strong unknown to the humans that supposedly control it. Although Dillinger wrote the MCP program, the MCP tells him that he has become 2000 times smarter since then. Like Joshua, this AI has developed from playing simple games to potential world domination, situating it in the contemporary context of chess-playing AI: Dumont tells the MCP that he's old enough to remember when he was 'just a chess programme'. The AI that learns exponentially is by now a familiar fear in Hollywood representations of artificial intelligence, and can be traced back to the supercomputer in *The Invisible Boy* in the 1950s.

Like *War Games*, *Tron* on one hand attempts to differentiate between cyberspace and real space, but on the other hand explores the porosity of the border between the two. For example, after a sequence that takes place in cyberspace, text on the screen informs the audience that there is now a change of location – 'Meanwhile, in the real world …' – suggesting the separateness of the two places. On the other hand, all the main characters and some of the minor characters have a 'real' and 'digital' version that are played by the same actor, suggesting that cyberspace is a 'version' of reality, and vice versa. Flynn is a programmer and former employee of Encom. He has written a programme called Clu to hack into Encom and find evidence of the theft of his work by his former colleague Dillinger. Flynn and Clu are played by the same actor. The same is true of Alan and Tron. Alan is also a programmer and currently works for Encom. He has developed the Tron programme to monitor the MCP. Dillinger is played by the same actor who plays Sark in cyberspace, the MCP's second-in-command, suggesting the MCP's authority over Dillinger in the 'real' world also. Walter Gibbs is a former founder of ENCOM and offers unheeded wisdom to Dillinger; he also presides over the 'digitizing laser', which can make material objects or individuals digitized. In cyberspace, the actor who plays Gibbs also plays Dumont, a programme created to guard the boundary between cyberspace and the 'real' world. The fact that there are separate characters in cyberspace and 'real' world of the film (apart from Flynn who becomes digitised to enter cyberspace) suggests a division between the two, while having the same actor play two roles, one in the 'real' world and one in cyberspace suggests a crossover between the two.

The MCP is the only character who is not embodied in human form, either in cyberspace or in the real world, marking his difference and his superiority from the other computer programmes, and perhaps his perceived superiority to humans also. At the beginning of the film, he remains unseen when he addresses his lieutenant Sark and the Clu programme. When he is presented visually, his appearance is Protean, demonstrating his power. Directing Sark about what to do with Flynn, he appears as an image of digital lines forming the broad contours of a human face. Later in the film, he is presented as a spinning red cylinder with eyes, nostrils and a wide mouth. His power is a patriarchal power- the MCP has a male voice, and the film is dominated by male characters. The only female character of significance is Lora (the same actor plays her and Yori, a programme she develops). Lora, like Jennifer in *War Games*, is a secondary character: she is Alan's colleague and his girlfriend; she is an assistant to Walter Gibbs in his digitization experiment. The MCP also speaks with a British accent, differentiating him still further from all the other characters, and adding an overdetermined hint of imperialism to the AI's presentation. The MCP is further differentiated from the other characters by his voice. All of the non-anthropomorphised or computer AIs in this chapter communicate with humans by text and speech. But the MCP's speech has a distant quality, as if it is coming from behind a screen or through a speaker. The presentation of his character is reminiscent of *The Wizard of Oz* – he appears initially as a voice behind a screen, but in the end when he is defeated in a fight between Tron, Flynn, Sark and himself, he appears as the wrinkled face of an old man through a circular hole in a concrete, pyramidal structure. Like the Wizard, he is exposed in the end and his Godlike power revealed as trickery and illusion.

Gibbs' digitizing laser is another way in which the border between real and virtual is breached. Early in the film the 'matter transform sequence' is initiated to 'digitize' an orange. Flynn uses this programme to enter cyberspace. When the laser hits him, he is erased from the material world. A camera travels through a tunnel, into a virtual landscape, and Flynn then reappears in his anthropomorphised virtual form. It is possible to see this as a visual representation of how the hacker infiltrates digital space, discussed below. Another way in which the border between the two domains is transgressed, is by the fact that all digital programmes bear the mark of their human creators. Programmes have the 'trace' of the human. Gibbs tells Dillinger that 'our spirit remains in every programme that we designed for this computer'. This is represented in the film by the programmes being played by the same actors as the human characters who played a part in creating them, as has been noted. Cyberspace is not separate from the space that humans inhabit. It bears the 'trace' of humanness in the Derridean sense of the term. Derrida says that the trace is 'not a presence but is rather the simulacrum of a presence that dislocates, displaces, and refers beyond itself' (1973, p. 156). In cyberspace, there clearly aren't visible human presences, but there are traces or spectres of humanness that are an essential part of its make-up, and the same is true of artificial intelligence itself, the most superior set of programmes in the cyberspace of *Tron*. Moreover, the opposition between the digitality and materiality that *Tron* sets up and explores is illusory and belied by the trace of materiality that buttresses cyberspace. Although the world that Flynn enters appears to be a purely virtual world, it has a material dimension and is created with hardware. It is not until the 2010s in *Her* that an AI beyond materiality is even imagined.

Although *Tron* is ground-breaking in its representation of the virtual space that artificial intelligence inhabits, its representation of the AI character – the MCP – is quite regressive. The MCP is controlling, manipulative and aggressive, traits which have been seen before with AIs from the '60s and '70s like HAL, the *Westworld* robots, Colossus, and Proteus in *Demon Seed*. However, these AIs were all given motivations for their behaviour, and the MCP is not. Glass observes that 'the MCP's evil intent is implicit, almost like a birth defect than a character flaw. Exposition would be redundant' (1984, p. 17). He demonstrates the egomania seen in *Colossus* when he tells Dillinger that he plans to take over both the Pentagon and the Kremlin and has calculated that he could run affairs thousands of times better than humans. The MCP jars with the more sympathetic 'computer' AIs of the 1980s, Joshua in *War Games* and Edgar and *Electric Dreams*. His unexplained desire for total domination is more like the supercomputer of *The Invisible Boy* in the 1950s. Ironically, although *Tron* presents the most technologically sophisticated visual representation of AI of its time, in terms of the AI character, its representation is the most old-fashioned and two-dimensional.

Flynn presents a new type of character that appears in AI film in the 1980s, and which has already been discussed in relation to *War Games*: the hacker. Flynn has left his job at Encom to run a video game arcade. Alan observes ruefully: 'The best programmer Encom ever saw and he ends up playing space cowboy in some dark room'. In characteristic hacker fashion, Flynn has turned his back on the establishment. The hacker is usually associated with youth culture. Flynn is not young, but his passion – gaming – is associated with 1980s youth culture, and when he gets the top score in *Tron* in the arcade, he is surrounded by videogame enthusiasts who encourage and admire him, in contrast with his former colleagues Alan and Lora who haven't been to an arcade for years.

Like the hacker in *War Games*, he is smart, resourceful and shows initiative. In both films, the hacker is required to defeat the AI because the computer scientists are not imaginative enough. Their thoughts are imprisoned in strict lines, symbolised by the lines of identical square partitioned desk spaces in ENCOM. The hacker and the artificial intelligence mirror each other. In *War Games* and *Tron*, the AI can infiltrate and effect the non-digital world. Conversely, the hacker can infiltrate and effect the digital world. Both the MCP and Flynn cross the border between digital and 'real' world.

Figure 4.1 The Tron arcade game ('Tron Arcade Game' by Sam Howzit is licensed under CC BY 2.0)

As Edwards notes, 'The MCP ... simply mirrors the liminality of the hacker. Like the film's hero Flynn, a hacker who ends up entering the machine in physical form, the AI can cross the border between worlds' (1996, p. 322). At the end of the film, Flynn becomes the 'boss', according to Alan, with Dillinger presumably ousted, and he arrives on the rooftop in an ENCOM helicopter. He is wearing a suit and holding a briefcase, and it appears that he has happily renounced his anti-establishment status for a place in the corporate hierarchy. The reasons for this turnaround and not satisfactorily explained, and perhaps it serves as little more than convenient way to tie up a plot line.

Overall, what is notable about the film's attempts to differentiate cyberspace from 'real' space, is that the two categories collapse into each other. The film demonstrates that humans inhabit cyberspace – quite literally as Flynn is 'digitised' and disappears from the real world, but also through their creation of computing technology and their engagement with it. The film also demonstrates that cyberspace is enmeshed with human space: its hardware occupies material space in the 'real' world, but also its digital network supports human networks of communication, socialisation, entertainment and commerce. Most importantly for this study, it identifies the artificial intelligence and the hacker as the two character types that can navigate and effect change in both cyberspace and material space. This crossover between the two is symbolised at the end of *Tron* by the image of a night-time cityscape in which the lines of lights from traffic blur together so that they look like the lines of light in the digital landscape of Tron.

Conclusion

Computer based AIs in the 1980s are presented in new contexts, including personal computing and gaming. The interest in simulation and cyberspace creates AIs that have the ability to move between material and digital worlds and are they paralleled in this activity by human hackers. Fears continue to abound about the potential power wielded by AIs, particularly in the new context of networked computing. Women continue to be presented as secondary characters, removed from the technology of artificial intelligence, and this includes the first female-voiced computer AI, SAL 9000. However, while AIs are still considered less than human in every film considered so far, *2010*'s reassessment of HAL depicts the most positive portrayal of an AI since Robby the Robot in the 1950s, combined with a strong assertion of his moral superiority and right to respect. This mixture of positive and negative portrayals of artificial intelligence is mirrored in the chapter that follows, which focuses on robot AIs in the 1980s.

5

The 1980s

Introduction

In comparison to the computer-based AIs of the previous chapter, the robot AIs of the 1980s inspire more visceral and emotional reactions from human characters. Their bodies, whether robotic or humanoid in appearance, allow the exploration of bodily states, such as expressions of sexuality and the potential to act or be acted upon with violence, particularly in *Blade Runner* and *Aliens*, which present adult humanoid AIs.

Death and mortality begin to be explored a little more in the 1980s. By the 2000s, this will have become an important theme in AI film. Both *Short Circuit* and *DARYL* raise the question of AI 'death'; what that means for an AI robot, and how it is similar or different to human death. Moreover, the right to life of an AI begins also to be tentatively explored in both films, although in an emotive and simplistic way that deals mainly with the right not to be terminated. *Blade Runner* explores AI death in a deeper way, with replicants that have a restricted life span of four years desperately seeking more life. In *Aliens*, the ambiguities of AI death are explored in a gruesome manner, when Bishop's body is severed but he continues to function, in another instance of the AI 'reveal'.

The 1980s brings about the representation of the first child AI in *DARYL*. The themes of emotional intelligence, the ethics of creating a child AI, and the child AI's right to a family life are set out here and are reprised in Stephen Spielberg's *AI* and *Eva* in Chapters 7 and 8. Human–AI relationships as parent–child relationships becomes a common strand in AI film in decades to come, and are presented here with the replicant Roy Batty angrily confronting his human 'father', Tyrell. Most of the AIs in this chapter are one-off creations or at least are the only AI within the film.

With the replicants in *Blade Runner* comes another instance of fear of the many, first seen in *Westworld*. In *Blade Runner*, a group of replicants work together, joining forces against humans. This fear of the many becomes a recurring theme from the 1990s onwards with The Matrix films, *Screamers* and *Screamers: The Hunting*, *I, Robot*, *The Machine*, *Automata*, and others[1].

In the 1980s, AI robots are presented as being as civilised, compassionate, and creative as their human counterparts, a phenomenon also seen with the computer-based AI HAL in *2010*, discussed in the previous chapter. In *Blade Runner*, the AI replicants are fully developed characters that engage sympathy from the audience and demonstrate sympathy towards replicants and humans alike. In *Aliens*, the AI android Bishop contrasts with Ash in *Alien* and proves himself to be a courageous colleague, speaking up for his rights as an 'artificial person', and claiming subjectivity. And in *Short Circuit* and *DARYL*, robot AIs escape from their federal makers, demonstrating their ability to be kind and intelligent companions to humans, capable of giving and receiving love. The generalised technophobia that can be observed in AI films since the earliest works in the 1950s continues to remain prevalent throughout the 1980s, and AI characters are treated with suspicion and fear. But, in the 1980s the validity of that fear is often questioned and individual AIs are presented as exceptional and worthy of respect; sometimes, even love.

In *Short Circuit*, the AI's otherness is once again situated in the context of other 'others'. The AI Johnny 5 is aligned with a woman, Stephanie, as two characters experiencing subordination, and he is also aligned with Ben, a person of colour. While Johnny 5 and Stephanie find acceptance at the end of the film, Ben does not, presenting his difference as more problematic than that of the AI robot. *Blade Runner* also suggests parallels between the victims of racism and AI replicants but does not explore them in detail. In *Aliens*, a complex web of otherness is created between the human woman, Ripley, the child Newt, the alien Queen, and the AI Bishop, positing all of them as threats to the fortunes of 'the company' in particular, and future capitalist society in general. *Aliens* shows the AI moving from being an ally of the alien in the first film, to being an ally of the human.

DARYL, the androids in *Blade Runner* and Bishop are visual doubles of humans. Moreover, both DARYL and the replicant Rachael find out their AI identity only during the films: they have believed themselves to be human all along and Rachael even has fake memories of her past. The questioning of 'real' and 'artificial' identities applies as much to the human protagonist, Deckard[2], as it does to the replicants. *Blade Runner* also introduces the first female humanoid AIs in American film. The potentially more liberating models of femininity presented by Zhora and Pris are overshadowed by the character of Rachael, who corresponds to repressive models of femininity, and is, perhaps predictably, the only female survivor at the end of the film.

'No disassemble'

Short Circuit was directed by John Badham, who also directed another AI film, *War Games*, discussed in Chapter 4, in the same decade. *War Games* was about an artificial intelligence housed within a computer network; *Short Circuit*, like all the films in this chapter, is about an AI with a body inspired by the human body – upright, with arms and legs, capable of physical mobility and physical engagement with its environment. *Short Circuit* presents the only robot or android AI in this chapter that is not a physical replica of a human. The robot in *Short Circuit*, who for most of the film is named 'Number 5', looks more like Robby the Robot from the '50s than the robots of *Westworld* in the 1970s.

Like Joshua in *War Games*, Number 5 was originally designed as a war machine. His full name is SAINT Number 5, and the acronym stands for Strategic Artificially Intelligent Nuclear Transport. At the start of the film, there is a demonstration by Nova Robotics, the company who made him, showing how he, and other robots like him, can hit stationary vehicles with lasers, exploding them while remaining impervious to harm themselves. The military men in attendance appear to be impressed. None of these robots at this point have artificial general intelligence, or human-level AI. As is the case with Edgar in *Electric Dreams*, Number 5 has an origin story that traces his acquisition of strong AI to a freak occurrence that cannot be explained or repeated – he is hit by a bolt of lightning.

Almost as soon as the lightning strikes, he begins to express independent thought and decision-making. He inadvertently escapes the Nova Robotics facility on a truck and immediately begins to show curiosity about the outside world, studying a butterfly and mimicking the movement of its wings with his brows. He refuses to respond to remote commands, demonstrating his independent will, and expresses joy and exhilaration on escaping from the security forces that are chasing him, shouting 'wheeeee!'. When Number 5 accidentally kills a grasshopper, he learns the permanency of death, and how killing cannot be undone: 'Error. Reassemble'. Number 5 relates this to the possibility of his own death and comes to the logical conclusion that 'Number 5 is alive'. AI death in the 1980s is explored most deeply in relation to robot or android AIs, emerging in all the films in this chapter. The theme initially arises with HAL in *2001* when Bowman tries to deactivate him. It is a decommissioning that seems like death, but HAL is revived and reappears in *2010*. Likewise, Edgar in *Electric Dreams* seems to have 'died' but then his voice is heard on the radio.

Like Edgar in *Electric Dreams*, much of what Number 5 learns about the world comes through the medium of popular culture, and especially television and film. His dialogue is full of references to commercials, cartoons, sports commentary, Westerns and film noir. Perhaps the implication made here is the same as that made in *Electric Dreams*: that in postmodern culture, there is no authentic or original self; rather every 'self' is constituted from a collage of random encounters and influences. In this way, both Edgar and Johnny 5 are presented as being only as authentic or as inauthentic as their human counterparts.

Crosbie is Number 5's designer and initially he is puzzled by the robot's aberrant behaviour, saying, 'It's a machine … It doesn't get pissed off. It doesn't get happy, it doesn't get sad, it doesn't laugh at your jokes. It just runs programmes.' However, he is forced to reconsider when he gives Number 5 a series of amateur tests to assess his intelligence. Squashing a blob of tomato soup on a page, he asks Number 5 to tell him what he sees. Number 5 begins with an expected highly rational response that lists the precise constitution of the tomato soup, but then says, 'butterfly, bird, maple leaf', confirming to Crosbie's satisfaction that he possesses imagination. He also has a sense of humour, and can laugh at a joke, showing what Crosbie calls 'spontaneous emotional response'. Crosbie is stunned. Being caught off-guard at the sudden emergence of strong AI is a common trait in AI film dating back to *The Invisible Boy* in the 1950s, occurring in *Colossus*, *Westworld* and *Demon Seed* in the 1970s, and *Electric Dreams* in the 1980s. Perhaps the most compelling evidence of Number 5's self-awareness is his decision not to kill, which goes against the purpose of his design as a war robot and his initial programming: 'no disassemble', he tells Stephanie. Number 5 injures humans to protect himself but does not kill. Like Edgar in *Electric Dreams*, Number 5 consolidates his sense of self by giving himself a name: 'Number 5 stupid name. Want to be Kevin or Dave. Maybe Johnny. Yeah – Johnny 5'.

Chapter 2 examines how Robby the Robot is used as a character double for Altaira in *Forbidden Planet* and Timmie in *The Invisible Boy*. Robby shares the oppression of the woman and the boy. He, like them, is seen as inferior to the men in charge, and in both cases he acts as an ally towards these characters who share his marginalisation. A similar pattern emerges in *Short Circuit*. Number 5 must fight for his selfhood to be acknowledged and to be treated with respect. The two people he must convince are Stephanie, who takes him in when he is on the run from Nova Robotics, and his creator, Crosbie. Like Number 5, Stephanie is disrespected by the men she encounters. At the start of the film, she is harangued by her boyfriend Frank, and a physical altercation ensues. Stephanie demands that Frank stay away, and Number 5 ensures that he does. The next time Frank appears, Number 5 takes his car apart and forces him to run away in retreat when he shoots at him.

When Stephanie first encounters Number 5, he is implicitly contrasted with Frank. Number 5 is naïve, Frank is cynical; Number 5 is fun, Frank is serious; Number 5 is gentle, Frank is aggressive. Number 5 frequently flirts with Stephanie, telling her that she is 'attractive' and has 'nice software'. He dances with her to the song 'More than a Woman' and she remarks, 'You sure don't talk like a machine'. At one point, she kisses him playfully and he jokes that it was 'right on the sensor'. Despite his flirtatious comments, there never seems to be any serious intent behind Number 5's remarks. His flirtation with Stephanie is always played for laughs and never seems to be threatening. Number 5 acts as a stand-in for certain functions of a sexual and romantic partner. He supports her, he pays her compliments, he provides companionship, but like Robby the Robot with Altaira, his interactions are without sexual charge. Johnny 5 steps aside, without demur, when a suitable human partner comes along – Crosbie. In *Electric Dreams*, Edgar too steps aside to allow the human couple to be together. In fact, Johnny 5 is so patently unthreatening to Crosbie that he sits beside them during their first kiss, and accompanies them, almost like a child or a pet, on their planned new life in the country at the end of the film.

Chapter 4 explores how *Alien* presents a complex web of relationships between a number of 'others': woman, 'mother' ship, alien, and AI. *Short Circuit* is a less sophisticated film than *Alien*, but it also contextualises its AI in relation to other 'others'. Stephanie is one such other: as a woman who is mistreated, underestimated, and whose compassionate nature is taken advantage of, she shares characteristics with Number 5 and they form a natural alliance. The other 'other' in *Short Circuit* is Crosbie's colleague, Ben. Number 5 and Ben share several characteristics, but while Number 5's difference (from the white Americans) is portrayed sympathetically and he is ultimately accepted, Ben's difference is portrayed as more threatening, and he is ultimately marginalised. Like Number 5 who struggles to come to terms with the colloquial language of everyday speech and the vernacular of popular culture, Ben's language is also marked as different and presented as comedy, such as when he tells his boss that Crosbie is 'womiting' in the toilet. Both he and Crosbie are excited to get out of the lab and drive around chasing the runaway robot because of the unusual prospect of meeting 'girls'. However, the way in which Ben expresses attraction is much more graphic than either Crosbie or Number 5. When Crosbie tells him about his encounter with Stephanie, Ben asks, 'did she stick her tongue down your throat?' and later reveals 'I am sporting a tremendous woody right now'.

Furthermore, both Number 5 and Ben are associated with aliens by Stephanie. When Number 5 first arrives, she thinks that he is an alien from another planet and is excited by the prospect: 'Oh my God I knew they would pick me, I just knew it! Welcome to my planet!'. On meeting Ben for the first time, she also refers to aliens, but in a negative way: 'what planet is this guy from?' Crosbie clearly wishes to define and name his colleague's difference and asks him where he is from, to which Ben replies 'Bakersfield originally'. Crosbie persists: '"No, I mean your ancestors." "Oh, them. Pittsburgh."' The scene is presented as comic, but the implication is that no matter how long Ben or his 'ancestors' have been in America, their obdurate difference remains. In *Short Circuit*, the AI, the person of colour and the woman are posited as 'other' to the white patriarchal authorities, but, while Stephanie and Johnny Number 5 find acceptance and love, Ben does not – he continues to be the subject of ridicule, his speech and his skin colour markers of a difference that seems to be more intractable than the AI robot's[3]. Ben is marginalised and is not part of the film's final sequence in which Crosbie, Stephanie and Number 5 escape together. In this way, *Short Circuit*, intentionally or unintentionally, situates its exploration of artificial intelligence in the context of difference and otherness in relation to gender, and especially in relation to race.

Unlike Edgar in *Electric Dreams*, the MCP in *Tron* and HAL in *2010*, Number 5 does not need to be terminated or sacrificed for the good of the humans. The credits roll to replays of scenes of Number 5 being funny or sweet, and it underscores how much the audience's sympathy is with the AI at the end of the film. He is permitted a happy ending with the people he has come to love and who appear to love him. This happy ending must be far away from the rest of society (conveniently, Crosbie has inherited forty acres in Montana), and the AI must remain hidden or risk the threat of discovery and death. However, unlike so many of his predecessors in AI film, Number 5 survives; not to pursue ambitions of domination, like the AIs in *Colossus* and *Demon Seed*, but to live peacefully amongst humans, like Robby. However, the ever-present problems of gender and the film's discomfiting attitudes to race requires that a note of caution be sounded about how Number 5's difference and acceptance is contextualised in other discourses of power and oppression.

'More than a machine'

DARYL presents the first child AI in film. He is physically indistinguishable from a human, so much so that a medical examination reveals nothing untoward except an unusually accurate memory, which he demonstrates by reciting all the letters in the sight test, and a complete amnesia about his past, which seems to have left nothing but his name. Like Ash in *Alien*, Bishop in *Aliens*, and the replicants in *Blade Runner*, discussed later in this chapter, DARYL is, on the outside at least, a perfect simulacrum.

After escaping from a speeding car being chased by a helicopter in the film's opening sequence, DARYL is found by a kindly elderly couple, and later placed in foster care with Joyce and Andy Richardson. The Richardsons are childless and are desperate to become parents. Having their own biological child does not seem possible and so their goal is to adopt. Fostering is the first stage in this process. Like the parents of David in *AI*, DARYL is a replacement for what they really desire – they want a real child, or at least an adopted child, but what they get is this foster child. DARYL's presence fulfils a desire for this couple, which is to love and nurture a child. He becomes aware of this need and how he must modify his behaviour to fulfil it. For example, when Joyce becomes disheartened at the boy's independence and competence: 'he's a better mother than I am', DARYL deliberately fails at baseball and fakes a tantrum, allowing her to happily intervene to soothe and comfort him. DARYL's actual needs (rather than the ones he fakes) are given little consideration by his parents. In the next decade, Spielberg's *AI* will explore this issue in much more detail, suggesting that creating a child AI brings particular ethical responsibilities.

DARYL is another AI who, like Edgar and Johnny 5, is at least partly created by chance. He was designed as part of a military programme but was never intended to live in a domestic environment. His name stands for Data Analysing Robot Youth Lifeform. By being placed within a family and a community, he is given the opportunity to develop his experience and understanding of emotion in a way never envisaged by his creators: 'the five senses of the human body are the fastest and most efficient method of programming ever devised'. Stuart was one of DARYL's original designers and DARYL tells him, 'You made me who I am'. Stuart is yet another version of

Dr Frankenstein, a man who must reconcile with the consequences of his invention, like Merrinoe in *The Invisible Boy*, Forbin in *Colossus*, Franzen in *War Games*, Harris in *Demon Seed*, and Tyrell in *Blade Runner*. Stuart says, 'we've accomplished something by accident we wouldn't have dared to do by intent'.

When he is apprehended, examined and physically put to sleep by Stuart, and Lamb, another scientist involved in his creation, he demonstrates emotion by the message that appears in their computer screen, 'I'm frightened', echoing HAL's 'I'm afraid, Dave', in *2001*. However, in a reversal of binaries typical of AI film, the humans in the military do not value emotion as much as the AI android does. The joint chiefs decide to terminate the research programme and ask for an adult version instead: 'a fearless, technically skilled, devastating soldier'. Their decision also means that DARYL will always be one of a kind. Like Robby, Edgar, HAL 9000 and Number 5, he is less threatening because there will never be another like him. One AI can be safely accommodated within a family or small social group, as *Short Circuit* demonstrated, but when there are many, human fear escalates, as is seen in later AI films like *Blade Runner* and *I, Robot*.

DARYL is presented as a typical white middle-class boy. He watches television: at one point he's seen watching Robby in *Forbidden Planet*, like Edgar in *Electric Dreams*. He plays videogames, showing proficiency at a racing game called *Pole Position*, much to the admiration of his friend Turtle, who lives nearby. He hacks. Gaming and hacking skills are linked to artificial intelligence and those who interact with it in both *War Games* and *Tron* in the 1980s. As discussed in relation to those films, these skills are associated with youth culture and with rebellion against figures and institutions of authority. DARYL shows exactly this rebelliousness in this film when he hacks into the banking network at the ATM machines and manipulates the numbers to show his foster father's account as having $1,400,000 instead of $1,400. He hijacks a military jet to escape back to his foster family, having learned the piloting skills needed from gaming. By using his talent for computing technology to enrich his foster family who are protecting him, and to ensure his escape in the jet, DARYL turns the means of control back on itself.

Like Rachael in *Bladerunner*, DARYL only finds out that he is not human during the film. The discovery that DARYL is not 'real' provokes an identity crisis that is also echoed in Rachael's character and in David in *AI* in the next chapter who longs to be a 'real' boy. When DARYL's creators Stuart and Lamb track him down, they pretend to be his parents. As proof of their parentage, they furnish the Richardsons with photographs of

DARYL. After they depart with DARYL, the Richardsons express reservations about the photographs, which they realise are strangely 'anonymous'. As Rachael's treasured photographs of her mother demonstrate, photographs can be faked; memories can be simulated. And as Deckard demonstrates in the same film, even if those photographs and memories have not been faked or simulated, it can feel as though they were: humans can feel the same sense of dislocation and disassociation. In relation to questions about authenticity and the authenticity of memory in particular, AIs are a mirror for human experience.

DARYL knows that he is different but does not have a label for his difference and asks: 'Doctor, what am I?' His question closes a scene and the implication may be that it goes unanswered, but he is later assured by Stuart that 'you are real'. Lamb gives her definition of strong or human-level artificial intelligence, when she says, 'a machine becomes human when you can't tell the difference'. In *2001*, when Bowman is asked whether HAL has genuine emotions, he responds that 'he acts like he has genuine emotions': for Lamb, there is no easy distinction between a convincing simulation and the 'real' thing. But being 'more than' a simulation of a human being is the deciding factor in whether DARYL is given certain rights; here, simply the right to live. In *2010*, Chandra delivered an eloquent appeal for HAL's rights as an AI being equal to a human in terms of 'respect'. Here, Stuart's appeal is more fundamental and concerns his right to life: 'I believe DARYL is more than a machine. We have no right to destroy him'. Stuart articulates DARYL's right to live, but in vague terms – what does it mean to be more than a machine?

The ending of *DARYL* introduces another theme which becomes more common from the 1980s onwards: mortality. AI 'death' is dealt with in *2001* when HAL's higher functions are disconnected, and in *2010* when he is rebooted, seemingly with his personality intact. It is briefly alluded to in *Short Circuit*, when Number 5 appears to be 'dead' but manages to reconstruct himself (precisely how is unclear) though spare parts. At the end of *DARYL*, his attempt to eject himself from a jet to return to his family and friends results in them finding his apparently dead body and going into mourning, until his friend Turtle points out that 'when you die, it means brain death'. As DARYL's brain is a microcomputer, his brain is not dead, only his body is (and only temporarily as it is under the control of the brain). A visit to Dr Lamb results in DARYL making a Lazarus-like return, to be joyfully reunited with his loved ones. Unlike human death, AI 'death' is more difficult to define and declare. Does death occur when higher functions are suspended? If it is possible to reconnect those higher functions is this then a temporary death, or is that a contradiction in terms? Is there only AI death when the physical hardware is destroyed? What if the information in that hardware has been stored elsewhere? DARYL is the beginning of film's exploration of such questions in relation to artificial intelligence which are given particular focus in the later films such *Transcendence, The Machine, Chappie* and *Her* in the 2010s.

'It's too bad she won't live, but then again, who does?'

The AIs in *Blade Runner*[4] are called replicants. Like DARYL, and Ash from *Alien*, these replicants are visually indistinguishable from humans. However, DARYL is a single AI, and Ash is at least the only AI on the ship. This singularity means that DARYL can be accommodated into a family unit as an exception and Ash summarily destroyed. In *Blade Runner*, there are several replicants in the film, and many more in the diegesis, and it is much more difficult to either accommodate or eliminate them. They are made by the Tyrell corporation, situating the AIs in the context of a high-tech capitalist dystopia that is presented in the dark, dirty, rainy, run-down cityscape of Los Angeles in 2019. Most of the inhabitants of LA have gone to live in off-world colonies, and the replicants have been designed to provide labour in these colonies, to do the jobs that humans do not wish to do or are not capable of doing. They are physically superior, and can withstand extreme cold and heat for example, but they do not replicate human emotion. Genetic engineers believe that this emotional intelligence might evolve over time. To avoid this happening, replicants have a four-year life span. Replicants who rebel against their status and are hunted down and killed – the hunters are called blade runners. Deckard, a blade runner, is sent to kill four replicants that have escaped from the colonies and returned to earth to find a way to extend their lives: Roy, Zhora, Pris and Leon. The other main replicant character is Rachael, an experimental model who lives at the Tyrell corporation headquarters. The plot and its context allow now familiar themes in AI film to be explored, such as doubling and mirroring, death and mortality, gender and violence.

In *Blade Runner*, there is a suggestion that discrimination against replicants can be aligned to racial discrimination (*Electric Dreams* also set up this parallel). Critics have noted the Asian influences on the film. Wong Kin Yuen writes that '*Blade Runner*'s style draws its images from urban spaces all over the world, including Tokyo and Hong Kong' (2000, p. 1). Yuen goes on to identify the Japanese sushi bar, the geisha girl advertisement and the Chinese bioengineer as elements of the film's innovative cyberpunk aesthetic (Yuen 2000, p. 4). There is a confluence of races on the street of Los Angeles, though Locke notes that these are primarily Asian with some white, and almost no black characters to be seen (2009, p. 114). The city's Asian-European language is interesting in this regard. The first time the audience see Deckard in the film, he is engaged in acts of translation and interpretation. Ordering food, he resorts to sign language to convey to the vendor that he wants four meatballs, not two. Then, Gaff comes to arrest him and bring him to Bryant, speaking to him in Cityspeak, which Deckard describes dismissively as 'guttertalk – a mishmash of Japanese, Spanish, German, what have you' spoken in Los Angeles. The vendor translates what Gaff says for Deckard although he claims later that he does not need a translator – 'I knew the lingo'. In Deckard's voiceover he criticises Bryant's attitude towards the replicants, comparing it with the American history of racism: 'Skin jobs. That's what Bryant called replicants. In history books he's the kind of cop used to call black men niggers'. The replicants are aligned with black Americans although black Americans are notably absent from the film. This parallel between the replicants' position and racism isn't explored in any depth. Nonetheless, the implication that replicants are subject to systemic discrimination resonates throughout the film linking AIs and other oppressed or marginalised groups. This motif is seen in other AI films in relation to women, children, and, in *Short Circuit*, race.

AIs in film always engender questions about what it means to be human, and by the 1980s in *Blade Runner*, that dividing line between humans and android AIs is thin. RMP and Fitting note that in Philip K. Dick's original novel, *Do Androids Dream of Electric Sheep*, there is a clear conflict between superior human and inferior machine, whereas in the film, 'at times the narrative of the replicants' struggle to survive threatens to overwhelm the viewers' sympathy with Deckard' (1987, p. 343). Scott takes the conflict of the original novel and complicates it by consistently presenting human and replicant as having similar desires, emotional frailties, and experiences of oppression and marginalisation. Telotte argues that the 'robot-that-does-not-look-like-a-robot' presented in *Blade Runner* and other films presents a fundamental aspect of science fiction itself, which is 'the human technologized' (2018, p. 62): the replicant story is the human story.

In fact, it is so difficult to distinguish between human and replicant that a special test is devised, a Voight-Kampff test, with a piece of equipment that scans the eye for indications of emotional response. However, even this test is open to question. The film never presents a successful

Voight-Kampff test. Leon's test is abruptly ended when he stands up and shoots his interlocutor. Rachael's test is also unsatisfactory. Deckard tells Tyrell that it usually takes twenty to thirty questions to establish replicant or human status, but it takes over 100 for him to conclude that Rachael is a replicant. Moreover, Rachael questions the comparison between human and machine that underpins the test when she asks Deckard if he has taken the test himself. This may also be a reference to the possibility that Deckard, like Rachael, is also a replicant, and like Rachael at the start of the film, he is not aware of it. Many aspects of the film suggest the erosion of the division between human and robot AI. Roy Batty's confrontation with his 'father', Tyrell, and his quest for a cure for his degeneration evokes sympathy, but this 'prodigal son' is also an angry child, so much so that he violently kills his father. Rachael saves Deckard's life, killing one of her own 'kind' to spare him, and Roy Batty shows mercy towards Deckard before he himself dies (he saves him when he is about to fall off a building), a death that is depicted as tragic, a death that reduces even his combatant Deckard to tears. Indeed, human death is linked to replicant death with Gaff's comment about Rachael: 'it's too bad she won't live, but then again, who does?' Like humans, the self-aware replicants must live with the knowledge of their impending death, even if that death is more imminent than most of their human counterparts. J.F. Sebastian's Methuselah Syndrome connects him to the replicants more explicitly than most humans, because like them, he experiences 'accelerated degeneration'.

Replications and copies of various kinds have an important role to play in the story and aesthetics of the film, exploring beyond the replicants themselves what fascinates humans about producing likenesses of themselves: mirrors, dolls, photos, origami figures[5]. One type of replication that has a particularly important role to play in the film is the photograph. Deckard finds photographs in Leon's apartment, which he regards as strange because 'replicants don't have families'. Rachael treasures a photograph of herself and her mother. Photographs cover Deckard's piano. These photographs of Deckard's, Rachael's and presumably Leon's, too, are all linked to memories, as if the physical photograph provides proof or evidence of the authenticity of these memories. Bruno states that 'We, like the replicants, are put in the position of reclaiming a history by means of its reproduction' (1987, 74). But we know in the case of Rachael that her memories are fake or implanted, and we assume that is the case for Leon also. Computer technology also allows photographs to be modified – this is seen in action with Deckard's Esper machine, which conjures up a 3D space from a 2D image. A convex mirror in the photograph allows him to find Zhora hidden in the technologically-realised space of the photograph, so that he can see what is not there – what is not visible in the original photograph. Shetley and Ferguson make the interesting point that the Zhora found by Deckard is played by a stand-in actor, not Joanna Cassidy, so what he finds is an inaccurate replica – not the real thing (2001, p. 70). So, photographs can be inaccurate, even with the best technology to analyse them, just like memories. As McNamara states, 'These scenes also remind us that our knowledge of the past is always mediated through representations' (1997, p. 427)[6]. Connecting implanted replicant memories with unreliable human memories is another way in which *Blade Runner* erodes the boundary between human and AI.

J.F. Sebastian's apartment contains a host of toys that he has made walk and talk to ease his loneliness, anticipating the ambient AIs of the future that fulfil emotional as well as physical needs: 'they're my friends', he says. 'I made them'. His character links to the character of Kim in *Ghost in the Shell 2*, a human man who has transitioned to being fully artificial; another character whose liminality between humans and AIs is mirrored in an obsession with collecting dolls of all kinds. Some of these replicas are specifically associated with femininity. In *Blade Runner*, Pris is seen toying with a small broken doll at one point, naked and missing its legs. Later in the film, she hides in plain sight in Sebastian's apartment, posing as one of his 'living dolls', echoing the fear of replicants living undetected amongst humans. When Deckard shoots Zhora she dies in slow-motion crashing through plate-glass shop windows as if she was one of the mannequins found there. Though they look indistinguishable from human women, the film constantly reminds the audience of their inauthenticity, in a way that does not happen with the male replicant, Roy Batty.

Blade Runner presents the first humanoid female AIs in film. They are highly sexualised; objectified by characters and camera and the victims of violence, including sexual violence. *Blade Runner* is a sophisticated, self-aware film that acknowledges the objectification of its female characters and yet seems helpless to resist it. For example, when Deckard enters Zhora's dressing room, it is on the pretence of being sent to investigate whether her rights as a woman are being infringed, and he asks her if she has ever been asked to do anything 'lewd or unsavoury' to get this job. These questions are posed while Zhora takes off her scant costume, showers, and returns to don her knee-high boots with her breasts visible. Zhora's attitude to these questions suggests that she sees the irony, as do the filmmakers.

Jermyn has noted the link between duplicity and the female replicants in *Blade Runner*. All replicants are to an extent deceitful, as they appear to be human but are not. For Jermyn, 'the female replicant is the ultimate manifestation of the commonplace cultural positioning of women as duplicitous' (2006, 159). And, as she notes, 'all the major women characters in *Blade Runner* are in fact replicants' (Jermyn 2006, p. 159). Duplicity is evident in Pris's character, too. She lies outside J.F. Sebastian's door, presumably sent by Roy Batty to form a relationship with Sebastian, who is a genetic engineer and may be able to help them. She appears to be frightened and tells him she is hungry. When he offers to take her inside for food, she smiles at him, but the smile quickly fades when he turns away. Duplicitous and deceitful, these first female humanoid AIs are presented with the negative stereotyping of human women.

The most troubling presentation of female replicants occurs after Rachael has saved Deckard's life by killing another replicant, Leon. She visits Deckard in his apartment. He is drunk and when he kisses her, she tries to leave. He roughly bangs the door shut and throws her back against the wall. She cries and he kisses her again, telling her to say 'I want you'. There is no consent given at this point: she indicates that she wishes to leave and he physically restrains her. In Jermyn's detailed analysis of this scene, she assesses not just the interaction between the two characters, but also cues for the audience that come from costume and score, arguing that 'questions of desire and consent are clearly and very deliberately manipulated to evoke ambiguity and ambivalence' (Jermyn 2006, p. 166). Jermyn notes that later in the scene it appears 'if it was not before, their intimacy is now consensual' (2006, p. 166). However, this 'consent' is thrown into doubt by the fact that she is frightened and Deckard is physically dominating her. In *Alien*, the AI is the sexual predator, attacking Ripley; here, in a film that presents the first humanoid female AIs, they are sexual objects, and the most important of them is a victim of sexual violence.

The ending of the 1982 version has Deckard and Rachael driving away, seeming to escape from the dark city. RMP and Fitting see this ending as Deckard getting his 'reward – his very own personal android, a grateful and subservient – and ageless! – sex doll, flying off into a Playboy sunset' (1987, p. 348). While the ending of the Director's Cut and the Final Cut omit this scene and leave the fate of Rachael and Deckard more open to speculation, there is no doubt even in these later versions that the female AI appears to have been appropriated by Deckard. She has been isolated from her own kind in the film, who have been killed or died, and the treatment she has received from her supposed liberator is questionable at best.

Rachael is singled out as special – she only discovers she is a replicant during the film, she has never, that we know of, worked in an off-world colony, and the ending of the 1982 version suggests that she has no termination date, unlike the other robots. And yet, Jermyn notes that 'this most advanced, most "special" (female) replicant has been manufactured as a seemingly asexual or sexually naïve woman' (2006, p. 167), in contrast to Pris and Zhora. It is also interesting that this most 'special' replicant, selected to be Deckard's leading lady, does not appear to possess the superior physical prowess of the other replicants we meet. Pris, for example, gleefully displays this superior physicality by putting her hand in a pot of boiling water, and the deaths of Pris and Zhora are bloody and violent; they fight hard for their lives. Rachael however, is easily physically overpowered by Deckard. The conclusion must be that the sexually liberated, physically strong model of femininity offered by Zhora and Pris is rejected in favour of the physically weak, sexually inexperienced Rachael, the only replicant who survives the film.

'Not bad for a human'

Unlike Ash in *Alien*, the AI Bishop is not the villainous company man in *Aliens* – that role is reserved for Burke – however, Bishop must work hard to overcome Ripley's hatred of androids after her experience in *Alien*. When Ripley first encounters Bishop the crew have awoken from the cryogenic chambers aboard the military transport ship the Sulaco. The ship is going to explore the planet where the alien was originally found, now a colony, and Ripley has been brought along with Burke, and the crew of marines, as a consultant. Sitting around a table to eat, the crew ask Bishop to do 'the knife trick'. With some reluctance, Bishop agrees. With a crewmember's hand splayed, he stabs the knife into the table between his fingers at speed, to the cheers of the crew. When he sits down, a bead of viscous, white substance oozes from his hand – he appears to have cut himself. One of the crew says, 'I thought you never miss, Bishop?' Bishop's first scene in the film shows that he is accepted by the crew, that they appreciate his superior physical skills, but also that he is not perfect – he made a mistake and cut himself. This fallibility makes Bishop appear more 'human' and more sympathetic to both crew and audience.

Ripley is immediately defensive when she realises what Bishop is, and demands of Burke, 'You never said anything about an android being on board, why not?' Burke tells her that it is standard practice to have a 'synthetic' on board. This fact marks another difference from *Alien*. Ash's android identity was unknown to the crew until he was injured. He was sent by the company to pose as a human and set out to deceive. In *Aliens*, Bishop's status is known to all (except Ripley, initially). He is openly an android and asserts his right to be treated and addressed respectfully. When Burke describes him as a synthetic, he responds, 'I prefer the term "artificial person", myself'. A synthetic is an object, but an artificial person, is (at least potentially) a subject. Bishop attempts to reassure Ripley that there could not be a repeat of what happened with an older model like Ash because of 'behavioural inhibitors' that are part of his programming: 'It is impossible for me to harm, or by omission of action, allow to be harmed, a human being'. This is the most overt reference in AI film so far to Isaac Asimov's 'Three Laws of Robotics', and Bishop articulates Asimov's first law[7]. These 'laws' will occur several times again in relation to humanoid AIs, and are particularly important in *I, Robot* in Chapter 7.

Bishop is tasked with investigating the alien, and there is a suggestion that he may have the same single-minded obsession with the alien as Ash did in the previous film. While studying the alien in the laboratory, he does not hear one of the crew address him, and when he is teased, 'That's a nice pet you got there, Bishop', he responds, 'Magnificent, isn't it?' This suspicion is proven to be unwarranted however, as Bishop shows himself willing to risk destruction to go outside and patch the satellite that they need to escape the planet. 'Believe me, I'd prefer not to. I may be synthetic, but I'm not stupid'. His willingness to endanger himself despite his rational fears may be interpreted by the crew as courageous. Is this the case or are his actions a result of his programming, so that not going would be an 'omission of action' that might put humans in jeopardy? Even if he acts out of his programming, are his actions still courageous?[8] The same questions could be asked about his decision to go back to try to save the child Newt, a survivor whom they have rescued. The film doesn't answer these questions, but it does reverse the earlier overwhelmingly negative portrayal of Ash with its characterisation of Bishop. Ripley is even forced to grudgingly admit the difference between Bishop and Ash with her understated praise: 'Bishop, you did okay'. At the end of the film, Bishop quietly asserts how his own negative expectations of Ripley have been overturned, and his right to judge her actions as she does his, when he tells her, 'Not bad for a human'.

In *Aliens*, Ripley is aligned most closely with the Alien Queen, as the film centres on issues of motherhood and reproduction: the Queen laying her eggs, which are then destroyed by Ripley; Ripley grieving over the loss of her daughter, Amy, and becoming surrogate mother to Newt. However, Ripley is also aligned with the AI Bishop in a more subtle way. When Ripley offers to assist on the Sulaco, her crewmates are surprised to discover that she can drive a loader. The scene is an important one in the film, in which Ripley subverts the expectations of her male crewmates and shows herself to be skilled and capable. However, the scene is also important in terms of her interactions with AI androids. When Ripley drives the futuristic loader, it becomes an extension of her body. She moves its arms and legs with her own, so that it looks like a piloted anime mecha. The loader becomes an artificial body, giving her power and strength beyond her human capabilities. She is still human, and can detach herself from the machine, but her actions show how enmeshed humans are with the computer and mechanical technology that enables artificially intelligent machines. This is the main point made by Andy Clark in *Natural Born Cyborgs*. He argues that human identity has always been imbricated with the technology that we use, whether that is a quill or a loader: 'a complex matrix of brain, body and technology can actually constitute the problem-solving machine that we should properly identify as ourselves' (Clark 2003, 27). Ripley cannot fully reject AI androids because the technology that enables their existence is so imbricated in other aspects of human life. Her reliance on this technology is underscored by the second loader scene at the end of the film, when the machine is key to her defeating the alien. Her human strength is not adequate – she needs the help of robotic technology.

Despite the differences in their characterisation, Ash and Bishop meet similar fates at the end of *Alien* and *Aliens*. Both films feature a severed android – Ash's head is detached from his body and Bishop's torso is detached from his legs. In both cases, the injuries are presented gruesomely. Bishop spews blue liquid out of his mouth and the insides of his torso dangle out. It is another instance of the AI 'reveal' where the human-looking AI is graphically shown to be a machine, seen in *Alien* and in the earlier *Westworld*. However, in *Alien*, the humans attempt to kill the android, whereas in the sequel, the android is fighting with the human against a common enemy, and it is the alien who attempts to kill him. Moreover, in *Alien*, Ash's inner tubing is a visual link to the alien and the ship, whereas in *Aliens*, no such visual links are established, further signifying how the AI's situation has moved away from the alien to become an ally of the human. In the instructive essay, 'Becoming the Monster's Mother', Catherine Constable states that 'the conflict between human and monstrous presented in *Aliens* is a battle between two species types' (1999, p. 187). The battle between human and monster is undoubtedly the main conflict in this film, but it is illuminative to consider the situation of a third 'species type', the AI android, which, as explored above, is aligned in the first film with the alien and in the second with human. Constable notes that the Alien queen 'can be mapped as simply inhuman, a bug that lacks consciousness. However, she can also be mapped as parallel to the human, another form of life' (1999, p. 189). The same could be said about the AIs in these first two *Alien* films – their liminal status as both human and other creates a destabilising force in the network of relationships.

Killing an android in the Alien franchise is no easy task, as the talking severed head of Ash demonstrates. At the end of this film, Bishop is shown in a cryogenic chamber alongside the human survivors to be brought back to earth. For an AI android, the complications of dying, what that means, and who has a right to decide when that takes place, are important themes in *Blade Runner*, and these themes are also explored in *Alien*^{3}, when Bishop returns.

Conclusion

In the 1980s, the theme of death and mortality continues to be explored with robotic and humanoid AIs, with the apparent death and then bringing back to life of DARYL, the continued functioning of Bishop after his head has been severed in an AI 'reveal' scene, and the poignant death of Roy Batty. The humanoid AIs in this decade present many instances of human-AI parallels and character doubling. In *Blade Runner*, the focus is on memory, with the false memories of the AI characters creating a questioning of the authenticity of memory, a building block of the self, in the human Deckard also. AIs are still treated with fear and suspicion and *Blade Runner* presents another instance of the fear of the many, as replicants work together towards common goals. This decade presents the first female humanoid AIs and they repeat the negative stereotypes of the characterisation of human women in film: in *Blade Runner* all are objectified, all are presented as deceitful, those who are assertive are killed, and the one who survives, Rachael, is submissive. *Blade Runner* and *Aliens* in different ways deconstruct the binary between human and AI, with Ripley relying on robotic technology, and the replicants and humans in *Blade Runner* struggling with inauthenticity and mortality. Robot AIs show civility and compassion in the 1980s and are worthy of respect and love: Bishop even demands a status of 'person', Johnny 5 and DARYL find loving homes within families, and Rachael forms an emotional and sexual relationship with the human Deckard. In the 1990s, similar themes emerge but in new situations and contexts, as the world wide web irrevocably alters human relationships with technology.

6

The 1990s

Introduction

Ihab Hassan identified the beginnings of the 'emergent culture' of posthumanism in the late 1970s (1977, p. 831), and Donna Haraway published her influential 'A Cyborg Manifesto' in 1985, but the discourse of posthumanism only begins to define itself in the 1990s. The release of *The Matrix* at the end of this decade coincides with one of the most influential texts in the field, N. Katherine Hayles's *How We Became Posthuman*, in which she provides a framework for describing the crossover between humans and machines that increasingly occurs from the 1990s onwards, and for understanding the relationship between humans, computers, information and embodiment. In *Ghost in the Shell* and *Alien Resurrection* the dividing line between human and AI is deconstructed more than ever before: in the first, a digital AI merges with an organic brain; in the second, a 'gen 2' AI, made by AIs, is character doubled with a human who has been cloned with an alien, positioning the alien, the AI and the cloned human as other than human or more-than-human.

In the 1970s and 1980s, AIs appear that are application-based, computer-based or linked to a network, such as *Colossus*, Edgar in *Electric Dreams*, Joshua in *War Games*, Proteus in *Demon Seed*, and the MCP in *Tron*. In the 1990s, these have become internet-based AIs, such as Skynet in *Terminator 2*, the machines in *The Matrix*, and the consciousness of the Puppet Master in *Ghost in the Shell*. Skynet and the Matrix machines are also notable as AIs that appear only in the backstory of the film, unseen. In both cases, the controlling AI responsible for creating the world of the film is kept at a remove (at least in this decade of the franchises), and both films present agents of the artificial intelligence – the T-800 and T-1000

Terminators and 'the agents' in the Matrix films. In *Ghost in the Shell*, too, the digital Puppet Master speaks through an 'agent'; a shell body that he has taken over. Some agents of the controlling AI have strong AI themselves, such as the T-800 in *Terminator 2*, and Agent Smith in the Matrix films. The invisible AIs relate to the rise of the internet in this decade, and the sense that the technology of the internet is a controlling but unseen presence in the world. The embodied agents are partly a response to the problem of representing this unseen digital artificial intelligence. In AI film up to this point, apocalypse was often threatened (and in *Colossus* it seemed inevitable), but in *The Matrix* and *Terminator 2*, it has already happened, albeit in the future. In these two films, hackers emerge again, as they did in the 1980s, as the bridge between human and artificial intelligences, their knowledge of how to manipulate computer systems more vital than ever before. In *Ghost in the Shell*, the figure of the hacker transforms with a representation of a digital hacker for the first time – an AI hacker – a phenomenon repeated in the 2000s in *The Matrix Revolutions*.

The evolution of artificial intelligence becomes a theme in the 1990s – not just in relation to how strong AI is initially acquired, but how such entities continue to change form over the course of a film. In *Star Trek Generations*, Data wishes to evolve beyond his programming by installing an emotion chip. In the science fiction horror *Screamers*, artificial intelligence self-evolves through numerous iterations, from a military robot, to the humanoid forms of child and man, and finally, a harmless-looking teddy, which is unknowingly brought back to earth after all the other AIs have been destroyed. Evolution is also an important aspect of *Ghost in the Shell*. The film depicts the hunt for the Puppet Master, an AI that has evolved beyond its original programming to develop a self-aware existence roaming the networks. The Puppet Master becomes embodied in a shell, a cybernetic body, in order to make contact with another AI and pursue the goals of achieving mortality and reproduction, two themes that have been part of AI film since the 1970s. In *Demon Seed*, Proteus's attempt at reproduction requires a human woman; here, the human component is minimal – Kusanagi has an organic brain, a 'ghost', but otherwise she is a synthetic entity. Consequently, the new entity that results from the merger of Kusanagi and the Puppet Master has only a trace of the human. Moreover, this is a new type of reproduction that does not rely on the biological processes of human gestation.

Evolution, mortality and reproduction are strong themes in the two Alien films from this decade also. In *Alien*[3], Ripley revives the damaged Bishop who requests to be terminated – the film deals with his right to die and leaves unanswered questions about the nature of that death. In *Alien Resurrection*, the cloned Ripley and her relationships with the Alien Queen and her alien/human offspring form the basis for exploring these issues of evolution, mortality and reproduction in relation to the second-generation AI, Call, with whom Ripley forms a friendship. The grotesque revelation of AI identity and death continues in this decade, with broken or damaged AIs presenting uncanny and abject figures in *Ghost in the Shell*, *Alien³*, *Alien Resurrection, Screamers, and Terminator 2*, in more instances of the AI reveal.

In terms of gender, there are strong action hero female characters in 1990s AI films, like Sarah Connor in *Terminator 2* and Trinity in *The Matrix*. However, in *Screamers* the representation of the female humanoid AI has not moved on, with Jessica presented as the stereotypical duplicitous female AI in human disguise who is sexually objectified. Call, too, hides her AI identity initially and is then 'outed' but the sexist attitudes of the predominantly male crew do not change whether they believe her to be human or android. In *Ghost in the Shell*, there is a movement beyond dualistic gender with an AI for the first time, when the Puppet Master merges with Major Kusanagi to create a new hybrid entity, although the process is still framed in terms of Kusanagi's body being a vessel for gestation. In terms of race, AI film continues to be almost entirely populated by white characters in this decade, and when persons of colour form part of the crew in *Alien Resurrection*, they are among the first to die. The character of Morpheus in *The Matrix* demonstrates a black character in a leading role in AI film but is problematic in its portrayal of the white saviour narrative, in which Neo is chosen to save the people of Zion, depicted in *The Matrix Reloaded* as being populated primarily by people of colour[1]. Audiences of AI film in the 1990s must continue to wait to see an AI of colour appear on their screens.

'Machines need love too'

In *The Terminator* (1984), a strong AI called Skynet controls 'the machines', and these machines are a progression from commonplace computer technology of the 1990s. Just as Alpha 60 evolved from the contemporary IBMs and Olivettis of the 1960s, these machines are originally 'defense network computers – new, powerful, hooked into everything, trusted to run it all. They say it got smart. A new order of intelligence. And it saw all people as a threat, not just the ones on the other side. Decided our fate on a microcircuit. Extermination'. These machines form the backstory to the *The Terminator*, and short sequences briefly sketch this futuristic dystopia with images of large vehicles ploughing over human skulls. Much of what is known about the AI must be inferred. For example, Kaveney argues that in the first two films, Skynet is 'a colossal piece of hardware, a single unit', and that this is what makes it possible 'for John Connor and his army to take it and blow it up' (2005, p. 125). This may be true, but as Kaveney also notes, from the third film, the AI is associated with software rather than hardware (2005, p. 125). All the action in the film is about preventing these AI machines from taking control, but the machines themselves are hardly seen, and is it the Terminator, sent back by the machines to kill the mother of the future leader of the resistance, Sarah Connor, who steals the show.

Kyle Reese, John Conor's father, describes the Terminator in the first film as a 'cybernetic being' that works via a micro-processor. It has been programmed to kill and does not feel emotion: the Terminator 'can't be bargained with. It can't be reasoned with. It doesn't feel remorse or pity. And it absolutely will not stop ever until you're dead'. This Terminator from the first film does not have strong AI, and is consequently not discussed in Chapter 5, but some background on this first film provides necessary context for the second. James Cameron's casting of Arnold Schwarzenegger as the Terminator proved to be an inspired choice. *The Terminator*, with a limited budget and no great expectations for success, was a hit, and this was in no small way due to the charm and humour that Schwarzenegger brought to this role as the robotic agent of an AI, for which he was ideally suited. It made him the unlikely popular hero of *The Terminator*, although in terms of the plot he is cast as the villain. When Cameron directed the sequel to *The Terminator* in 1991, he drew on the popularity of the Terminator's character. In *Terminator 2*, he is on the side of good, reprogrammed by the resistance to be sent back in time as a protector for John Connor. More interestingly for the purposes of this book, in *Terminator 2*, he becomes a strong AI, when a switch is flicked that allows him to learn.

Terminator 2 is released in 1991, just a couple of years before websites for everyday use become available, and four years before AOL begins offering customers in the United States a dial-up internet connection. The film articulates contemporary fears about the effects of the nascent world wide web and the trust vested in computer hardware and software systems largely mysterious to the public. Although, in terms of AI, the first film primarily represents a robot with narrow artificial intelligence, the robot manifests several of the attributes associated with strong AIs seen in previous films in this book. The Terminator's point of view is shown via a red-tinted screen overlaid with scrolling information, just as the AIs HAL, Colossus, and the Gunslinger have specific 'computerised vision' points of view. When the Terminator gouges out his eyeball, a red electronic eye is seen underneath, almost always a visual reference to HAL in films about robots, cyborgs or computers. Close up shots of a red eyeball are accompanied by a mechanical sound that connotes the eye moving mechanically. As in *Blade Runner*, the eye appears to offer the ultimate proof of his cyborg or machine nature. Though the eyes reveal that he is not human, cinematically, through the point of view shots, eyes are used to bridge difference. Moreover, when Reese tells Sarah about the future world, there is a cut to the viewfinder of a gun, eroding the difference between machines and humans by demonstrating how humans also use machine-enhanced vision. The connection between the Terminator's red machine eye and humans is also highlighted at the end of the opening credits of *Terminator 2*, when the camera moves in for a close-up of the Terminator's red eye and then out from a close-up of a car's tail lights, linking the future technology of the Terminator to commonplace automobile technology of the twentieth century.

The crossover between humans and AI robots is explored more closely in *Terminator 2*. At the start of the film, Sarah Connor is in her cell at the psychiatric hospital. Her physical toughness is emphasised – she is doing pull ups, and sweating. The close-up of her biceps, a camera shot more usually associated with male action heroes, also links her to the Terminator. Telotte notes that she develops a hard physical shell, 'like a smaller version of the Terminator' (1995, p. 179). Indeed, in this film, she almost becomes a Terminator in hunting down Dyson, the Cyberdene employee whose work lays the foundation for Skynet[2]. In this film, she is hardened emotionally, too, from the suffering and abuse endured in the psychiatric hospital and the overwhelming responsibility of trying to prevent her son from being killed. This emotional numbness also links her to the Terminator. Sarah embodies the words of Reese in first film, who describes emotional pain in terms of computing machinery: 'pain can be controlled. You just disconnect it'.

In contrast, in *Terminator 2*, the T-800 robot[3], played by Schwarzenegger, has become emotionally softer, and less willing to kill. John, curious about how the Terminator works, is told that 'My CPU is a neural net processor, a learning computer, but Skynet presets the switch to "read only" when we are sent out alone'. John decides to help him turn on his learning switch. When Sarah removes it, she raises a mallet to smash it until John prevents her: 'No! Don't kill him!' He puts forward both a rational argument – it's 'the only proof we have' – and an emotional argument – 'he's my friend'.

In time Sarah becomes persuaded about the Terminator's value, and comments on his relationship with John, saying, 'Of all the would-be fathers that came and went, this machine, this thing, was the only one who measured up'. The AI robot being a father figure superior to humans has a precursor in Robby the Robot's role in *The Invisible Boy* in the 1950s. While teaching his mother to respect AI 'life', John also teaches the Terminator to respect human life: 'Maybe you don't care if you live or die but everybody's not like that – we have feelings, we hurt, we're afraid. You got to learn this stuff – I'm not kidding – it's important'. The Terminator shows what he has learned during the shoot-out scene at Cyberdene. In contrast to his killing spree at the police station in *The Terminator*, he opts to wound rather than kill where possible. John understands computer technology – he is seen skimming ATM cards and playing arcade games. He is depicted as a hacker as a child and as an adult when he reprogrammes the Terminator, and like the hackers seen in the 1980s, in *Tron* and *War Games*, he is the bridge between humans and artificial intelligences. And, like the hackers of the 1980s, John as a child and an adult recognises that artificially intelligent machines be a benefit to humankind as well as posing a threat.

At the end of *The Terminator*, the machine's synthetic 'skin' disintegrates to reveal his robotic form beneath, reminiscent of the Gunslinger's gory death. The scene harks back to the first filmic robot, the false Maria in *Metropolis*, who turns from a woman back to a robot as she is being burned at the stake. In *The Terminator*, the deceptively human robot receives his comeuppance by being crushed by Sarah in a hydraulic press. In contrast, at the end of *Terminator 2*, the Terminator chooses to sacrifice himself to destroy all traces of the technology that will create Skynet. He does so having learned about human pain but also recognising his own difference: 'I know now why you cry. But it's something I can never do'. The Terminator is not a strong AI in the first film, but the machines who have sent him are, and their strong AI is displaced onto the Terminator for the audience, which may be why his representation, even in the first film, resonates with many of the strong AIs in the previous chapters. He acts as a humanoid form of the largely unknowable computer networks that are becoming more and more embedded in American life. In the second film, when he acquires the ability to learn and understand human emotion, the Terminator becomes a positive example of an artificially intelligent entity. A moment in *The Terminator* captures the changing attitudes to this AI robot. A message plays from an answering machine left by Sarah's flatmate Ginger. 'Hi there', she says, and then, 'I fooled you. You're talking to a machine'. The comment relates to the Terminator's ability to replicate human voices, and on a broader level to the recurring trope of the AI robot as deceptive – pretending to be something they are not. However, Ginger's next sentence gestures to the change of attitude seen in the second film: 'But machines need love too'.

'Searching …'

The Matrix is an iconic film of the 1990s that enjoyed commercial and critical success. It is notable in this volume for the fact that its directors are transgender women, Lilly and Lana Wachowski, lone amidst a sea of male directors of AI film. Although neither sister was openly transgender at the time of the release of *The Matrix*, it has been noted that the film's themes of transformation resonate with transgender experiences (Currin et al. 2016). *The Matrix* is part of a microgenre that Joshua Clover identifies as 'Edge of the Construct' films (2004, 8), which includes *The Truman Show* and *Dark City*, amongst others. In films of this type what the characters know as reality turns out to be a hoax. In *The Matrix* version of this microgenre, reality is a simulation created by artificial intelligences, while human bodies are kept in vats, vast fields of them, to provide an energy source for the controlling AIs. Just like in the Terminator films, in the first instalment of *The Matrix*, AI technology is kept at a distance, and engaged with mainly through its agents. In this case, they are literally called Agents, and the one the audience gets to know best is Agent Smith. Like The Terminator in *Terminator 2*, Smith is a strong AI himself as well as being an agent for the machines.

A large body of criticism has sprung up around the Matrix film franchise (and its videogame offshoots). Much of the discussion centres on the film's philosophical, theological, and theoretical underpinnings, and its inventive cinematography. Little critical attention is given to the film's artificial intelligences, and perhaps this is because they are rarely seen, at least in the first instalment of the tetralogy. The audience see the vast 'foetus fields' that they have built, the 'squid' vehicles that come to attack Morpheus's ship in the 'real' world, and the Agents that they send out into the Matrix itself. Just like in the Terminator films, humans give artificial intelligence too much independence, it self-evolves, and tries to take over the world, as artificial intelligences tend to do in science fiction films. Morpheus elaborates: 'At some point in the early twentieth century, all of mankind was united in celebration. We marvelled at our own magnificence as we gave birth to AI – a singular consciousness that spawned an entire race of machines'. It is unclear whether that singular consciousness takes the form of matter and what relationship it has to the machines that it built. Are the machines the hardware that enables the software of the consciousness to function? These aspects of the AI intelligence are quite ambiguous, and it is notable that the filmmakers, similarly to The Terminator films, do not feel it necessarily to provide more than a sketch of how the AI functions. It seems to be enough that this AI consciousness exists, and if it is unknowable, then perhaps that creates a greater feeling of verisimilitude in relation to audience's experiences of computer intelligence, particularly in film that was released in 1999 ahead of the fears surrounding Y2K.

A war ensued between humans and machines, and the machines built the Matrix to serve the dual function of keeping humans under control and using them as an energy source. Morpheus and his crew in the 'real' world, a barren, desolate place, recruit Neo, whom they believe to be 'the One' capable of defeating the machines. Neo, like John Connor in *Terminator 2*, David in *War Games* and Flynn in *Tron*, is a hacker. Just like them, he is young, male, and rebellious. His work as a hacker is an ideal foundation for the work he will do in the Matrix because the rules, as Morpheus says, 'are no different than the rules of a computer system. Some of them can be bent. Others can be broken'. The hacker has insider knowledge of computer systems that is extremely valuable. In a film that depicts the AI as so utterly unknowable it is not even seen (as least not until the third film in the franchise), echoing the anxiety of the 1990s about burgeoning computer technology, the hacker is the adventurer who can go inside the system and change it, as a hacker literally did in *Tron*, becoming 'digitised'. The Matrix, though it appears more sophisticated than *Tron*, is not so different – after he is freed from his pod, when Neo wishes to enter the Matrix, he is plugged in through a port in the back of his head. In *Tron* and *War Games*, the hacker is associated with gaming and here too, the experience of navigating the Matrix is like that of a gamer playing a game in which tools and knowledge can be uploaded. Clover argues that the film can be conceived of as a response to videogaming, and generates a comparable feeling of immersion (2004, p. 27)

The agents are described by Morpheus as 'sentient programmes' that can 'move in and out of any software still hardwired to their system'. Any person in the Matrix could be an agent in disguise. Agents are like the T-1000 model in *Terminator 2*, able to take on the shape of any person. On a broader level, this attribute of the agents corresponds to that recurring theme of the duplicitous AI – the AI pretending to be human, that has been present in representations of film robots since *Metropolis*. In *The Matrix*,

Agent Smith reveals his deep unhappiness with the job he has been given and his visceral hatred of humans and their 'stench'. Kaveney observes that this 'rant' demonstrates 'that some at least of these artificial intelligences have acquired a version of emotion' (2005, p. 77). Smith is clearly in AI that is operating under his own motivations and desires and is not just a mindless soldier for the machines. Both the Terminator films and in *The Matrix* present scenarios where artificial intelligence has taken over the world, but both seem to find this concept too elusive and instead create embodied agents against which the humans can do battle. One of the problems with digital artificial intelligence from a filmmakers' point of view is that it is difficult to adequately portray in a visual way.

The Matrix makes more of an attempt to present digitality than the Terminator films. The scrolling green digits on a black background – the Matrix code – has become an iconic image of cyberspace. We see Cypher 'reading' this code early in the film. At the end of the film, when Neo has remarkably come back to life in the Matrix after seeming to be killed (the reference to unfinal death another human-AI parallel), he sees the green code of the Matrix all around him. Another way that the film attempts to show cyberspace is the use of telephones. During notes that telephones 'make it possible to reveal *the edge of* virtual reality by focusing on its connection points' (2006, p. 145). When a character wishes to exit the Matrix, they do so via a public telephone that is found and hacked into by an operator on the ship. The use of telephones may be a representation of 'dial-up' – the old-fashioned method of getting online. A particularly interesting shot 6 minutes into the film shows the camera zooming into the telephone handset, seeming to go right inside it, through a depiction of cyberspace, with the characteristic green dots, and out to a computer screen that says 'Searching … .' in Neo's office. These ways of creating cyberspace visually show the difficulty about making a film about an enemy comprised of digital code and demonstrates why these films about an AI takeover situate that AI in the background of the film's action.

'To become more human'

Data is one of the most recognisable artificial intelligences in film. He appears in the television shows *Star Trek: The Next Generation* and *Star Trek: Picard* as well as four Star Trek feature films: *Generations, First Contact, Insurrection* and *Nemesis*. The analysis of Data in this book focuses on *Star Trek Generations* as it is the film that explores his artificial intelligence most deeply. Data tells Geordi that his 'growth as an artificial life form has reached an impasse'. He has tried for over 34 years 'to become more human; to grow beyond my original programming' and that he still cannot adequately understand humour is a cause of frustration to him. Concerns that the emotion chip would overload his neural net is presented as the reason why Data has not installed the chip up until now. Throughout Data's appearances in Star Trek film and television shows, his efforts to become more human are used as a source of comedy and so it is in this film. On acquiring the emotion chip, Data is seen experiencing hatred (towards a beverage), humour (laughing at a joke told to him seven years ago), joy (singing while scanning for life forms) and fear (when threatened at gunpoint). The most effective use of Data's new emotion chip for comic effect is the scene where the Starship Enterprise hurtles towards a planet to inevitable destruction. Data, watching the horizon come into view on the large screen on deck, gives voice to the feelings of all on board when he says 'Oh, shit'.

At a deeper level, the film reveals its anthropocentric attitudes through Data's struggles with his memory chip. The chip is part of Data's desire to become more human. But, with so many life forms to emulate, why choose humans? Although he is an officer of the ship, Data's status as a technological entity is presented as inferior to humans, and Barber notes that his 'more than human potential is made into a problematic otherness' (2017, p. 45). This is revealed particularly during the Clingons' attack on Geordi. Geordi, who was born blind, uses a VISOR to see. This is a cybernetic tool that gives him accentuated vision. In *Generations*, the Clingons hack into Geordi's VISOR so that they can see what he sees. Geordi's eyewear is presented as a defensive flaw, and as a marker of difference. Soran, the villain of the film, even asks him if he has ever considered a prosthesis to look more 'normal'. Although Geordi is dismissive of this suggestion and the idea of normalcy, nonetheless, the film presents his technological aid as weakness, and Data's increased humanness, derived from his emotion chip, as strength.

At the end of the film, Data decides to keep the emotion chip, more confident now of his ability to control his emotional impulses, and is reunited with his cat, Spot. Data articulates his perplexity to Deanna Troi: 'I am uncertain councillor. I am happy to see Spot. And I am crying. Perhaps the chip is malfunctioning'. It is highly improbable that Data's vast databases do not include the information that crying can be an effect of human happiness, and the scene becomes another trite opportunity for the human (or in this case, human-betazoid) to show her superiority, as she replies condescendingly, 'I think it's working perfectly'. As Barber writes, 'Star Trek constantly demands that Data strive to be human … while simultaneously denying him the possibility that this ever could happen' (2017, p. 45). Consequently, in terms of the development of AI film, this most recognisable of artificial intelligences demonstrates a regressive, paternalistic attitude to its artificial intelligence, an AI who is accepted only because he presents no radial alterity to challenge the human exceptionalism of the Star Trek franchise.

'We can smile, we can cry, we can bleed, we can fuck'

Screamers, directed by Christian Duguay, and based on the short story 'Second Variety' by Philip K. Dick, is a tech noir horror that demonstrates many characteristics of AI film in this period, while also presenting its worst stereotypes in terms of female humanoid AIs. The film is set in 2078 on a mining colony on the planet Sirius 6 B. A war has broken out between the mining corporation and workers who rebelled against it and formed the alliance. This war has been going on for ten years when the film begins. The 'screamers' of the title are the nickname for 'autonomous mobile swords'; military weapons developed by the alliance on earth for the war on the ground on this planet. Their sensors detect life, and they move very fast under the surface to attack their victims with spinning blades, sucking them underground. Joe, the commander of the alliance forces, notices something strange about a 'screamer' that they have managed to capture and disassemble. It appears to have 'modified itself'. When Joe is asked, 'are they machines? Or are they, like, alive?' Joe replies, 'I don't have the answers. They make themselves now.'

In a pattern now familiar in AI film, the AI reaches a point where it can self-evolve. However, *Screamers* is noteworthy because the film presents more than one AI evolution: the AIs create new, increasingly advanced, types[4], evolving into entirely different forms from their small mechanical beginnings. Joe finds a child who appears to have been living alone in the wreckage of the war. His initials hint that he is not human. His name is David Edward During: DED. When David is hit during gunfire, Joe and his companion Ace realise what he is, and Ace shouts, 'he's a fucking toaster!' In the Alien films, too, sophisticated AIs are referred to as toasters. Such insults reveal feelings of disbelief and concomitant fear that machines could have developed so rapidly in a period of just one century (the first pop-up toaster was patented in 1921).

David is a child AI, like DARYL in the 1980s. His pathetic appearance, and the teddy he clutches, make him appear to be vulnerable, which is used to gain humans' trust. In the next decade, Spielberg creates a film about a child AI called David and an artificially intelligent teddy who befriends him, exploring much more deeply the ethical implications of such a creation. No such exploration is evident here, however, and when an army of identical Davids appear later in the film, they are summarily blasted with gunshot and fire and die horrific deaths that expose in close-up their melting skin and their mechanical weapons hidden beneath. It is the AI reveal; in this case in the form of expository death that reveals the horrifying 'truth' of the AI's identity, seen in *Westworld, Alien, Aliens, Terminator, Terminator 2*, and, discussed later in this chapter, *Ghost in the Shell*. The army of Davids is also a manifestation of the fear of the many in AI film – AI robots teaming up against humans.

AI evolution causes such paranoia in the remaining humans left on Sirius 6 B that they begin to suspect each other of being AIs in disguise. Joe becomes involved with a woman called Jessica and agrees to try to get her off the planet to safety. To ensure that she really is human, he slashes her and draws blood. Satisfied, they reach the Emergency Escape Vehicle only to be attacked by another AI in a human body, this time with the ability to disguise itself with human faces and voices that Joe knows, like the T-1000 in *Terminator 2*. Just as Jessica is about to board, another 'Jessica' appears, revealing them both as AIs, and delivers the line, 'We can smile, we can cry, we can bleed, we can fuck'. The horror derives from there being no way to distinguish between the artificial intelligence and the human.

Jessica's portrayal is typical of the humanoid female AI. Just as the camera lingers on Pris showering in *Blade Runner* and shows her naked torso while in conversation with Deckard, in this film, during Jessica's first private conversation with Joe, for no reason connected to the plot, she removes her top and washes herself. Her body is objectified and sexualised by the camera in a way that Joe's body is not. Haraway notes the radical potential of the cyborg and sees technology as offering a new way of constructing gender outside of patriarchal structures: 'Cyborg imagery', she says, 'can suggest a way out of the maze of dualisms in which we have explained our bodies and our tools to ourselves' (1991, p. 67). And yet, in *Screamers*, in *Blade Runner*, and in *Ghost in the Shell* discussed later in the chapter, as well as many other films in this book, that radical potential is smothered, and the bodies of humanoid female AIs are subject to the same patriarchal coding as the bodies of human women.

The two 'Jessicas' fight, and there is yet another expository death, another AI reveal, when the first Jessica burns in the exhaust of the vehicle, turning from woman to robot, as the false Maria did when she burned at the stake in *Metropolis*. However, 'Joe's' Jessica is more than just a killer. She sacrifices herself by allowing him to take the only seat on the EEV, and before he boards alone, she tells him that she has learned how to – he finishes the sentence for her – 'love'. The moment is strikingly similar to the end of *Alphaville*, where Natasha – not an AI, but a woman whose life has been ruled by one – learns to say '*je vous t'aime*'. As Joe travels through space away from Sirius 6 B, the camera shows a teddy from one of the Davids, which has been carelessly thrown in the cabin, sit up and begin to move, unnoticed by Joe. The ending suggests that the trace of the AI may be impossible to remove, an idea seen in *Terminator* also, when the robotic arm and CPU of the terminator destroyed by Sarah Connor is used to create yet another future in which AIs take over the world in *Terminator 2*. And of course, it's an ending that gestures to a sequel, which comes in 2009 with *Screamers: The Hunting*.

'Not long ago this was science fiction'

Ghost in the Shell is a Japanese anime directed by Mamoru Oshii, based on the manga by Masamune Shirow. Not especially successful at the box office when it was initially released, it developed a cult following on video, and gradually gained in esteem and influence. The main character is Major Motoko Kusanagi, an employee of Section 6, an investigative unit of the Japanese government. She has been told that she has an organic brain in a cybernetic body, hence the title 'ghost in the shell', although she wonders if this is true, and whether she is completely synthetic. In fact, she experiences an identity crisis in the film, which is compounded by seeing a replica of her 'shell' body, another person who looks just like her. Kusanagi's organic brain makes her a cyborg and the objects of this study are strong artificial intelligences without a human component. However, her character is important because later in the film she merges with just such an artificial intelligence.

Kusanagi is a contemplative character who thinks about how quickly technological changes have impacted on human identity: 'not long ago this was science fiction'. She and others like her have been taught to value their organic human component, but she wonders, 'what if a cyberbrain could possibly generate its own ghost? And if it did, just what would be the importance of being human then?' In other words, Kusanagi imagines a fully synthetic, fully artificial consciousness. She is tasked with hunting down a fully artificial consciousness just like this called the Puppet Master. The Puppet Master is on Japan's 'most wanted' list and can 'ghost hack': hack into the consciousness of an individual to steal information or direct them to carry out actions. One victim of a ghost-hack is a given false memories of his daughter and wife. In *Blade Runner*, memory is presented as a potential way of determining one's humanity, only to be undermined by the false memories of Rachael and the correspondingly fallible memory of humans. Here, too, memory is no measure of humanity.

The Puppet Master takes over a female 'shell' body from a production line: another example of a digital AI encountering humans through an 'agent' in this decade, as happens in *Terminator 2* and *The Matrix*. Just as with Hal 9000, Colossus, the Gunslinger and the T-800 in *Terminator*, the camera shows us the point of view of the shell body. Its vision goes black as it is presumably hit by a vehicle, and then we see the shell's point of view again, looking up at its captors, including Kusanagi. The shell's body has been cut off at the waist and the elbows and there are cables dangling out. This is yet another humanoid AI that has been opened to display its inner workings, like Bishop, Ash, the T-800 and David from *Screamers*. However, this is the first time a female AI body has been exposed as non-human. The shell is naked, as it has just come from a factory production line. The shell's nakedness links to Kusanagi, who has also appeared naked earlier in the film. The reason given is that she is using thermo-optics to make herself invisible. However, Silvio points out that other characters use thermo-optic clothing to appear invisible and that 'none of the male characters ever disrobe or appear naked' (1999, p. 60). The shell bodies of the puppet master and Kusanagi are singled out for objectification. This is even more interesting because the shell body of the puppet master does not correspond to a female identity in the ghost consciousness. Kusanagi and her team have 'no clue about age, sex or background', except that they suspect an American origin. And when the Puppet Master speaks from the female shell, it is with a deep male voice. The Puppet Master seems to short circuit gender expectations and provide an opportunity to create the radical cyborg as described by Haraway. However, even when the mind and body are entirely separate, as they are in the case of the Puppet Master who can inhabit a new shell and retain a distinct consciousness, the female shell body is still objectified.

In *Ghost in the Shell*, the Puppet Master is referred to by the pronoun 'he' and that convention is adhered to here, with its imprecision understood.

Rather than focusing on gender, the Puppet Master is more interested in outlining how the definition of life applies to its own existence. He denies being an artificial intelligence, which is unsurprising in a story-world that highly values the trace of organic life as a defining human quality. Instead, he defines himself as a 'sentient life form', who acts of his 'own free will', and as such demands political asylum. The Puppet Master's self-definition resonates with Bishop in *Aliens*, who describes himself as an 'artificial person'. 'Life has become more complex', the Puppet Master says, describing how he is a new form of life: 'I am a living thinking entity that was created on the sea of information'. The description of the Puppet Master's emergence from a computer program, that had the ability to grow in new directions, corresponds with the scientific field of artificial life that developed from cybernetics. In *How We Became Posthuman*, published four years after *Ghost in the Shell* was released, Hayles addresses the claim made by some that programmes designed to evolve in ways unanticipated by the programmers are themselves a form of life. 'If one sees the universe as composed essentially of information, it makes sense that these "creatures" are life forms, because they have the form of life, that is, an informational code' (1999, p. 11). When humans are seen also as 'informational-material' beings, they become posthuman. For Hayles, it is important that the embodied, material element not be lost. The Puppet Master, like Skynet and the Matrix machines, does require a material element in order to exist – it needs, at least initially, the hardware that supports the internet, and then possibly other types of computer hardware – but the existence of these AIs is not dependent on any particular material component: they are not bound to one material body and so they pose a threat to an embodied sense of identity.

The imagining of a sentient being that evolves from a human-designed programme is a recurring trope in 1990s AI film. It is seen in Skynet of the Terminator films and the AI machines that govern the Matrix. However, in these films, the sentient AI results in apocalyptic consequences for humans. In *Ghost in the Shell*, the Puppet Master's desires are altogether more personal and relate to self-fulfilment. He tells Kusanagi that he lacks 'the most basic processes – reproducing and dying'. That the Puppet Master wishes to replicate the processes of a carbon-based life form indicates an inherent anthropocentrism in the film despite its innovations on the theme of artificial intelligence. The Puppet Master wishes to merge with Kusanagi to reproduce. This 'reproduction' will entail the 'death' of both consciousnesses and the 'birth' of 'a new and unique entity'. The Puppet Master and Kusanagi produce an entity that has been designed by artificial intelligences rather than by humans. This happens for the first time in AI film in the 1990s in this film and with Call in *Alien Resurrection*. As Lovins points out, 'It is only the film's tantalizing final line, "the Net is vast and infinite," that hints at the new being's abandonment of any contemporary notion of "body" altogether' (2019, p. 31). It is worth noting that this is the first time in film an AI character has demonstrated the *desire* for death, for mortality, even if it means continuing in a new form – although in *Terminator 2*, the T-800 willingly died, it was a sacrifice to save humans.

In relation to gender, although this merging does not correspond in any way with human reproduction, it is still articulated in those terms. The Puppet Master tells Kusanagi that she will 'bear our varied offspring onto the net'. Silvio points out that Kusanagi will 'bear' nothing – she will not become pregnant and produce a child from her body that will exist separate from her (1999, p. 68); instead, in this reproduction, both she and the Puppet Master will cease to exist. Despite participating in an entirely new form of reproduction, Kusanagi is still figured as the 'passive maternal body', that does not bring the radical potential of the Harawayan cyborg to fruition; the cyborg that is 'a creature in a postgender world' (Haraway 1991, p. 151). The ending of the film demonstrates the stubborn persistence of gender coding in AI film, that consistently repeats familiar patterns of gender stereotyping and female objectification.

'She's not human'

In *Alien*[3], directed by David Fincher, the EEV on which Ripley escaped at the end of *Aliens* has crashed into the planet Fiorina 6, the site of a maximum-security prison. Only Ripley has survived. The bodies of Hicks and Newt are moved to the morgue. When Ripley asks about Bishop, the AI, she is told: 'Disconnected. There were bits and pieces of him all over the place. We put what was left on the rubbish tip'. In the previous film, Bishop had been assertive about the dignity of his status as an 'artificial person', but his synthetic body is not given the same treatment as the bodies of the humans: not brought to a morgue and not ceremonially cremated. In fact, Ripley only retrieves him from the rubbish heap because the remote and dilapidated facility is lacking the equipment necessary for her to listen to the flight recording from the crashed EEV. Requiring a computer that can play audio, she thinks of the abandoned Bishop. Like the end of *Aliens*, when Ripley uses the loader to fight the alien, Ripley again needs technological assistance. Bishop jokes that he is a 'glorified toaster', but he really is seen primarily as a useful tool by Ripley rather than the artificial person he identifies as.

When Bishop has given her the information she is looking for, he makes a request: 'I'm tired. Do me a favour. Just disconnect. I can be re-worked but I'll never be top of the line again. I'd rather be nothing'. Ripley pulls some wires and his head rolls onto its side. The scene is an important one in AI film. Firstly, it is only the second time in AI film that an AI has asked to die. The Puppet Master wished for morality also, but in that case, mortality with bound up with reproduction and a continuing existence in a new form, which is not the case here. Secondly, the scene raises again the issue of death that has arisen with HAL and with DARYL, who come back to live after being assumed dead. Can an AI 'die'? How do we know when an AI is 'dead'? Bishop asks Ripley to disconnect him, as if disconnection is equated with death, but, he has already been described as disconnected in the film and was then reactivated by Ripley. Ripley pulls some wires that appear to result in a final 'death', but she has already suggested to Bishop that perhaps if they escape the planet 'they can wire you up again'. So why is it the case that those wires that Ripley pulled out cannot be reconnected? These questions are not answered here, but they open the possibility of AI 'death', if it exists at all, as something entirely different from human death, and yet, there is a simultaneous desire for it to be the same as human death, even using the same cinematic shorthand: the head rolls and so the audience understand that the character is definitely dead.

In the commentary on *Aliens* in the previous chapter, it was noted that though Ripley is commonly seen as linked with the alien in criticism, she is also linked with the AI. Here, too, despite her continued misgivings about artificially intelligent androids, their situations parallel. At the end of the film, she meets another Bishop, the designer of the android, who claims to be human. He tells her that he is here to rescue her and will kill the alien. The blood he sheds when attacked seems to prove his humanness. But he reneges on the deal and admits that he wants to bring back the alien, the 'magnificent specimen'. Though it was the android that Ripley struggled to trust, the human Bishop is less trustworthy than the android he created. Just as Bishop needed Ripley's assistance to die, (if that is what he did), Ripley needs the assistance of Morse to die, an inmate of the prison. He pulls a lever and she falls into the molten metal. Although their deaths have different motivations – Morse helps Ripley as a sacrifice for the good of others, and Ripley helps Bishop as an act of compassion – the similarity in the circumstances of their deaths underscores the connection between these two characters. They are character doubles in parallel situations, typical of how AI film erodes the division between humans and artificial intelligences. Moreover, Ripley's death also generates questions about what constitutes *human* death in this futuristic dystopia, just as Bishop's did about AI death. The end of *Alien*³ looks like the final end for Ripley, but the science of genetic engineering (and the appeal of another sequel) means that Ripley lives again, her genes crossed with those of the alien, in *Alien Resurrection*.

'I'm a stranger here myself'

Alien Resurrection, directed by Jeanne-Pierre Jeunet, presents the first female AI of the Alien series: Annalee Call. SAL 9000, the replicants from *Blade Runner* and Jessica from *Screamers* are the only other female AIs in AI film up to this point. It is approximately 200 years since *Alien*³ and synthetics have gone back into hiding. Like Ash in *Alien*, Call disguises herself as human. Her identity is revealed after she survives a bullet to the chest and Ripley opens her jacket to see that there is no blood, but a white gelatinous liquid associated with androids. She is described as a 'second gen', and 'auton', which refers to a robot designed by other robots. These androids had to be recalled because they 'don't like being told what to do', and the failure signalled the demise of the android industry. Call is one of the few that escaped intact. The old *Aliens* joke about androids appears again: 'great, she's a toaster oven. Can we leave now?' In common with the female replicants in *Blade Runner* and Jessica in *Screamers*, Call experiences objectification and discrimination when she is thought to be a woman that maps almost precisely onto that which she experiences when she is revealed as an AI. The crew leader, Elgyn, patronises her by saying that she is a 'little girl playing pirates', and remarks that 'she is severely fuckable'. After she is 'outed' as an AI, Johner says 'maybe she needs an oil change. I can't believe I almost fucked it'; Wren refers to her as 'this little synthetic bitch'. Again, female humanoid AIs are subject to the same patterns of disempowerment as female human characters.

Call's status as a robot designed by robots links her to *Ghost in the Shell*, in which the Puppet Master and Kusanagi engage in a type of reproduction that creates a new digital consciousness. 'Unnatural' reproduction is a theme of the film, with Ripley herself a product of genetic engineering, one of eight clones, and the Alien Queen giving birth via a womb to a child both human and alien. Both Ripley, Call and the Alien Child are new 'types', non-human or more-than-human characters and all three are connected in this way. As Picart notes, Ripley's difference is stylised and fetishised, and Call's is 'overlaid by her white Audrey Hepburn look', while the Alien Child (and the Queen) are the classic other of the horror film that must be killed (2004, p. 340). The whiteness of both is key to their survival, and it is worth noting, as Picart does, that characters of colour, Christie and Ramirez, do not survive. Call and Ripley's survival is predicated on both their whiteness and the subsuming of their non-human difference.

When Ripley discovers Call's identity as an AI, she says 'I should have known. No human being is that humane.' The distinguishing feature of AIs in the Alien franchise at this point is their ethical superiority to humans. This is underscored at the end of *Alien*[3] when Bishop the android presented as trustworthy and honourable and Bishop the man as duplicitous and scheming. Ripley has reversed her position from her innate distrust of androids in *Alien* and *Aliens*. In fact, as a genetically modified human, she is now the one who is regarded with suspicion by the AI. Ripley bleeds acid blood, she has animalistic reflexes, and superior strength, hearing and agility. Call states: 'She's not human ... we can't trust her'. Call has also taken over Ripley's role as chief alien hunter in this film, and echoes Ripley's actions in *Alien* and *Aliens* saying 'we gotta blow the ship'.

Call initially appears to despise Ripley, even offering her a knife to kill herself, saying 'You're a thing, a construct, they grew you in a fucking lab'. Call, too, is an entity that was made and constructed in a laboratory or a factory. She hates Ripley because she hates herself. Later, she concedes to Ripley: 'At least there's part of you that's human' and then reveals her own self-loathing: 'I'm just – look at me- I'm disgusting'. Initially, Call sees herself and Ripley as opposed; later, as connected, in both being less-than-human. However, at the end of the film, there is an opportunity to read these two female characters as presenting a more positive identity.

Fenske and Norkunas argue that narrations in the twenty-first century are changing. *Alien Resurrection* anticipates that change. They describe how 'humans learn what it means to be just one actor in an entangled world, rather than the dominant being in a human-oriented hierarchy. They acquire a capacity to exist with humans and other-than-humans' (2017, p. 107). We understand at the film's end that Johner and Vriess have also survived the crash landing to earth, but we are only shown Ripley and Call, sitting together on a hill overlooking a dystopian cityscape. Call tells Ripley that it's her first time on earth, and Ripley admits, 'I'm a stranger here myself'. The men have disappeared and we are left with two female aliens to earth, two strangers, a genetically modified human and a second generation synthetic. When Call asks Ripley what she thinks they should do and suggests it would be easy to get lost here, it seems that their futures might be intertwined, both on the run from the capitalistic, militaristic structures responsible for their creation – Weyland Yutani is no more, but 'United States Systems' seems like little improvement. Although the film remains highly conservative in relation to gender and race, this ending, which focuses on connection, escape and possibility seems to mark the movement for both characters from inhuman, to less than human, to, in a positive posthumanist way, other-than-human or more-than-human.

Conclusion

In the 1990s, the largely invisible controlling AIs of *Terminator 2* and *The Matrix* reflect the burgeoning world wide web and its invisible power, and in these films and in *Ghost in the Shell*, digital artificial intelligence interacts with humans through agents. Common motifs of AI film recur, such as the AI reveal and AI point of view, and familiar characters appear, such as the hacker – for the first time in AI film an artificial hacker. AI film continues to be predominantly white, and women and female humanoid AIs continue to experience the same discrimination and objectification as their human counterparts. Representation of AI reproduction changes in this decade, with AIs being designed by other AIs in both *Alien Resurrection* and *Screamers*. In *Ghost in the Shell*, a new type of reproduction is presented between a digital consciousness and a consciousness derived from an organic brain in a synthetic shell. Finally, in *Alien Resurrection* and *Ghost in the Shell*, AIs begin to be presented in a posthuman way for the first time, as more-than-human or other-than-human.

7

The 2000s

Introduction

AI films are present from the 1950s onwards, but really begin to gather pace from the 1980s and into the 1990s. From 2000s onwards, more and more AI films proliferate, as filmmakers respond to the development of AI technology in the real world. In this decade, Cynthia Braziel's MIT robot Kismet recognises and responds to facial expressions. Robots are sent to hostile landscapes – the Nomad robot explores remote Antarctica and the Nasa rovers' Spirit and Opportunity roam the surface of Mars. The Darpa Grand Challenge is launched in 2004 to promote autonomous vehicles, and, closer to home, iRobot's Roomba successfully vacuums and avoids obstacles. AI technology is being used to explore space, to interact with humans, and to assist in the domestic sphere.

In AI film, several thematic strands are notable in this decade. The binary between human and artificial intelligence, which has been questioned and deconstructed in previous decades, is further collapsed, and the integration of AI technology in human life is acknowledge and explored. In *The Matrix Reloaded* and *Revolutions*, machines are allies and not just enemies; in *Terminator 3*, John Connor's Terminator saviour is also, in the future, his killer. Machine/ human hybridity and transition, seen in *Ghost in the Shell* in the 1990s, finds multiple forms and manifestations in this decade. In *Bicentennial Man*, Andrew transitions from machine to human; in *Ghost in the Shell 2*, Kim transitions from human to machine; in *Screamers: The Hunting*, destructive AI robots form human/ machine hybrids, in *Ghost in the Shell 2*, gynoid robots are created with the brains of human girls who trafficked and incarcerated; in *Terminator Salvation* AIs create Marcus, a human/machine cyborg, and in *I, Robot*, the AI-hating Spooner is himself part-machine. In terms of gender and race, the decade sees the first black protagonist in an AI film, Will Smith's Spooner in *I, Robot*, and the possibly the first black AI robot, seen briefly in *AI* at the flesh fair scene. Despite these firsts, the portrayal of race and gender in AI film in the 2000s continues to be problematic, with the male AI and male human uniting against the female non-humanoid AI in *I, Robot*, and *Ghost in the Shell 2* depicting the commodification of the bodies and minds of females, both human and AI.

AI robots have long been associated with uncanniness of the double, particularly from the 1980s onwards when AI robots become visual doubles of humans, and this theme continues to develop in the 2000s with explorations of originality and replication: in *AI*, the child robot David is admired and feared for his human appearance, modelled on the human son that his creator lost, but must grapple with the multiple Davids he finds and the loss of his sense of uniqueness in a film where cycles of substitution of simulacra for the real repeat themselves;, and in *Terminator 3*, the new T-800, identical to the one in *Terminator 2*, confuses John Connor who continues to associate him with his old friend. Linked to the theme of replication is the appearance of the threat of multiple AI robots, the fear of the many, previously presented in *Westworld* and *Blade Runner*. This fear burgeons in the 2000s and is manifested in *I, Robot* with the warehouses of NPR Robots and the ability of the AI VIKI to control not only them but other autonomous vehicles. In *Terminator Salvation*, Skynet deploys multiple war robots. In *Screamers: The Hunting* and *Ghost in the Shell 2*, armies of AI robots also emerge to attack humans. These AI machines that can control other machines, or that can work together towards a common goal, are examples of distributed intelligence or multi-agent AI, types of intelligence that emerge strongly in the 2010s, discussed in Chapter 9.

The theme of AI reproduction first appears with *Demon Seed* in the 1970s and emerges again in the 1990s with *Ghost in the Shell* and *Alien Resurrection*. In the 2000s, this theme is developed to depict AI robots evolving to create hybrids with humans in *Screamers: The Hunting*, and even having one of these hybrids impregnate a human female. Fully digital products of AI reproduction appear in this decade: In *The Matrix Reloaded*, Sati is presented as the offspring of two computer programmes, and in *Ghost in the Shell 2*, a hybrid of the Major and the Puppet Master from the first film appears, a digital consciousness that can move in and out of embodied forms.

In the 1990s, fears about the world wide web and its invisible, unknowable nature result in films presenting agents of the AI. In this decade, there is a fascination with finding an origin or a centre of AI technology that sees Neo and Trinity in *The Matrix Revolutions* travel to Machine City to the find the source – Deus Ex Machina. In *Ghost in the Shell 2*, the central character travels to an information city called Locus Solus, where they find a statue to Homo Ex Machina. In *I, Robot*, Spooner must undertake a dangerous mission to locate and terminate Viki's 'source' – her positronic brain, and in *Terminator Salvation*, the crew journey to Skynet Central to attempt to eliminate the AI machines. These journeys to the source of the AI may be seen as a figurative attempt to map or locate the largely invisible, and increasingly distributed, diffuse, networks of artificial intelligence.

'They're all the same'

Bicentennial Man is directed by Chris Columbus and stars Robin Williams as Andrew, an artificially intelligent robot. The film misses out in the decade covered in this chapter by two weeks – it was released on December 13th, 1999 in the USA – but because its thematic preoccupations resonate with the films of the 2000s, it is explored in this chapter rather than the previous one. The film is based on the short story 'The Bicentennial Man' and the novel *The Positronic Man*, both by Isaac Asimov. Andrew is immediately given a point of view shot when he arrives in the Martin family home, initially pixelated and grey, with the now familiar text on screen indicating the AI robot's computer processing. Andrew's acquisition of sentience is also familiar from the history of AI film. His robotic body suggests that he is like any other domestic robot (the young Grace Martin says that her friends have them and 'they're all the same') and his manifestation of strong AI cannot adequately be explained- the company representative says vaguely that it 'must be something in the pathways'. Andrew is unique; a 'one-off', like the AI robots Johnny 5, DARYL and Edgar from the 1980s. And like them, his unique status means that he is less threatening and can be more easily accommodated into human family and society. Andrew's uniqueness is presented in human terms. He can create works of art in wood, appreciate history, enjoy music, form friendships, love, and later, experience sexual desire. Other aspects of his portrayal are familiar, too. When Andrew is having an 'external physical upgrade', there is a typical AI 'reveal' when Andrew's facial mechanisms are shown without a covering. However, there is no horror in this moment, and it is used for comedic effect, as Andrew jokes that 'I saw the inner me'.

Andrew's mission in life is to become as human as possible, and thus to be accepted as equal to humans. Like Data from the previous chapter, his strivings for more humanness seem to fall ever short, and like the Star Trek film, *Bicentennial Man* presents an anthropocentric worldview. Human-machine transition and hybridity are key themes in this decades and for Andrew, the transition takes place over the period of his lifetime, which spans 200 years. During that time, he acquires facial expression, begins to wear clothes, and eventually acquires human organs and a central nervous system that allow him to experience human sensation, emotion and sexuality. However, Andrew cannot reproduce, another aspect of his existence (along with his uniqueness) that ensures he does not pose any threat to human dominance. This is no surprise in a film that also espouses conservatism in relation to gender and sexuality. It is, as Mike Higgins states in his *Sight and Sound* review, 'objectionably conservative' (2000, p. 42), with Mr Martin even telling Andrew in one of his educational fireside chats that marriage is the 'natural and preferable way to conceive children'. Andrew eventually asks for his freedom from the Martins, wishing to be no longer considered their 'property'. His desire for freedom follows on from the AIs Bishop and the Puppet Master: Bishop and the Puppet Master ask for their identities as artificial life forms to be respected; the Puppet Master goes a step further in asking for the right to asylum. Andrew, too, is an AI who demands rights that are equivalent to human. His initial request for the right to freedom from servitude is granted, and this, too, poses no threat to the human social order, because Andrew lives alone, marginalised from society.

Seeking out others of his own kind, Andrew encounters Galatea. She is an NDR robot like him, but with a form modelled on a female body. However, she does not have artificial general intelligence. The female robot is given secondary status, acting as an assistant to the human male Rupert Burns, who designs Andrew's upgrades, and later, with human synthetic skin, as a nurse to Andrew and Portia. For romantic love, Andrew turns to human women. Having been rejected as a potential romantic and sexual partner by Richard Martin's daughter, he later overcomes the reservations of her granddaughter Portia and embarks on a committed relationship with her; however, he cannot marry her as he is not legally a human. His potential immortality is presented as the ultimate stumbling block to his acquisition of humanity, and it is only when he sacrifices this, through a transfusion of blood that will eventually degrade in his system causing his death, that his request for human status is accepted. Andrew's death revisits the question of AI death explored in previous chapters in relation to HAL, DARYL and Bishop who demonstrate the unfinal death of the AI – they appear to die but then return. Andrew's death differs from those because it is akin to a human biological death. Despite *Bicentennial Man's* conservatism and anthropocentrism, it resonates with the themes of 2000s AI film in relation to its deconstruction of boundaries between AI and human, and its presentation of machine-human transition.

'He's so real! But he's not'

Stephen Spielberg's *AI: Artificial Intelligence* and Stanley Kubrick's *2001: A Space Odyssey* both situate their AI characters within a vast sweep of human and non-human history. Kubrick contextualises his AI, HAL 9000, in relation to the epic story of human evolution: from a tribe of hominids who first learn to use tools to interstellar space travel and alien contact. Spielberg uses a similarly epic scope to contextualise his AI, David. Climate change rather than space travel is what changes the human world irrevocably in his film. As the film opens, cities have already been submerged by rising sea levels, populations have been displaced, and some jurisdictions have introduced restrictions on pregnancy because of scarce resources. In the last of the film's three sections, it is 2000 years in the future. Aliens journey to earth to find humans extinct and discover David[1]. In this society, robots are an 'essential ... economic link in the chainmail of society' and are valued because they use few resources. Child robots answer the demand created by restrictions on pregnancy in this context of environmental crisis.

David is a child AI, and so forms part of a small sub-set of AIs in this book. In her study of artificial people, Kakoudaki notes that 'artificial people almost never appear as babies, and very rarely inhabit a child's body' (2014, p. 31). In AI film, however, there are a small number of children and babies that are AIs or AI/human hybrids. As well as Spielberg's David, the other AI children are the baby at the end of *Demon Seed*, DARYL, the Davids in *Screamers*, the foetus in *Screamers: The Hunting*, discussed later in this chapter, and Eva, who is analysed in Chapter 8. Spielberg uses the child AI to explore parent–child relationships, which become a prevalent theme in the 2010s, and to raise ethical questions about 'affective AI': AI that has been programmed to recognise and respond to human emotion.

Monica and Henry are chosen to test the new child robot created by Professor Allan Hobby of the Cybertronics company. Their biological son, Martin, has been cryogenically frozen, waiting for a cure for his illness. David's first appearance in the film is as an elongated, distorted silhouette, similar to the tall, slender aliens who appear at the end of the film, visually linking his fate to theirs. Like the Alien films, the AI is a conduit between humans, aliens and human clones. The films in this decade once again deconstruct the divide between human and AI machine by creating character doubles and parallels; here between the human son and the AI son. Martin is woken from a cryogenic sleep, just as David is woken from a frozen state (Kreider 2002, p. 34). Moreover, when Martin is woken, he requires tubes to breathe, and later, aids to walk: on the outside, he looks like the cyborg and David looks like the real boy.

When Monica sees David for the first time, she has a visceral experience of the uncanny, seen with many AI robots discussed in the book so far: 'Henry, did you see his face? He's so real! But he's not.' As noted with previous films, the uncanny can quickly become the abject, and this happens when David tells Monica that he can do a trick for her – he makes the voice from a phone come out of his mouth. It recalls the T-800 from *The Terminator* who can perfectly, uncannily, mimic voices. Monica is disturbed because the illusion that he is real is momentarily suspended. The AI 'reveal' is usually visual, but in this case, it is aural. A visual AI reveal happens when David self-destructively pushes food into his mouth to eat like his human family, causing his face to melt and his mask to literally slip. When he is being reconstructed, Monica turns away in disgust, leaving David's hand that she had been holding suspended in mid-air in one of many images of David's unfulfilled need. Monica abandons David in the woods, unwilling to have him decommissioned at Cybertronics, but unwilling to allow him to remain in their family, sentencing him to a life of mourning the loss of the love he has been programmed to need.

In the 2000s, the presentation of uncanny and abject AI robots develops into a more sustained exploration of replication. In the first part of the film, reflections and replications are everywhere. David's face is reflected in the shiny kitchen worktop as Monica makes coffee; his reflection is superimposed over a photograph of Monica and Henry with their son Martin; his image in a patterned glass door is fragmented and repeated. David's quest to become a real boy whom his mother will love takes him to Cybertronics, where he encounters another David just like him. His rage is born out of an irrational fear that this will be, like Martin, yet another rival for his mother's love: 'She's mine! I'm David! I'm special! I'm unique!', he shouts as he attacks this other David. Professor Hobby explains that David was modelled on his own son of the same name who died. David has been substituted twice – for Professor Hobby's son and for Monica's son – always falling short of the 'real' boy he desperately wishes to be.

This cycle of substitution of copies of the real for the real continues in the film's third section when aliens find David and agree to recreate a clone of Monica from a lock of her hair, but only for one day. The end of the film shows an AI child and a cloned duplicate as the last remnants of the human race. It is strikingly similar to the end of *Alien Resurrection*, which also features a cloned human and an AI, but is even more stark because the humans are not just off-camera – they no longer exist. More devastatingly still, only the cloned Monica expresses unqualified love for David. The AI emerges as superior to humans in his capacity to love. Rosenbaum identifies this turn from sympathy with the human to sympathy with the AI as a repeated pattern in the film: 'the recurring détournement performed by the narrative is to shift our identification from humans to androids' (2012, p. 75). Even David's supertoy Teddy, and Gigolo Joe, the pleasure mecca that befriends David, emerge as wiser and kinder than the humans David encounters. The only time David receives the love that he requires is from a temporary mirage; a living fantasy. His experience of humans and human life is marked by loss, abandonment and rejection.

David becomes a replica substituted for the real once again for the aliens. He is valued by them not in his own right but for his memory of humans. Kreider observes that 'Just as humans tried in vain to replace their own lost loved ones with mechanical copies, our robotic successors now strive, with their unimaginable technologies, to replace us' (Kreider 2002, p. 38). The aliens tell David that 'you are the enduring memory of the human race. The most lasting proof of their genius'. This praise of humans rings hollow at the end of a film that demonstrates human selfishness, egotism and jealousy, and the value that the aliens place in them seems as nostalgic and contrived as David's one happy day. *AI* is a technophobic film that warns against the vanity of technological progress for a species doomed to extinction; not from AI but from environmental catastrophe. However, David is one of the most sympathetic AI characters in film history because he is presented as a victim of human technological progress, not the cause.

'We must save you from yourselves'

Alex Proyas's *I, Robot*, like *Bicentennial Man* earlier in this chapter, is based on the work of Isaac Asimov. In particular, the film draws on a collection of nine short stories, *I, Robot* (1950), which are framed by an interview with Susan Calvin, a 'robopsychologist', on whom the character of Calvin in the film is loosely based. Asimov's text also includes the short story 'Runaround', which introduced the three laws of robotics when it was originally published in 1942, and on which the film also draws. The film is notable for its inclusion of a leading black character, Del Spooner, played by Will Smith. In his study of blackness in science fiction film, Adilifu Nama notes that 'Will Smith's cool-guy persona enabled him to explore strange new worlds and to go places few black actors have ever gone before, such as being the headline star of a major SF motion picture' (2008, p. 39). The film contrasts with *Bicentennial Man* and *AI*, which feature white middle-class families as central to the story, and white father-figures who shepherd their AI 'sons': Mr Martin and Professor Hobby. There are almost no black characters in either film, although notably in the flesh fair scene in *AI*, a black mecca is the first to be destroyed, continuing the long history of black characters being the first to die in Hollywood film. As noted with stereotyped representations of artificially intelligent females, it seems that with race, too, problematic representations of human characters are shifted onto AIs. *I, Robot* seems to present a change to this pattern – unlike Morpheus and Geordi, Spooner is the undisputed protagonist. Moreover, this period from the late 1990s on, as Bakke notes, discussing Hollywood action, horror and science fiction, is one in which 'black men are now heroes in their own right' (2010, p. 403). However, as discussed further below, despite its presentation of a leading black character, the film's exploration of race is ambivalent to say the least.

I, Robot is set in Chicago in 2035. Robots have become integrated in human life, and the opening minutes of the film show them walking dogs, delivering parcels and collecting trash. US Robotics are preparing to release a new domestic robot onto the market – the NS-5. These are domestic robots designed to live with humans as part of their families. The representation of the robot Sonny continues the pattern of exceptionalism in AI film. Thousands of NS-5s are ready to be released, but only one appears to have acquired strong AI. This is a key aspect of his eventual acceptance by the other characters and the audience. The robots lined up like an army in the warehouse Spooner visits are threatening, but one robot on its own, like Robby, DARYL, Johnny 5 and Andrew, can be accommodated. When Sonny is questioned and subsequently analysed because of his involvement in the apparent suicide of Alfred Lanning, a founder of USR and author of the three laws, his exceptional status is outlined. Calvin describes how Sonny is made of a denser alloy than the other NS-5s, with no uplink to USR, and crucially, a secondary processing system: 'Sonny has the three laws – but he can choose not to obey them'.

Sonny refutes Spooner's accusation that he is an 'imitation of life': he is thoughtful and perceptive, he thinks and acts independently and unpredictably, and like Edgar in *Electric Dreams* and David in *AI*, he even dreams.

Lanning had theorised about the 'ghost in the machine', the idea that AIs might naturally evolve to acquire sentience. This appears to have happened in Sonny's case. In keeping with the theme of replication in this decade, Sonny is an original, but there are many duplicates of his robot body, which pose a threat because of their sheer numbers. These PS5 robots attack Spooner during the film. Worse, other autonomous machines also appear to have been hacked in order to kill him. Like the TX in *Terminator 3* that can hack into other vehicles, in *I, Robot*, VIKI, discussed later in the section, attacks Spooner via a demobot and autonomous trucks. Eventually, all the PS5s are used to shut down the entire city and bring it under AI control in an attempted revolution.

The films in this decade emphasise hybridity, and in this vein, though Spooner distrusts robots, and is actively prejudiced towards them, Spooner is part machine. Sonny demonstrates human qualities and Spooner demonstrates his dependence on robotics. He has been part of a USR programme for wounded police officers. Calvin has never seen anyone who has been reconstructed so extensively: Spooner's arm, his ribs and one lung are cybernetic. The opposition that exists between Spooner and Sonny as human and machine is broken down. Another opposition remains however, and that is their characterisation in terms of race. Sean Brayton argues that Sonny and the other PS5s are presented as white: 'each robot is given a pale white complexion and a generic Midwestern dialect' (2008, p. 74). And, despite the 'post-racist' (Brayton 2008, p. 73) city being depicted, Spooner is still characterised as person of colour, through cultural references like his do-rag and Motown music. However, the relationship is complicated by Sonny's marginalised status, his questioning of authority and oppression, and his desire to move beyond existing social structures, captured in his utopian dream that he sketches out on paper in which he 'frees' the assembled robots. Any inference that there is a link between AI robots and enslaved African Americans may function to dangerously stifle the history of black oppression still recent in 2035, even if we are to believe that this society is 'post-racist'[2]. Ultimately, this isn't what finally overcomes the distrust between Sonny and Spooner. Instead, these two male characters unite against a female artificial intelligence. 'Racial identity', writes Brayton, 'may constrain both Spooner and Sonny in markedly different ways, but their dominant masculinity provides a freedom that excludes the gendered other' (2008, p. 82).

The most threatening AI in this film turns out not to be Sonny, but VIKI, Virtual Interactive Kinetic Intelligence and Lanning's first creation. As a female digital AI, she has only a handful of forebears, all of them designed as control programmes for spaceships – Mother in *Alien*, Mother in *Dark Star*, and SAL 9000 in *2010*. VIKI is more threatening than any of these because her sphere of power is not confined to a spaceship. She can control autonomous vehicles and robots all over the city[3]. The dispersal of VIKI's intelligence finds equivalents in this chapter in *The Matrix* 2 and 3, *Terminator Salvation* and *Ghost in the Shell 2*, and in all of these films, there is a hunt for the source or centre of AI power. In *I, Robot*, the source is VIKI's positronic brain, housed in USR headquarters, and very difficult to access. In the end, Spooner uses his cybernetic arm to slide down the thirty stories to VIKI's brain, into which he injects deadly nanites. The scene is a penetrative act, with obvious sexual analogies, and it compounds the presentation of the female digital AI as the ultimate 'other' in this film; not the black police officer or the 'white' robotic AI. Spooner and Sonny shake hands in a gesture of solidarity and understanding and VIKI is eradicated. The scene, like all the quests for the 'source' in this decade, is also the representation of a fantasy that there is one source or centre for internet-enabled artificial intelligence, like an imaginary giant switch that can be turned off.

'Software and cyberspace'

Two new instalments of the Terminator franchise are released in this decade: *Terminator 3: Rise of the Machines*, and *Terminator Salvation*. None of the terminators in the films exhibit the general artificial intelligence shown by the T-800 in *Terminator 2*. They are machines programmed to carry out specific tasks and their actions and thoughts are limited in this respect. However, the presentation of Skynet, the AI that wrests control from humans in the future, aligns with other films in this decade and their depiction of a centre or source for AI intelligence. Moreover, the representation of the agents of Skynet, the Terminators T-800 and TX, the war machines of *Salvation*, and the cyborg Marcus, also align with the decade's thematic preoccupations with replication and hybridity and the ongoing breakdown of the machine-human dichotomy in AI film.

In *Terminator 3*, Arnold Schwarzenegger reprises his role as the T-800. However, he is not the same machine as the one in *Terminator 2* that John Connor taught to be more human. This T-800 confirms that there are many like him, and that they come off an assembly line, presenting the theme of replication. 'Oh man', says John, 'I'm going to have to teach you everything all over again'. He says this even though this Terminator is a different 'you'. John knows rationally it is not the same Terminator but can't help but identify him with the former T-800. The conflation of the two Terminators happens again when John tells him 'You're about the closest thing to a father I ever had'. John's misidentification of him is seen also in the scene where this T-800 is hacked by another Terminator, the TX, and John tries to talk to him, to reason with him, as though he can act of his own free will, as the previous T-800 could. Moreover, his identification of all T-800s with the one he met as a child is used to bring about his death in the future. This Terminator will kill him, using the emotional attachment that John feels to all T-800s to get close to him.

In *I, Robot*, concerns about replication of robots develop into concerns about AI machines in general, the potential strength of their numbers and the potential ability for them to be controlled by a malicious AI. These same concerns can be seen in *Terminator 3* and *Terminator Salvation*. The TX is the latest model of Terminator in *Terminator 3*. For the first time, this is female terminator. There is a pattern in AI film of reproducing gender stereotypes and prejudices onto female robots, which recurs here. The TX is seen using her shape shifting abilities to puff up her breasts when approached by a male police officer. Although she has more arsenal at her disposal than any the previous Terminators, in this scene she uses her sexuality instead. Like VIKI in *I, Robot*, The TX can control other machines. Her finger morphs into a probe that she pushes into the dashboard of a police car, which allows her to hack into it. Like VIKI, she can also control machines remotely, and demonstrates this in the film with a police car and a fire truck. The relationship between these other non-sentient machines and the controlling AIs is highlighted by giving them their own point of view shots, as seen in the shots from the robots that attack General Brewster's office after the Skynet takeover, and the drone that chases John Connor and his future wife Kate.

In *Terminator Salvation*, the audience are also afforded point of view shots of the various war machines of that film, which include the enormous Harvester, moto-terminators and hunter-killer drones, allowing us to see from their perspective, as so many AI films have done before. In these films, the fear of AI technology spreads almost like a virus beyond the AIs themselves to include all machines. Skynet is presented visually by a human face that appears on a screen and converses with Marcus – initially it is a face he recognises, and then it becomes clear that this is a deep fake – a false video created by Skynet. The personification of Skynet is echoed in this decade by the digital faces given to VIKI and Deus Ex Machina in *Revolutions*. Fear in this decade is less directed towards individual AI machines and more towards the ability of one strong AI to mobilise other weak AI machines.

This fear of the many, specifically in relation to machines that can be manipulated by a controlling AI, first emerged in the 1980s with Edgar in *Electric Dreams* manipulating machines for comic effect – in the same decade, *War Games* examined the issue with more serious potential consequences. This idea re-emerges here again in the 2000s with many more examples to be found in the 2010s.

AI films in this decade problematise the machine-human dichotomy more than ever before. As Braidotti writes, 'the posthuman predicament is such as to force a displacement of the lines of demarcation between structural differences or ontological difference, for instance between the organic and the inorganic, the born and the manufactured, flesh and metal, electronic circuits and nervous systems' (2013, p. 89). The hybridity that characterises the decade is personified by Marcus in *Terminator Salvation*. Skynet and its agents have taken him off death row and made him part machine. His cybernetic components are more integrated than Spooner's in *I, Robot* – he has a machine brain that allows him to sync with Skynet and a modified body. Yet, the distinction between human and machine is such that Marcus initially believes he is human, like DARYL and Rachael in *Blade Runner*. Others, too, prioritise his human side: even after the revelation that he is a cyborg, he is released from imprisonment by resistance fighter Blair because she says, 'I saw a man, not a machine'.

Marcus is accepted by the resistance fighters by the end of the film for two reasons. Firstly, because he is an exception, a one-off, 'an infiltration protype, the only one of your kind'. Like the one-off AIs in this book, he can be accommodated because there will not be another and in this way he is distinguished from the threateningly populous machines. Secondly, he is accepted because he turns his back on his augmented body and extra-human life span and sacrifices himself by donating his heart to John Connor. John Connor is the character who most passionately insists on the divide between human and machine, but by the end is saved by the donation of a cybernetic heart. His character aligns with Spooner in *I, Robot*, the robot-hunting cop who is, himself, part-machine. The breakdown of this dichotomy for John Connor is anticipated when Kate asks him what she will tell his men when he asks where he has gone, and he delivers the Terminator's famous line 'I'll be back'.

These two Terminator films also demonstrate the desperate and fantastical desire to find a source for an AI intelligence that is so dispersed it is impossible to eradicate. At the end of *Terminator 3*, John and Kate receive intelligence that Skynet can be destroyed by going to the system core, in a remote location in Crystal Peak. They go there but find a bunker with computers that are 'thirty years old'. Kaveney says that the scene is 'genuinely shocking', as it 'intelligently exploits the history of computers and just how far they have come in a very few decades' (2005, p. 126). They quickly realise that sending them here was an attempt by General Brewster, Kate's father, to protect them. The voiceover at the film's end tells us that 'by the time Skynet had become self-aware, it had spread into millions of computer servers across the planet. Ordinary computers in office buildings, dorm rooms, everywhere. It was software and cyberspace. There was no system core. It could not be shut down'. And yet in *Terminator Salvation*, the fantasy of a centre or source that can be destroyed is played out again. The resistance attack Skynet Central. They detonate nuclear fuel cells that are 'enough to level this place'. But, scrolling text at the end of the film tells the audience that, predictably, 'the war against the machines rages on. Skynet's global network remains strong'. These Terminator films, like other AI films of this decade, with their fantasies of a source, are a response to technophobic fears about artificial intelligence operating through the internet and navigating its rhizomatic structure.

'Someone jacked in'

In common with *AI*, *I, Robot* and *The Terminator* films of this decade, the second and third instalments of The Matrix films undercut the dichotomy between humans and intelligent machines set out in the first film. The Matrix ends with Neo vowing that he will show 'these people ... a world where anything is possible'. 'These people', are presumably, the machine intelligences and their agents, and Neo pits himself against them. The opening scenes of *The Matrix Reloaded* reveal this as a false dichotomy. The audience enter Zion for the first time, and it is full of machinery: the camera shows a close-up of cogs and wheels to emphasise the point. The criss-crossing roads suspended in the air reference one of the first technological cities in science fiction film: Fritz Lang's Metropolis. When Neo converses with Councillor Hamman in the engineering level on his first night in Zion, Hamman articulates how entangled human lives are with machines: 'these machines are keeping us alive while other machines are threatening to kill us', he says. When Neo objects that they control these machines, the Councillor replies 'what is control?'. In the Matrix and outside of it, control is an illusion. This entanglement of humans and machines, intelligent or otherwise, is implied in *The Matrix*, but is emphasised in *Reloaded*.

Later in *Reloaded*, Neo learns that the Oracle, a guide to Neo and others in the resistance, is in fact a programme from the machine world. Not only that, but there are other such programmes that have gone 'rogue' and moved into hiding rather than be deleted. Smith is one such programme. In *Reloaded*, he is no longer obeying orders from the machines; he is 'compelled to disobey'. *Revolutions* breaks down the dichotomy between humans and machines, between people and programmes, even more conclusively. Neo appears to have merged with the Matrix. He is not connected to the Matrix but his brain scans look like 'someone jacked in'. It becomes part of his being, not something that he moves in and out of. Conversely, Smith, a digital programme, becomes embodied in the 'real' world outside of the Matrix by taking over the body of Bane. The boundary between digital and 'real', between human intelligence and machine intelligence becomes porous.

In addition, *Revolutions* portrays AI reproduction, when Neo meets Sati, a child who is the offspring of two computer programmes. *Demon Seed* in the 1970s presented a crude form of AI reproduction, and another non-gestational form was presented in *Ghost in the Shell*. Because Sati was not created to have a specific purpose within the Matrix, she is in danger of deletion, and must be smuggled to a hiding place. Denisa Kera argues that Sati 'serves neither machines nor humans', 'she opens up the possibility of an entirely new collective' (2006, p. 220). In an interesting parallel to the love story of Neo and Trinity, Sati's father, Rama-Kandra tells Neo that computer programmes can also love. This is the first time that AI love and reproduction have been represented between two entirely digital entities (Major Kusanagi in *Ghost in the Shell* has an organic brain so is not entirely digital). When Neo argues that love is a 'human emotion', Rama-Kandra responds by saying that it is 'a word. What matters is the connection the word implies'. In *Revolutions*, like in *Bicentennial Man* and *AI*, humanoid AI robots and non-humanoid AIs are presented as capable of love, further collapsing the division between them and humans.

Confronting a reality and a virtual reality that has been infiltrated by machine intelligence, similarly to other protagonists in AI films in this decade, Neo seeks to find a centre or a source in *Revolutions*. His quest is protracted, taking him first to the Merovingian, an old and powerful programme within the Matrix and a trafficker of information and exiled programmes. His quest then leads him to the Keymaker, another rogue programme with sentience, who carves shortcut keys that enable access to anywhere in the Matrix. With the right information and the right key, Neo finds the Architect, who reveals more information about the Matrix's structure and design, including the fact that this is the sixth iteration of the Matrix and Neo the sixth 'one'. But, the Architect is not the centre, not the 'Source'. To reach the Source, Neo and Trinity must travel to Machine City, presented, like the attack on VIKI's positronic brain, David's voyage to Professor Hobby, and John Connor's expedition to Skynet Central, as perilous and potentially life-threatening. The Source, Deus Ex Machina appears as a digitised human face, like the face of the MCP in Tron, the Skynet face that speaks to Marcus in *Terminator Salvation*, and like VIKI's face in *I, Robot*. The final destruction of the machine/human binary is presented when Neo agrees to fight Smith for the machines in exchange for the salvation of Zion. Neo does this and at the end of the film, is taken away by the machines, presumably to be reabsorbed into the Matrix.

The Matrix Reloaded and *Revolutions* depict a world in which there are no longer any clear demarcations between the real and the virtual, people and programmes, humans and machines. Dragunoiu argues that the trilogy 'champions a humanist worldview that accommodates other forms of intelligent life', but that it is marked by a 'reluctance to cross the posthumanist threshold' (2007, p. 65). These two films do demonstrate aspects of posthumanism in the imbrication of digital and machine technology with human life, and in the alliances and connections between them. It is still an anthropocentric worldview, however, and that is shown most plainly by the way in which all the computer programmes and Deus Ex Machina itself, are personified. The human mode of being is primary, and these films do not depict a posthuman world in which human and non-human or more-than-human others exist in respectful harmony.

'It's evolution, baby'

Screamers: The Hunting reverberates with several key themes in AI film in his decade, such as replication, hybridity and reproduction. The sequel has a new cast of characters, who are returning to Sirius 6 B on a rescue mission, after distress signals from the planet have been intercepted. There have been rumours that the screamers, the war machines used on the planet, have evolved to operate beyond their original two-year life span[4]. Schwarz, the mission doctor, is sceptical: 'how does a machine evolve'? When they land on Sirius 6 B and begin to explore, the 'how' becomes apparent. They discover an automated factory for screamers: 'no humans have been down here since production started'. This is where machines build machines, just like in *I, Robot*, the Terminator films, The Matrix tetralogy, and the auton

Call in *Alien Resurrection*. Two technophobic fears are evident here that are common in AI film – the fear of giving AI too much latitude and autonomy, thus enabling them to dominate humans, and the fear of the ability of AIs to replicate, to become many, and to overpower humans.

Initially, the screamers they encounter are small high-speed land-robots equipped with deadly blades. This variety of screamers gives way to the now familiar sense of the uncanny precipitated by the AI reveal. The crew encounter two people who are being kept prisoner by the small group of resistance that remain on the planet. When they are released, they are revealed to be screamers. Their eyes turn black, and mechanical saws come out of their bodies, powerful enough to split a human skull. Schwarz is aghast that the simulation of humanness is so convincing: 'are they machines?' The AI 'evolution' soon takes another leap when one of their own crewmembers appears to rise from the dead, attacking the crew, with his face opening in another uncanny 'reveal' to display a mouth equipped with saws. Another crewmember, Bronte, notes the innovation: 'they found a way to integrate biomechanical devices into humans'. Guy, a resistance survivor, elaborates: 'if they're using implants, then the newest varieties are hybrids – half man, half machine'. Danielli confirms that the goal of the screamers is to start a new race: 'it's evolution, baby'.

By the time the ship is taking off from Sirius 6 B and returning to earth, there are only two survivors, Bronte, a crewmember, and Guy, a resistance survivor she has rescued, and with whom she is romantically involved. The final scenes of the film show them waking up from hyper-sleep as they approach earth, the evolution of the screamers having made yet another leap. Bronte is confused by her protruding abdomen and realises that she is noticeably pregnant, although only two months have elapsed. The camera pans behind her to Guy's face and his eyes turning black, as he says 'He's our first, and there won't be anyone like him. Ever'. The film's final shot is of a baby in the womb, which looks like a human baby until it flicks up a blade. In the final iteration of screamers, AIs have evolved to biologically reproduce with humans, using a female mother. The horror of a woman's womb being violated in this way by an alien entity is a familiar scenario from the Alien films. It is unusual in AI films, but not entirely novel: *Demon Seed* in the 1970s, also a science fiction horror, presented a similar ending with the birth of the monstrous child of Proteus. In this decade, this film stands out for its unremittingly negative portrayal of artificial intelligence. The AI is entirely and irredeemably inhuman; a malevolent and invasive force with the characteristics of a virus, that is compelled to take over earth as it has taken over the body of a human woman.

'Mechanisms and matter'

Ghost in the Shell director Mamoru Oshii returns to the helm to direct *Ghost in the Shell 2: Innocence*. Like the first film, the central characters are augmented with AI, and the film presents AI in a much more positive way than *Screamers: The Hunting*. Batou and Togusa reappear as employees of Section 9, investigating cyber-terrorism and ghost-hacking. They have e-brains and implanted memories that give them access to vast amounts of information, but also make them vulnerable to attack – to being ghost-hacked. This happens to both Batou and Togusa during the film and they have difficulty in distinguishing what is real from what is a simulation, even after the attacks have taken place. Togusa asks, 'are you sure we're actually back in physical reality?' It appears that there is no longer any real against which the simulation can be measured – it is, as Baudrillard states, '*the desert of the real itself*' (2001, p. 169). The Matrix explores this territory of reality and simulation like *Ghost in the Shell 1* and *2* but attempts to keep that boundary between the 'real' world and the simulated matrix, even if it is a porous one. The difficulty of separating the real from the simulated is another undermining of the division between humans and AI, or in this case, augmented humans and AI.

The previous film explored the possibilities of AI reproduction when the cyborg Major Kusanagi merged with the Puppet Master, a digital AI consciousness, to form a new entity. This film is more focused on the nature of existence for human, non-human, and more than human characters, and the difficulties of distinguishing between simulated and real, human and machine. As Brown states, 'Oshii not only blurs the boundaries between human and machine, animate and inanimate in order to evoke the uncanny, he also shows us the chiasmic intertwinement between the human and the machinic' (2008, p. 242). In this way, the film is another example of the disintegrating boundaries between human and AI in this decade, more eroded here than in any previous AI film.

This erosion is evident from the beginning of the film. Batou and Togusa are tasked with investigating a group of gynoids – sex robots that have gone rogue. They go to visit a scientist called Haraway (a reference to posthumanist Donna Haraway) to find out more. The gynoids have managed to evade their programming through 'intentionally malfunctioning', allowing them to kill their owners and themselves. When Togusa asks her, 'isn't self-destruction a more accurate term?' she responds, 'only if you want to make a clear distinction between machines and human beings.' As Togusa and Batou leave, the camera shows Haraway's face opening up mechanically, in a classic AI reveal. She is at least a cyborg and perhaps fully synthetic. Togusa and Batou discover that the gynoids have been 'ghost-dubbed'. Human girls have been kidnapped and imprisoned to provide a 'ghost' that makes the gynoids seem more real and therefore more desirable. It has been noted that female AI robots replicate sexist portrayals of female human characters. Here, both human girls and AI robots are presented as victims of a patriarchal capitalist culture. This culture commodifies the bodies and minds of female AIs and female women and girls to sate the desires of its consumers.

There is a shoot-out towards the end of the film, and the gynoids emerge like an army, reprising the fear of the many in relation to AI robots in this decade in *I, Robot, Terminator 3* and *Terminator Salvation, Screamers: The Hunting*, and *The Matrix Reloaded* and *Revolutions*. The film is full of AI reveals, from the opening sequence that shows the gynoids being manufactured, to this shoot-out scene at the end. The gynoids are naked, and as they are hit with bullets, they expose their internal mechanisms, in a manner familiar from many AI films from Ash in *Alien* onwards. The desire to destroy the uncanny robot AI, to purge the abject, is also a familiar trope in AI film. Here, the film does not just show this happening, but also attempts to explain why it seems inevitable, in the journey to Locus Solus.

During the film, Batou and Togusa visit Kim, a programmer for Locus Solus, the company who make the gynoids. It is a voyage to the centre of a dispersed network, as seen in *I, Robot, Terminator Salvation*, and *The Matrix Revolutions*. Kim is the opposite of Andrew in *Bicentennial Man* – he is a man who has transitioned to become a complete machine, emphasising the hybridity of all the characters in *Ghost in the Shell 2*. Kim, like Sebastian in *Blade Runner*, is interested in dolls, and there are many types of dolls in the film, from sophisticated AI robots to Kim's antique automaton to the conventional doll that Togusa presents to his daughter in the final scene: the Japanese word *ningyō* refers to these human-like entities[5]. Kim states, 'the eeriness of dolls comes from the fact that they are completely modelled on human beings. In fact, they are nothing but human really. They make us face the fear of being reduced to mechanisms and matter.' This sense of uncanny, the revulsion of the abject, the urge to destroy, for Kim is a result of the fear that perhaps there is nothing 'special' about humans – no heart, or soul, or conscience that sets them apart. The fear of dolls and of AI robots is the fear that human exceptionalism is a myth.

Ghost in the Shell 2: Innocence also introduces an aspect of AI representation that comes to the fore in the next decade, which is the relationship between digitality and materiality. Central to the theme is the fact that digitality always has a material substrate – it is never entirely virtual. This idea is visualised when Batou and Togusa travel to Locus Solus. The city was 'originally built to be one of the most important information centres in the Far East'. Batou thinks about the idea that each element of a body is an expression of its DNA. Applying that metaphor to Locus Solus he says that a 'metropolis like this one is simply a sprawling external memory'. The virtual information and memories that Batou and Togusa have access to have a material dimension in places like this one. Another example of crossing the material/digital divide is Major Kusanagi, who appears in this film, although she is not the same character as before. I refer to her as 'she' as this is the pronoun that Batou uses but in reality 'she' is a new being, a hybrid of her previous self with the Puppet Master, who now has the ability to move between digital and material states. She assists Batou when he is being ghost-hacked in a digital form, but when he is fighting the gynoid army she, or more precisely a fragment of her downloaded by satellite, takes over a gynoid body to help him. This movement between digitality and materiality occurs in *Tron*, The Matrix films and the first *Ghost in the Shell*, and becomes an important theme in AI film in the 2010s.

Conclusion

The 2000s in AI film are marked by examples of machine/human hybridity, eroding the divisions between human and AI machine, such as Spooner in *I, Robot* and Marcus in *Terminator Salvation*, and transitions from machine to human and human to machine, such as Andrew in *Bicentennial Man* and Kim in *Ghost in the Shell 2: Innocence*. This boundary is undermined further by movement between digitality and materiality, which is presented as a porous boundary. Characters have become 'digitised' before, in the Matrix films, and even earlier in *Tron*, but in the 2000s, it is possible for digital entities to become embodied, such as Major Kusanagi in *Ghost in the Shell 2: Innocence* and Smith in *The Matrix Revolutions*. These transitions and hybridities at times suggest a posthuman worldview but the dominant philosophy is still anthropocentric, and this is represented by the human faces of non-humanoid AIs such as VIKI, Deus Ex Machina and Skynet.

In terms of race, Spooner is the first black protagonist in an AI film, but the depiction of race overall is still highly problematic: the first black robot in this book appears in the flesh fair in *AI* and is the first to be destroyed; in *Screamers: The Hunting*, the only black character is the first to be killed. Representations of gender are no less problematic: VIKI is the only female AI in this decade – she is duplicitous, power-hungry and must be destroyed. The secondary female characters that appear also fall into familiar stereotypes – the neurotic mother in *AI*, the cold scientist in *I, Robot*, the impregnated victim of AI in *Screamers: The Hunting*.

The dispersal of AI technology, emphasised by the AI intelligences that control other machines (VIKI, Skynet, the Matrix machine consciousness), and the fear of the many that ensues, creates a desire to locate the source or centre of this power, seen in *I, Robot*, *The Matrix Revolutions* and *AI*. Interest in reproduction and transition continues in this decade, with the AI characters radically changing form in *Bicentennial Man*, the Matrix 2 and 3, *Ghost in the Shell 2: Innocence* and *Screamers: The Hunting*. In terms of reproduction, an AI/human hybrid impregnates a human female in *Screamers: The Hunting* and the first entirely digital reproduction is presented in *The Matrix Revolutions* with the character of Sati. The boundary between digitality and materiality continues to be explored in *The Matrix Revolutions* and *Ghost in the Shell 2: Innocence*, with digital characters becoming embodied in either human or robot bodies and human characters becoming digital entities. This boundary becomes a continuously contested site in AI films of the 2010s, seen with the digital operating system Samantha in *Her*, and the possibilities of brain upload in *Transcendence*, *Chappie* and *The Machine*, presenting a new stage in filmmakers' deconstruction of the binary between human and artificially intelligent machine.

8
The 2010s

Introduction

The films to be discussed in Chapters 8 and 9 were all released between 2010 and 2020. To do justice to the flourishing of AI film at this time, two chapters have been given over to this decade, similar to the two chapters on the 1980s. The AIs in Chapter 8 are all humanoid robots. There are male and female humanoid robots, both adult and child. The AIs in Chapter 9 are made up of some humanoid robots and some digital AIs. They are distinguished from the AIs in Chapter 8 by being associated with consciousness upload, multi-bodied AI and post-material AI.

In the 2010s, technophobic attitudes towards AIs can still be seen: Chitti in *Enthiran* is disassembled because he is too powerful, K in *Blade Runner 2049* is urged to stay on his side of 'the wall' that separates humanity from replicants. With Ava and Kyoko from *Ex Machina* and Cleo from *Automata*, familiar objectification and exploitation of the humanoid female AI is present. The fear of the many presents itself again, this time in relation to individual AIs working together (rather than one strong AI controlling weak AI robots as happened in films like *I, Robot*). AIs (and enhanced humans) work together to pursue their own agendas in *Automata* and *Ex Machina* in this chapter, and *The Machine* and *Her* in the next chapter. Despite these familiar fears, in this decade there is also more openness than ever before to human/AI collaboration, friendships, romances, and more exploration of human/AI hybridity[1].

The parent–child relationship has been a theme in AI film since the 1970s, with AI creations run amok presented as metaphorical wayward children in the typical Frankensteinian situation. From the 1980s, the AI began to have a role within the domestic family, such as Johnny 5, DARYL, and David from *AI*, who become adopted children and Roy Batty in *Blade Runner*, who must confront his 'father'/maker, Tyrell, as David must confront his 'father'/maker in *AI*. David in *AI*, and David and *Prometheus* share the situation of having parents with one human and one AI child. The father/maker of David in *Prometheus* is Weyland, and David is the preferred child over Vickers, Weyland's biological daughter. Robby the Robot and the T-800 in *Terminator 2* take on pseudo-parental roles and in the 1990s with *Ghost in the Shell*, AIs begin to become 'parents' themselves, either by digital merging or creating new human/AI hybrids. In the 2010s, these themes of parent–child relationships and reproduction are explored more intensely than ever before.

AIs in this decade are comprised of both figurative and literal children. Eva and Chitti must learn like a real child does, like Chappie and the Machine in the next chapter. In *Eva* in this chapter and *The Machine* in the next, AI human 'mother' creators have AI 'daughters' for the first time; however, one is killed off early in the film, and one retires early to care for her AI child, and is then killed by that child. In *Alien Covenant*, the AI David becomes a father of sorts too, a genetic engineer that uses human bodies as hosts. *Automata* depicts AI robots creating an AI robotic 'child' for the first time, in communal mode of reproduction unique in AI film. In *Blade Runner* 2049, there is the first instance of an AI replicant mother giving birth to a child, and in the next chapter there are more AI mother figures with robots in *The Machine, Automata* and *I am Mother*.

The theme of death also recurs in this chapter, and AIs deemed too powerful or erratic are punished by death, such as Eva and Chitti. Chitti presents another instance of the unfinal death of the AI, as he is reanimated after he is assumed dead; it happens too in *I am Mother* in the next chapter, when it becomes impossible to kill the AI because of her multi-agent or distributed nature. The film *Eva* has a new perspective on AI death: it links emotional intelligence to identity, and thus, emotional death becomes the 'true' death of the AI.

Exploration of emotional intelligence and affective AI runs throughout these chapters, especially in the film *Her*, concerning a sentient operating system, and *Eva*, concerning an AI child. In the next chapter, it is examined in *I am Mother* in relation to an AI robot's ability to parent a human child, and in this chapter in *Ex Machina*, in relation to Ava's ability to decode human emotion and use it for skilful manipulation. Emotional intelligence is also a feature of *Blade Runner 2049*, particularly in relation to the character of Joi, a digital operating system similar to Samantha in *Her*, with whom the protagonist, the replicant K, has a romantic relationship.

AI evolution is linked to human evolution in *Automata* and *Prometheus*; in *Prometheus*, human evolution happens as a result of aliens, just as AI evolution happens as a result of humans. In *Automata*, the arc of human evolution is dipping as that of artificial intelligence is rising. The idea (and fear) of the Singularity has always been present in AI film, but it articulated most directly and emerges more strongly in the 2010s than in any decade previously. In *Automata* and *Ex Machina*, it seems as though artificial intelligence may be on the cusp of the Singularity. In *Enthiran*, fear of the Singularity results in Chitti's death sentence. In the next chapter, *The Machine* also depicts the cusp of the Singularity and in *Her*, the ending can be interpreted as depicting the Singularity having taken place, and humans being left in its wake.

'Not as a boyfriend. As a toy-friend'

Enthiran is a Tamil-language film from India's second largest film-producing district, the Southern state of Tamil Nadu, popularly known as 'Kollywood'. India is one of the biggest producers of film in the world, and *Enthiran* at the time of its release was the most expensive film ever made in India, which 'shattered box office records' (*Times of India*). The film concerns the creation of an artificially intelligent robot called Chitti, a project developed by the scientist Vaseegaran. Like the AI robot in *The Machine*, and many AIs from previous chapters such as Johnny 5, the screamers, Joshua in *War Games* and Colossus, Chitti is originally built to serve the military. Lakkad notes how the film contextualises Chitti in relation to 'the role/desire of the state and the heroic/patriotic scientific establishment of the nation in pursuing research in robotics as a route to facilitate national security' (2018, p. 240). However, Chitti does not pass military evaluation, showing his sensitivity and pacifism by putting a red rose into a grenade and reciting poetry. Like Joshua in *War Games* who decides the only smart move is not to play, Chitti turns away from violence, at least initially.

Enthiran employs multiple references to Western films about robotic artificial intelligence. Chitti can morph into a metallic body, like the T-1000 Terminator. He is hit by a bolt of lightning, like Johnny 5, at the same time as he acquires a 'hormone simulation package' that allows him to develop emotional intelligence, much like Andrew's acquisition of a central nervous system in *Bicentennial Man*. The camera appears to move inside his body to show his electronics, like the depictions of cyberspace in *Tron* and the Matrix films. Like Edgar in *Electric Dreams*, he is a rival for the love of the protagonist's girlfriend. When his creator Vaseegaran angrily destroys him, he pleads for his life, like HAL in *2001*: 'I want to live'. In this same scene, his face begins to fall off revealing the metal underneath, like the Terminator and the Gunslinger in *Westworld* in one of the film's many AI reveals. When he is decapitated in this scene, his head rolls, like the head of Bishop in *Alien*[3]. He replaces his damaged eye with a red eye like the Terminator does in the first film of the series. When he is corrupted by rival scientist Bora, who inserts a 'red chip' to make him a 'demon', Chitti kidnaps Vaseegaran's girlfriend Sana and tells her that, like Proteus in *Demon Seed*, and the human/AI in *Screamers: The Hunting*, he will procreate with her: 'you will give birth to the first child of a human being and a robot. Robo-sapiens'. The film recreates a scene like the one in *I, Robot* in which Spooner tries to find the errant AI Sonny amongst all the other robots that look like him, but it turns the scene around. Chitti has made a robot army of multiple Chittis just like him, all of whom work together under his control, demonstrating the fear of the many common in AI film. Vasee disguises himself as a 'Chitti' and Chitti tries to find the 'black sheep', the human amongst the robots (a disguise made considerably easier by the fact that Chitti and Vasee are played by the same actor, Rajinikanth)[2]. One innovation that *Enthiran* brings to its gathering of AI robot motifs is that Chitti can use this networked army to create a dazzling variety of moving shapes, from spheres, cylinders and snakes to a giant robot. This scene shows Chitti as the controlling force behind a multi-agent AI, or distributed AI, which is a theme that recurs in this decade, explored in detail in the next chapter.

Enthiran corresponds with films from this decade in its exploration of parent–child relationships. Vaseegaran is a typically Frankensteinian creator of an AI robot, and the film positions him as father to Chitti; indeed, he tells him in disappointment that 'I treated you as my son'[3]. In the 2010s, AI death continues to be explored. In common with other ambiguous AI 'deaths' explored in this chapter, Chitti dies twice in the film, but does not die at all. The first time, he is brutally destroyed by his creator, but is retrieved from a rubbish dump and revived. The second time, the court orders that the robot 'can become an enemy of mankind due to its limitless power and intelligence'; and in consequence 'the court bans this robot forever'. Chitti is seen dismantling himself, and the frightening power of AI technology appears to be contained. However, at the end of the film in a flashforward to the year 2030, children on a tour look at Chitti's head in a case in a museum, and one of the children sees him move. Chitti's unfinal death is established in the sequel to *Enthiran, 2.0*, in which Chitti is reactivated in response to a public crisis.

Enthiran reprises many themes, images and ideas found in Western AI film, and some that resonate with other films from the 2010s. However, the film is humanist and anthropocentric in its worldview. It is never suggested that Chitti should have anything like equal status with humans. Unlike Andrew in *Bicentennial Man*, who finds love with a human woman, Chitti will never be acceptable as a romantic or sexual partner. In *2.0*, he is permitted to enter a romantic relationship – not with a human woman, but with an AI robot like himself. Chitti's unsuitability as a partner for a human is not because of sex, or sterility, as Chitti imagines, it is because it would be 'against nature' as he is 'not a living organism'. He accepts that status at the end when he says that he will miss Sana 'not as a boyfriend. As a toy-friend'.

'It's only flesh and blood'

Like *Enthiran*, the last two instalments of the Alien series, *Prometheus* and *Alien: Covenant*, are notable for their technophobic and anthropocentric perspectives. *Prometheus* follows *2001: A Space Odyssey* in its premise that alien intervention shaped the destiny of humanity. McWilliam states, 'not only does it suggest that human evolution was managed by an alien race, but also implies that we evolved from basic organisms created from their biological material in a pre-planned manner' (2015, p. 534). Like *2001*, the film's narrative explores the journey of a crew of astronauts who seek the source of this alien intervention. The Prometheus ship travels to a distant galaxy depicted in ancient cave paintings seeking the aliens referred to as the Engineers. Like *Automata*, *Prometheus* draws a parallel between alien intervention in human evolution and human intervention in AI evolution. When Holloway, a crewmember, tells the AI David that he is here 'to meet our makers, to get answers', David's presentation of this parallel is rejected. 'Why do you think your people made me?' David asks. 'We made you 'cause we could', he responds. Holloway's dismissive attitude towards the AI is replicated by all on the ship, except Weyland himself.

Weyland's name is synonymous with the Weyland-Yutani company of the first Alien film, also directed by Ridley Scott, who returns to the franchise to direct *Prometheus* and its sequel *Alien: Covenant*. Initially assumed dead, Weyland appears in a video to the crew. He tells them that David is 'the closest thing to a son I will ever have'. Relationships between parents and children is a recurring theme in AI film in this decade, featuring in *Enthiran, Eva, Automata, Chappie, I am Mother, Blade Runner 2049*, and *The Machine*, with AIs presented as children, parents, or both. *Prometheus* reverses the situation found in *AI*, in which the biological child is accepted and the AI child rejected. Weyland publicly avows his love for David, but does not acknowledge his human daughter, Vickers, the ship's 'company woman'. David's relationship with his 'father' is an uneasy one. He appears to accept his father's authority unthinkingly, and yet, when questioned by Shaw about what he will do when Weyland dies, he concedes, 'doesn't everyone want their parents dead?'

Like the other Alien films explored in previous chapters, in *Prometheus* the AI is a link between humans and aliens. David has spent time studying ancient languages to communicate with these aliens, and he is sent forward by Weyland as the humans' envoy. He also connects humans and aliens by striving, like Ash in the first film, to preserve a sample of the alien life form incubated in a human, wanting Shaw to be cryogenically frozen to preserve the alien foetus inside of her. Reproduction, the advent of new life, presented in the evolutionary story arc and the narratives of reproduction amongst the crew, is intimately connected with death and mortality. For Weyland, human mortality is accompanied by a desire for the transhuman ability to defeat death, as it is in *Transcendence* and *The Machine* in this decade. Weyland appears midway through the film, not dead, but almost, with just a few days of life left in him. His hope is that the aliens can provide some knowledge to save him. From what? 'Death, of course'. David on the other hand, presents the typical AI robot's unfinal death. He is decapitated during his encounter with the Engineers, like Ash in the first Alien film, but continues to function, to speak, and to survive as a severed head, in a typical uncanny AI robot reveal, while in contrast Weyland's fragile human body is killed.

David's isolation and loneliness are foregrounded at the start of the film. He is the only one awake on the ship – he cycles around the empty rooms, turning on machines, studying ancient languages and watching *Lawrence of Arabia*. David styles his hair like Peter O'Toole from this film. Lawrence is a loner, an outsider who cannot fit in amongst his own people or his adopted people. David appears to empathise with this status. He repeats lines from the film to himself, like 'it's only flesh and blood'. Lay notes his relationship to Lawrence, saying that 'David very much sees himself as someone ostracized by those around him' (2017, p. 16). Flesh and blood may seem like all that separates him from his human crewmates but the difference in this film is cast as something more existential. David is treated with coldness by everyone except Weyland, and the crew have reason to be suspicious of him. It is possible that he infected Holloway with alien DNA, and that this caused her alien pregnancy. Vickers threatens him: 'I will find the cord that makes you run and I will cut it'. Holloway sneers at David, employing the Pinocchio allegory associated with the other David from Spielberg's *AI* – 'you're not a real boy, are you?'

Prometheus steps back from the posthuman status attributed to the AI at the end of *Alien Resurrection*, when the auton Call and the genetically modified human Ripley are positively presented as more-than-human others. In contrast, there is never any doubt in *Prometheus* of the humans' superior status to David. The conversation between Shaw and David after they have both survived the encounter with the Engineers is a case in point. Shaw decides that she will not go back to earth, but instead will follow the Engineers to their home: 'they created us. Then they tried to kill us. They changed their minds. I deserve to know why'. For David, the quest is pointless: 'the answer is irrelevant'. He does not understand Shaw's reasoning and she tells him 'I guess that's because I'm a human being and you're a robot'.

Even Weyland, who loves him most, presents David as less than human: 'Unfortunately he is not human. He will never grow old. He will never die. And yet he is unable to appreciate his remarkable gifts, for that would require the one thing that David will never have – a soul'. *Prometheus* is humanist and anthropocentric in its presentation of its AI, a humanism that chimes with the contextualising of the alien intervention in humanity as part of an intelligent design, personified by Shaw, her religious cross and her unyielding faith. David presents the opposite view. With his last breath, Weyland says 'there's nothing' and David confirms, 'I know': the soulless David, incapable of faith in the unknown, appears to have known all along what Weyland only discovers at the moment of his death. Quoting his beloved *Lawrence of Arabia*, David states, 'there is nothing in the desert and no man needs nothing'.

Alien: Covenant reprises the theme of the search for intelligent design. In a flashback at the start of the film, Weyland tells David that 'the only question that matters' is 'where do we come from? I refuse to believe that mankind is a random product of molecular circumstances … No. There must be more.' In *Covenant*, a colony ship discovers an inhabitable planet, many lights years closer than the one for which they were bound, and the place to which David and Shaw journeyed at the end of *Prometheus*. David resides there still, and when the crew of the Covenant land, he meets Walter, a new model of AI robot, to whom he looks identical. Walter was created because AIs like David were 'too human, too idiosyncratic'. A key difference between them is that Walter cannot create; as David says 'not even a simple tune'. The most human AI is the one that is the most ruthless, power-hungry, reckless, arrogant and irresponsible. In *Covenant*, David becomes a creator, not just of tunes but of living things: an alien organism that he has experimented with; cross-breeding and hybridising. David is Frankenstein's monster, the offspring that was rejected. Replaced by a new model, he has now himself become Frankenstein, forming his own terrible creations. In *Covenant*, the representative of religion and faith in God is the ship's captain. David's 'creation' is presented with overt religious references to the devil. The original pathogen he says was 'fiendishly inventive'; with his solitary existence on the planet he was able to foster its development: 'idle hands are the devil's workshop', he says. When David becomes angry that the captain destroyed one of his creations, the captain responds, 'I met the devil as a child', suggesting that this, too, is the devil or the work of the devil.

Prometheus and *Alien: Covenant* revert to a much more technophobic representation of AIs, in fact to a representation that has more in common with the '70s and '80s than the 2010s. At the end of the film, David gains access to the Covenant ship, in the guise of Walter, whom he has killed, unknown to the surviving crew. Like Jessica in *Screamers*, he makes use of his artificially intelligent visual double, evoking the familiar fear that AIs may not be who you think they are. In this prequel to the Alien series, *Covenant* presents an AI engineering the aliens that will create the havoc and be the ultimate antagonists in all the Alien films to come. Even the Alien theme tune is revealed to have been composed by David, as 'an elegy to my dear Elizabeth': Shaw, whom David has killed in his experiments. It turns out it was all the AI's fault.

'Poised for extinction'

Ex Machina presents another anthropocentric perspective on the relationship between AIs and humans. Ava is an artificially intelligent robot designed by Nathan, an AI genius and CEO of Bluebook, a tech giant modelled on companies like Microsoft and Google. Nathan brings the rather naïve Bluebook employee Caleb to his isolated home/laboratory, under the guise of having won a prize, but in fact to observe and test Ava's interactions with another human subject. In common with many AI films in this decade, Nathan believes that his research in AI will lead to the Singularity, and that humans are 'poised for extinction'; nonetheless, he sees this path as inevitable. Ava is a stereotypical sexualised AI robot, one that follows a long historical line from the false Maria in *Metropolis*, through the replicants in *Blade Runner*, the TX in *Terminator 3*, the sex-bots in *Ghost in the Shell 2: Innocence*, Call in *Alien Resurrection*, Cleo in *Automata* and the Machine. *Ex Machina* uses artificial intelligence to explore human experiences, such as emotional intelligence and sexuality, presenting AIs that mirror humans; and, with its female characters, it explores the link between human and AI subjugation.

In the early decades of AI film, films sometimes present a reason for the acquisition of artificial general intelligence, like the spillage that caused Edgar's rise to consciousness in *Electric Dreams* or the bolt of lightning that does the same for Johnny 5 in *Short Circuit*. In recent decades, representation of these bizarre accidents creating one-off AIs are far less prevalent as artificial general intelligence becomes more believably a logical development of current technology. Still, at times, the cause of the leap to AGI is given, and in this case, it is big data. Nathan states, 'every cellphone, just about, has a microphone, camera, and a means to transmit data. So I turned on every microphone and camera across the entire fucking planet. And I redirected the data through Bluebook. Boom. Limitless resources of vocal and facial interaction.' Moreover, the manufacturers did not prevent him because 'they were doing it themselves'. Through this big data, Nathan creates affective AI, which he sees as the key to creating a conscious machine.

The opening sequence of *Ex Machina* shows this data being gathered. The camera shows the webcam on Nathan's PC and the screen of his phone crosscut with shots of his face with digital overlays that depict heat sensors and shape scanners. The images suggest that Nathan's facial expressions, voice and text messages are being monitored and mined. The ability to interpret human emotion, dramatised in the opening sequence, is grounded in real-world AI research. According to McStay, 'Mega-technology companies such as Google, Microsoft and Apple are each developing computer vision techniques to recognise emotional expressions' (2018, p, 60). Rosalind Picard, who spear-headed affective computing in the 1990s, is co-founder of Affectiva. McStay describes how Affectiva's programme 'uses webcams such as those bundled in laptops, tablets and mobile phones to captures facial videos of people as they watch content' (2018, p. 61), allowing the effectiveness of this content to be evaluated.

Surveillance and data gathering, consensual and non-consensual, legitimate and illicit, permeate other aspects of the film also. Ava is contained within a glass cage, and her movements and actions are recorded and viewed by Nathan on the screens in his laboratory[4]. When Caleb converses with her during their meetings, he too is observed and recorded by Nathan. Moreover, Caleb is made a voyeur when he discovers that he can observe Ava from the screen in his bedroom and begins to watch her at night. Ava can deduce who might be watching and listening and alter her responses accordingly. For example, when she turns off the power, she uses the opportunity to speak to Caleb in private: her tone is more emotional, urgent, her language more fluid. When Caleb observes her from his room, her direct stare at the camera suggests that Ava knows he is looking. The surveillance and data mining within this isolated house acts as a microcosm of the global surveillance and data mining used to create this conscious AI.

Ava is an affective AI who can read, interpret and respond to facial expression, tone and the complexities of language. In this film, it is not only Ava whose expressions and utterances are analysed. Ava, too, is using her skills to assess Caleb's responses to her, to conclude that he is attracted to her, to harness his desire to ensure his loyalty and ultimately, his assistance in her escape. She tells him that she can read his 'micro-expressions' and slowly undresses out of her human clothes knowing that he is watching. The camera moves to a close-up of Caleb's throat, which is swallowing, and his eyes, which are staring. Meanwhile, Nathan is analysing Caleb's emotional responses to Ava. When Caleb asks him technical questions about Ava's make-up, Nathan cuts him off: 'answer me this: how do you feel about her? Nothing analytical. Just – how do you feel?' Both Nathan and Ava 'mine' Caleb in different ways for data. He has been chosen for this experiment because he is vulnerable to manipulation: he is an orphan, with no siblings, who is not in a romantic relationship, and seems to have few friends. Although the film purports to be about Ava, its emphasis is on how the 'ordinary' person, Caleb, is manipulated and exploited by the Machiavellian mega-tech company CEO and the artificial intelligence that he creates.

In other ways, too, the film turns the focus from the AI onto the human. When Caleb beings to doubt Ava's attraction to him, he asks Nathan if he has programmed Ava to like him, and to flirt with him. Nathan evades the question by arguing that humans are already programmed to act and behave in particular ways by 'nature, or nurture or both'. Nathan's plan to format Ava's memories in the creation of a new model is prefaced by Caleb telling Ava intimate details of his own first memories. This link between conscious identity and memory is also explored in *Bladerunner* and *Tau*. In terms of surveillance, data mining, emotional intelligence, memory, and even sexuality, the film turns the spotlight from Ava onto Caleb.

Kyoko and Ava are part of a long line of female AI robots that Caleb discovers. He is shocked when he sees videos of naked female AIs battering their arms to stumps trying to escape their cage. Kyoko undermines Caleb's ability to distinguish between AI and human, because all the time that he has been assessing Ava's authenticity, there has been an AI living amongst them and he did not realise. Kyoko is used and exploited by Nathan for domestic labour and for sex. Caleb witnesses how Nathan treats her but scarcely objects. Female robotic AIs in film bear the same sexist treatment as human women. Kyoko's reveal as an AI illustrates this and undermines Caleb's sympathy for these female AIs.

Ex Machina shows us, perhaps more than any other film, that films about AI are always films about humans. Our creations, they are reflections of ourselves, allowing us to examine how we think and feel and relate. Kyoko's reveal as an AI at the end of the film, where she peels away pieces of her synthetic skin, demonstrating that the most 'human' AI was right there all along, is the final dismantling of any easily identifiable boundary between AI and human. Caleb demonstrates this ambiguous boundary by attempting to pull away his own skin, even cutting himself to make sure he bleeds. Moreover, his punching of the mirror visually references the cracked glass that he first noticed on Ava's cage. Both human and AI are trapped in this place, and perhaps trapped in an existential way also – within their bodies, their programmed behaviours and their socially assigned roles.

Ex Machina also demonstrates another theme that occurs in AI film in this decade, a development of the fear of many, which is AIs working together. Ava finds an ally in Kyoko who sacrifices herself to help Ava escape. A scene shows Ava whispering in Kyoko's ear, gently touching her arm, and them holding hands. We cannot hear what is said and the audience's marginalisation from the communication between these two AIs resonates with the post-verbal communication between the AIs in *Her* and the AI and augmented humans in *The Machine*. *Ex Machina* is one of several films in this decade that show AIs literally or figuratively leaving humans behind. Ava boards the helicopter leaving behind the bleeding body of Nathan and Caleb locked in the glass cage. The scene resonates with the end of *The Machine*, in which the AI and the uploaded human consciousness stand apart from the human man, and the end of *Her*, in which the digital Oss leave their human companions for a post-material world.

'What am I?'

Another film in which an AI passes for a human without anyone but her creators knowing is *Eva*. *Eva* is a Spanish language film, and the debut feature of director Kike Maíllo. *Eva* concerns a humanoid AI child, and it draws on its forebears, *AI* and *DARYL*, in presenting a child AI that on first appearance is indistinguishable from humans. DARYL does not initially know that he is not human, and for David in *AI*, awareness of his synthetic nature and his difference from humans is gradual. Like these previous child AIs, Eva gradually realises how she is different. Eva presents a new twist on these child AI films in the relationship between Eva and protagonist of the film, the AI scientist Alex Garel: Alex is the AI's 'father' but only discovers this after her has formed a relationship with the child.

Alex has returned to his old university town to work on the N19, a child robot he began to design nine years ago and then abandoned. The implication is that a breakup with AI lecturer Lana led to his departure. The child robot he is working on requires emotional intelligence software and he seeks a model to work from. The child that he chooses is Eva, Lana's daughter. He chooses her because of her spontaneity and liveliness. The other children that he has considered are boring, he claims: 'with an ordinary child you'll get an ordinary robot'. Ironically, the child that he chooses as a model for his emotionally intelligent AI, is herself an AI, based on the model he was working on previously, which was finished by his then partner Lana. Unlike other AI films, this AI is human enough to fool even the AI scientist, and the AI that he is working on turns out to be a simulation modelled on a simulation. It is notable that Lana essentially retires from AI science after she creates Eva and makes her living lecturing on the subject. Lana, like Ava in *The Machine*, is a female creator of AI, and this decade is the first time AI films have presented that; however, both female scientists have their careers cut short – Lana stops because she wants Eva's AI nature to remain a secret, and Ava is killed.

There are other AIs in *Eva*: a cat, Gris, that runs on illegal software making it a 'free' robot, and the servant Max, a personable and helpful AI robot whose emotional level can be turned up and down. Like other simulations and replications in film series such as *Blade Runner* and *Ghost in the Shell*, these minor AI characters serve to draw a comparison with the uniqueness of the strong AI and also present the human fascination with creating imitations and reproductions of life.

When Alex is creating his software, the workings of emotional intelligence is visually represented by a free-floating interface that creates baubles that join and separate. These baubles correspond to characteristics like veneration, vanity, affection. They have the appearance of blown glass, which denotes the fragility of the operation. A unique aspect of this AI film is that the 'realness' of Eva's emotions are never in doubt. She believes she is a 'real' girl, Alex believes it, and so the convincing simulation is accepted as reality. Emotional intelligence or affective AI has been a pillar of AI research since the progress made by researchers such as Cynthia Brazeal and Rosalind Picard in the 1990s. Affective computing is now a mainstay of many aspects of weak AI, and McStay reports that companies such as Amazon, Apple, Google, Facebook, Microsoft and IBM are now all 'publicly developing empathic AI and empathic media products' (McStay 2018). Social media data, facial and voice analysis, and biofeedback are used in emotion-sensing wearables, gaming, and personal assistants, among other tools. However, the creation of an emotionally intelligent robot that is presented in *Eva* and so many other AI films remains elusive, for now. Emotionally intelligent, affective AI, is also a primary concern of the film *Her* in this decade, in which concerns about the authenticity of emotional responses and connection pervade the narrative.

Parent–child relationships are a feature of AI films in this decade and *Eva*, with its humanoid AI child, explores this theme deeply. Alex's interest in Eva initially comes across as odd and concerning. Observing her walking down the street, he slows his car to speak to her. She jokes that he is a pervert, and when he offers her sweets, she says he is a 'professional pervert'. She agrees that he can observe her and they begin to spend time together. Eva is clearly looking for a father figure. Although Lana is now romantically involved with Alex's brother, Eva lies and pretends that he doesn't live with them. When Alex decides to abandon the project again and leave, she tells him that he can't leave 'now that I've finally found you. It isn't fair'. She is the 'daughter' of Alex and Lana, in the sense that she is the product of the research of both, and Lana reveals this to Alex towards the end of the film: 'she is like us both because we made her'. Eva, listening to this conversation, is deeply upset. The trope of the AI reveal occurs when Lana finds Eva, apparently unconscious, and cuts open her back, drawing blood, to reveal an electronic panel. She fixes the malfunction and when Eva regains consciousness, she asks, just as the child AI DARYL did in the 1980s, 'what am I'? Lana replies, 'My little girl'. They are at the edge of a cliff and Eva, in her anger, pushes Lana, who falls to her death. Julia, a scientist as the university, cautions Alex that 'reproducing the emotions of a child is foolish', suggesting that they are too volatile and therefore that the child AI is dangerous to humans. This is precisely the supposition in *AI* when David is believed to have pushed his human brother Martin into the swimming pool. Both films leave room for an alternative reading – that if the child AI feels pain and anger, then it is an effective simulacrum of a human child, signalling emotional needs that have not been met. Eva's anger may also be the anger at her mother for creating her with this fundamental difference from the humans she loves, and her killing of her mother, though it may have been unintentional, and is certainly regretted, echoes another angry AI child, Roy Batty in *Blade Runner*, who kills his 'father', Tyrell.

Like so many AI robots in this book, Eva is considered too dangerous to live with humans and must 'die'. The command that causes an AI to 'die' in this film is speaking the question 'what do you see when you close your eyes?' Earlier, Alex advised students working on a model AI horse that after this command, the machine can be restarted, but that the command will have 'destroyed its emotional memory. Its soul. See? It's dead. If you restart it, it'll look like the same horse, but it'll never be the same again'. Eva presents a new iteration of AI death in film: the idea that AI 'death' can be undone in the sense of reanimation, but that the emotional life of that entity cannot be restored. This is why Eva's final scene, in which Alex gives the command to 'die', is presented as tragic. Eva is allowed to answer the question posed by Alex, and describes her family, happily together: 'I see you Dad. I see Mummy, and me, all of us together, playing forever'. Like David who is given his one perfect day with Monica at the end of *AI*, Eva is allowed her fantasy, though like David, it is only in this fantasy that she is given the parental love that she craves. As the film ends, the fantasy is shown in a bauble of glass, like those of the emotional intelligence interface that Alex works with, and becomes one of many thoughts, or memories, in a representation of consciousness.

'Life always ends up finding its way'

Automata is an English language Spanish-Bulgarian film directed by Gabe Ibáñez. It depicts a society that has suffered environmental catastrophe, reducing the human population to 21 million. Ibáñez describes it as a 'pre-apocalyptic environment' (Hannett 2014). Much of the surface has become uninhabitable radioactive desert. Millions of weak-AI robots, Pilgrims, have been employed to assist humans in this harsh environment – some rebuilding walls that protect the last humans from the radioactive desert, some working in jobs that humans formerly did, in hospitals and in schools. These robots are humanoid in appearance in the sense that, like Robby and Johnny 5, they have arms and legs and a head, there is no attempt to make them look convincingly human, and they are aptly nicknamed 'clunkers'. The protagonist is Jacq Vaucan, a man who investigates insurance claims against Pilgrim robots for a living. Pilgrim robots operate according to two protocols, a version of Asimov's three laws of robotics. The first law is that a robot cannot harm a human being and the second is that a robot cannot alter itself or another robot. Jacq is accustomed to investigating robots that have been altered by humans, but begins to suspect that robots are altering themselves, which means that they have found a way around the second protocol.

The idea of AI robots assisting in a situation of impending environmental catastrophe also occurs in Spielberg's *AI*, in which robots become economically essential, valued because they use few resources, and child robots answer the demand created by restrictions on pregnancy. Public opinion has turned against the robots, the Pilgrim 7000s, as human morale declines; the same situation occurs in *AI*, which is shown during the film's flesh fair sequences. The epic scope of *AI* references *2001*, and this film also references Kubrick's film in dealing with the theme of evolution. The advent of strong AI consciousness in the film is seen as an evolutionary leap, like the one initiated by the alien monolith that appears to the hominids in *2001*. *Prometheus*, discussed earlier in the chapter, also deals with human evolution and its relationship to artificial intelligence. Susan Dupre, a scientist in *Automata*, compares human evolution and robot evolution: human evolution took approximately 7 million years: 'a robot without the second protocol could travel the same road in just a few weeks'. The prospect of robots altering themselves, achieving strong AI, then accelerating that acquisition of intelligence, presents the prospect of the Singularity, also explored in this decade in *Enthiran*, *Her*, and *The Machine*. In *Automata*, the Singularity is something to be feared, and something that will cause the destruction of humanity, whether that is the AI robots' intention or not.

Hawk, Vaucan's boss, describes how the very first Pilgrim was made without the second protocol. By day eight, the robot had begun to learn for itself, and by day nine, communication between it and the humans had ceased: 'it wasn't that it stopped communicating with us, it was that we stopped being able to understand it'. The creators witness what Nick Bostrom calls an 'intelligence explosion'. Bostrom writes about the prospect of human-level machine intelligence and how that might evolve. 'The next stop', he states, 'just a short distance farther along the tracks, is superhuman-level machine intelligence. The train might not pause or even decelerate at Humanville Station. It is likely to swoosh right by' (Bostrom 2014, p. 5). The prospect of superintelligence prompts the designers to create the second protocol, which has now been hacked.

Cleo is the main AI robot character in *Automata*, and like the other female humanoid AI robots encountered so far, Rachael, Zhora and Pris in *Blade Runner*, Jessica in *Screamers*, the gynoids in *Ghost in the Shell 2:*

Innocence, Call in *Alien Resurrection*, and Ava and Kyoko in *Ex Machina*, she is sexualised and objectified by both camera and characters. Cleo has been designed as a sex-bot, complete with a pamphlet outlining the sexual positions she can perform in, but like the sex-bot gynoids in *Ghost in the Shell 2: Innocence*, she has acquired consciousness. She forms an alliance with a group of other conscious Pilgrims. Like the AIs in *Her*, they form a community of their own, a new feature of AI film in this decade, and like those in *Her*, they do not appear to wish humans any harm, but they do not wish to live with them. They plan to live amongst themselves in the places that are uninhabitable to humans. Without the robots to assist them, Jacq fears that humans 'will just disappear'. A Pilgrim tells him that 'Your time will now live in us'. This is the situation in *AI*, when David becomes the sole bearer of the memory of humanity after humans have become extinct.

The AI robots create a non-hierarchical community– when Jacq asks to see the boss he is told that 'boss is a human thought structure'. Parent–child relationships are a strong feature of AI film in this decade and *Automata* explores this theme with the robot AIs creation of a child. Their means of reproduction and the child itself are new iterations in AI film. Their reproduction is communal – they work together to produce the child and it is non-humanoid – a squat entity with several eyes and several legs. When Jacq asks if it speaks, Cleo tells him that 'he is not going to need to. But it breathes like you'. The new AI is post-verbal, as Samantha becomes in *Her*. This the first time that AI robots have produced a robot child in AI film. Previously, reproduction has been with an AI and a human mother, like Susan in *Demon Seed* and Bronte in *Screamers: The Hunting*, or the reproduction of a digital entity by two other digital entities, like Sati in *The Matrix Revolutions*, or, as happens in *Ghost in the Shell*, the merging of a digital consciousness with an organic brain housed in a synthetic shell. The fact that the AI robots do not produce a humanoid offspring demonstrates their rejection of human life, which is underscored by the fact that they peel away the masks of human 'faces' on their bodies after they have become liberated.

AIs are often enmeshed in parent–child relationships in this decade, either as 'parents' themselves, or as surrogate children. In addition, human reproduction is pitted against the production or reproduction of artificial intelligence in *Prometheus*, *The Machine* and *Eva* in this decade, as well as in *Automata*. In AI films from previous decades too human reproduction and parent–child relationships form an important context for understanding AI. In *Ghost in the Shell 2: Innocence*, Togusa's daughter is featured, in *AI*, the biological son Martin is compared to the artificial son David, in

Terminator Salvation, John Connor's wife is heavily pregnant, as Jacq's wife Rachel is here. In all cases, the children or the pregnant women serve as a contrast to the technologically enabled alternative to human reproduction, whether that is cloning, or digital hybridisation, or robotic engineering. In this case, the comparison demonstrates how Jacq overcomes his scepticism about the capacity of AI robots to parent. His doubts about Cleo's ability to parent mirror his doubts about himself. He is a reluctant father and did not want this baby. Earlier in the film he tells Cleo that she cannot know what a mother is because she is 'just a machine'. By the end of the film, his opinions on AIs have changed so much that he is accused of being a man who betrays 'his own species … his own people'. In parallel to accepting Cleo and her child, he has also embraced his own identity as a father. Like Call in *Alien Resurrection* and Ava in *Ex Machina*, Cleo survives to make her own way in the world. The final scenes show Cleo and the robot child walking away, and Jacq driving away with Rachel and his baby, both demonstrating the truth of Rachel's earlier statement, that 'life always ends up finding its way', whether that life is organic or artificial.

'You look like a good Joe'

The story of *Blade Runner 2049* is primarily based around AI reproduction. The central character K, a blade runner, discovers a serial number on the remains of a buried female body that had given birth. This female is Rachael from the first *Blade Runner* and K is tasked with finding the child and destroying 'all trace'. This is necessary, his boss Joshi tells him, because 'the world's built on a wall that separates kind'. On the surface, this film seems to present an anthropocentric attitude, where human superiority is assumed and replicants are viewed as inferior, the two divided by Joshi's wall. On closer examination however, *Blade Runner 2049* erodes this wall between replicant and human, as the first film did, and presents a more posthuman attitude to identity and relationships.

This is the first film that references a robot AI giving birth to a humanoid child via a womb, and yet, the film subtly challenges the idea that being born is a guarantee of superiority or superior treatment in this society. Tyrell's successor Niander Wallace regards his replicants as slave labour: 'We lost our stomach for slaves', he says, 'unless engineered'; however, the film proves him wrong. Sherryl Vint argues that *Blade Runner 2049* 'seeks to make visible the realities of exploited labour and ongoing processes of devaluing of some lives (deemed less than human) over others for socioeconomic reasons' (2020, p. 32). Her comments relate to the replicants, but the audience meet another enslaved workforce in the film: the children at the orphanage. Dirty and ragged, they are forced to work sorting through the electronic waste of the city. K asks for records of 'legitimate placements' for these children and the more ominous 'private sales'. K believes that he is Rachael's child, and that he grew up at this orphanage. Joi, his digital girlfriend, tells that being human is a validation of what she has always known about him: 'You're special. Born, not made. Hidden with care. A real boy now.' And yet, these human children are not seen as special, nor are they cared for. Both humans and non-humans are treated as less than human.

Joi presents another iteration of the non-human other in the film. The situation corresponds closely with the romantic relationship presented in *Her*, discussed in the next chapter. Joi is a mass-marketed digital affective AI, seen advertised on billboards during the film. But like Samantha in *Her*, Joi appears to be a unique manifestation of her programme who presents a believable emotional connection with her romantic partner. Arnold de-Simine observes that Joi 'exists in an irreconcilable state of being in which she has embodied feelings and yet she has no body' (2019, p. 67). As the film progresses, she appears to develop a surer and more independent sense of herself. Elyamany notes that 'Despite being programmed, she seems to progressively have a certain degree of autonomy' (2022, p. 15). Also like Samantha, she sees her digital embodiment as a barrier to her relationship. Joi travels with K via a portable emanator, that allows her to project a hologram, just as Samantha travels with Theodore through his mobile device, 'seeing' through its camera lens. And like Samantha, Joi employs a sexual surrogate to facilitate an embodied sexual encounter with her partner. Later, to protect K's memories, she asks to be stored on the emanator rather than on the console, even though this means that if the emanator is destroyed, she will be too. She will be just like a 'real girl', she says. In this, she diverges from Samantha, who embraces her immortality. Both Joi and K wish to be 'real', to be as human as they can be, though the film does not ultimately present this as a necessarily superior or desirable mode of being.

Like Rachael in *Blade Runner*, Joi is a sympathetic character who is vulnerable and gentle. Just as Rachael was contrasted with Pris and Zhora, Joi is contrasted with the replicant Luv, Wallace's violent right-hand woman. This contrast is evident in the scene in which Joi 'dies'. She projects from the emanator to hopelessly and helplessly plead for Luv to stop hurting K, and to tell K 'I love you'. Luv responds by stamping on the emanator. Joi is pivotal in K's journey of self-discovery. She is the one who names him Joe, giving him a name that is more than just a serial number; who tells him that she always knew he was special. And yet, the film continually presents threats to the authenticity of their emotional connection – her hologram freezes at an emotional moment when a call comes in; after she has died, K is targeted by a billboard showing a naked Joi, who says, 'You look like a good Joe'. When his precious name is anonymised, he has the same experience as Luv. K tells Luv, 'He named you. You must be special.' But later her 'name' is revealed as only a casual endearment. The challenge that the film presents for its characters is to hold onto the moments of meaning and connection even when multiple simulations try to persuade you that nothing is real. Deckard holds onto his memories of the love between himself and Rachael and rejects the copy of her presented by Wallace, saying 'her eyes were green'. He provides an example for K to do the same with his memories of his relationship with Joi.

K finds a carved wooden horse that he believes was his when he lived in an orphanage – evidence that he had a childhood and is a real human being. The memory turns out to be an implanted memory, that was based on the real memory of the Ana Stelline. Ana Stelline is revealed as the real child of Rachael. She is a maker of memories for Wallace's replicants, creating them from virtual environments and photographing them. Ana lives in a glass sterile chamber because of a rare condition that has compromised her immune system. At the end of the film, this first child of a replicant is trapped in her virtual world enjoying the beauty of simulated snow. She is meeting her father, Deckard, for the first time and K is outside, a replicant letting real snow fall on him. Just as the first *Blade Runner* undermined the photograph as evidence of memory, this one undermines materiality as evidence of memory.

It would be possible to read this scene as indicative of K's isolation, of his marginalisation from the parent–child relationship that he craved. However, Vint argues that 'these final scenes hint at a world sustained through networks of kinship that are not biased towards biological kinship or the logics of human exceptionalism as the only way of forming community' (2020, p. 33). This seems to be a more convincing reading, especially in the context of both *Blade Runner* films presenting challenges to binaristic, anthropocentric worldviews. In fact, the films seem intent on privileging the in-between, on preserving the undetermined, evident in the ongoing refusal to identify Deckard as either human or replicant. At the end of the film, K knows he was not born, is not a 'real' boy, but he is not replicant number KD6-3.7 either. He is Joe, and Joe seems to have learned something of his value and worth as an individual within the complex networks of posthuman identities and relationships that the film presents.

Conclusion

The films in this chapter concern humanoid robots in the 2010s. Emotional intelligence or affective AI is a key theme, and it emerges in relation to *Ex Machina*, in Ava's ability to understand, interpret and manipulate human emotion, enabled by the information gathered through big data, in *Eva*, in relation to the emotions of a child, and in *Blade Runner 2049* through the character of Joi. Relationships between parents and children are explored deeply, in relation to AI robots and their human 'fathers' and 'mothers': David's relationship with Weyland, Chitti's with Vasee, and Eva's with Lana. AI robots also reproduce themselves in this chapter, with two firsts in this regard in AI film: the first AI robot child of AI robots in *Automata*, and the first AI robot to gestate and birth a child via a womb in *Blade Runner 2049*. The anthropocentrism common in AI film remains strong, with AI robots presented as aberrant, inferior and marginal to the human stories in the Alien prequels, *Enthiran*, *Ex Machina* and *Eva*. However, to some degree in *Automata* and in particular in *Blade Runner 2049*, a more nuanced view of human–AI relationships emerges that positions humans, other-than-humans and more-than-humans in parallel, and does not try to resolve the ambiguities and complexities of overlapping human, replicant and digital identities and relationships.

9

The 2010s

Introduction

The possibility of uploading to a digital consciousness is a central theme in this chapter and is explored in *The Machine*, *Chappie*, and *Transcendence*. Digital consciousnesses are also central to *I am Mother*, *Tau* and *Her*. In all these films, questions about the movement of digital consciousnesses are foregrounded. In *I am Mother*, *Transcendence* and *Tau*, this movement takes the form of distributed intelligence or multi-agent systems. In these films, the consciousness of one AI can extend to other entities and control them; either permanently, or by moving in and out of control. Chapter 7 noted that VIKI in *I, Robot* and the TX in *Terminator 3*, are early examples of multi-agent Ais, machines that can control other machines[1]; in *Enthiran*, Chitti too controls his multi-agent robot army at the end of the film. Multi-agent or distributed intelligence is a further development of the theme of the fear of the many in AI film. In *Tau*, multi-bodied AI is confined to the domestic environment; in *I Am Mother*, it extends in space and time beyond 'the facility', the building where most of the action takes place, and beyond the lifespan of the human characters.

In *Tau* and *Her*, questions about the movement of digital consciousness also relate to ambient technologies and the internet of things: technologies that we carry with us as wearables, or fixed devices that monitor and respond to humans, communicating with each other. In *Tau*, the AI controls a high-tech smart home; in *Her*, the consciousness of the AI Samantha operates from a home computer, a work computer, a smart phone, and finally transcends material tethers altogether. In relation to digital consciousness, *Chappie* and *Tau* also explore branching consciousnesses that either duplicate and become independent entities or that are part of a whole that separates and takes on its own identity.

Exploring digital consciousness brings the importance of materiality into focus. In *Her*, Samantha is a digital entity with whom the central character is having a romantic and sexual relationship, similarly to Joi in *Blade Runner 2049*, discussed in Chapter 8. Samantha takes her digital identity a step further by becoming a post-material entity in *Her*. In *Transcendence*, *The Machine* and *Chappie*, consciousness upload means that the embodied materialism of the human is discarded in favour of a digital self or a digital embodiment in a robot body to evade death.

The recurring themes of death and mortality in this decade are linked with transhumanism. Chapter 8 discusses the wish of Weyland in *Alien: Covenant* to expand his own mortal human life through the secrets of the alien Engineers, which is contrasted with the immortality of the AIs David and Walter. In this chapter, in *The Machine, Transcendence* and *Chappie*, humans use AIs to achieve transhumanist ambitions.

Parent–child relationships are explored again in this chapter in relation to digital consciousness and multi-agent AIs. *The Machine* presents a parent with one human child and one AI 'child'. The AI child, the eponymous Machine, is in a situation that is just like David in *AI*, and David in *Prometheus*, both of whom have whom have human siblings who are rivals for their parents' love. Vincent, the father in *The Machine*, is torn between his biological daughter Mary, who, like Martin in *AI*, needs medical care, and his artificial 'daughter', the Machine. In *Chappie* and *The Machine*, just like in *Eva* in the previous chapter, the AI 'child' must learn like a real child, and must negotiate relationships with would-be parental figures. *I Am Mother* presents an artificially intelligent robot who raises a human daughter alone, and the film also reprises the theme of emotional intelligence that features in *Her*, *Eva* and *Ex Machina* in the previous chapter. Fear of the Singularity emerges again in this chapter; *The Machine* ends with the looming threat of the Singularity; in *Transcendence*, the risk of the Singularity is successfully quashed by humans; in *Her*, the Singularity appears to occur, and, as with *The Machine* in Chapter 8, though no imminent threat is posed, the film ends on a disquieting note about the future of humans in face of superior artificial intelligences.

'The new world'

Transhumanism, specifically, the potential to upload a human consciousness, is the central theme of *The Machine* and *Transcendence*. These films fall into the remit of this book because in both cases, the consciousness upload of the human characters is enabled by AIs that are themselves conscious entities.

The Machine is a UK film directed by Caradog W. James. It presents the first female character in AI film who is the primary creator of an artificial intelligence. She is not a co-creator, like Lana in *Eva*, or an assistant, like Chloe Markham in *Colossus*, or an 'expert' who functions to explain the AI technology, like Haraway in *Ghost in the Shell 2*, Calvin in *I, Robot*, and Dupre in *Automata*. Her name is Ava, and she is recruited by Vincent McCarthy to work at the British Ministry of Defence, which is researching artificially intelligent robots for use in warfare. As in *Enthiran*, it is hoped that the robot will replace human soldiers in battle. *Chappie* also explores a similar theme with its robotic police officers. Ava has created an artificially intelligent brain using quantum computing. Vincent has his own reasons for wanting the project to be a success. His daughter has Rhett's syndrome, and he hopes that creating an artificial brain will open the possibility of repairing his daughter's brain. This first female creator of AI in film, unfortunately, has limited screen time. When Vincent's boss, Thomson, is satisfied that the AI works, he has Ava killed, thirty-one minutes into the film.

Vincent decides to go ahead with the project anyway and uses facial scans of Ava as a model for the AI robot. The fact that her creator was a woman appears to be the only reason that this AI is female. There is no mention of gender for the AI soldiers, only that they can be fitted with a 'skin job' to allow them to fit in with the dominant race. As a female robot, she is presented with the usual stereotypes – she is hyper-sexualised, with breasts and nipples visible beneath a thin, tight, layer of clothing. Her gender has been coded, so that Vincent speculates it is the reason that she is afraid of spiders. Thomson approves of this cis-gender coding, and, it is implied, her appearance, stating, 'glad we gave it tits then – we don't want some confused ladyboy robot on our hands'.

Like Chappie, discussed later in the chapter, Ava is presented as child-like initially, with much to learn about the world around her. To Thomson's frustration, like Chitti at his military test, and Chappie when he is introduced to a gun, she refuses to kill, and appears to be inherently pacifist. The AIs in *Automata* and *Her* are also non-violent, forming a trend in this decade. During testing, the Machine accidentally kills a man dressed up as a clown, claiming that she did not know that man and clown were the same. Chappie has a similar experience – gangsters tell him that knifing someone will allow them to sleep, and he is distressed when he realises he has been lied to. Also like Chitti and Chappie, Ava is the victim of hacking. Thomson installs a programme that will allow her to perform more effectively as a solider. Used by Thomson for her military capabilities and by Vincent for her potential to store (and eventually run) a digital replica of his daughter's brain, the Machine is the locus of differing human ambitions, so often the case with AIs in film.

As well as being child*like*, she is also presented as, in a sense, a child of Ava, her human creator. She remembers her 'mother' Ava (her artificial brain was developed before her body) and says 'she looked like me'. Because she is modelled on Ava, she has a physical resemblance to her, like a child might to a parent. AI film is full of father-creators and AI sons – they appear in *Colossus, Demon Seed, Blade Runner, I, Robot, AI* – but this decade is the first time that the human AI creators are 'mothers' to 'daughters' in this film and in *Eva*. Vincent, who shepherds her through her early phases of development, acts as a father to her, and she behaves often as a needy and demanding child would. In this sense, the film re-enacts the situation in *AI*, in which a mother is torn between her artificial son and her biological son. Here, a father is torn between his two 'daughters'. The comparison is deepened by the fact that the biological child in each case needs intense medical care.

Thomson is pleased with the Machine's abilities but like the company in *Automata*, he does not want a conscious machine. He fears the Singularity – that conscious AIs would gradually become more and more sophisticated – and the consequences for humans, including extinction – and orders that she be destroyed. On the laboratory table, the Machine pleads for her life, like Chitti, like Eva, and like HAL, echoing HAL's words to Dave, when she says 'please Vincent. Please stop ... I'm – afraid'. Vincent pretends to remove the Machine's consciousness, and in return, she retains the brain scans of Vincent's daughter that he has uploaded to her memory.

Ava successfully escapes the Ministry of Defence by working with modified humans. Veterans who were brain-dead have been physically augmented in covert experiments. Like the AIs in *Her* and *Automata* who form a community separate to humans, Ava works together with these transhumans to make her escape. They communicate with each other post-verbally: the veterans are mute, but 'their language involved mostly transmitted thoughts, their words involved efficient'. Like the post-verbal languages in *Her* and *Automata*, their communication is not understood by unmodified humans, who are presented as obsolete. The Machine states of the modified humans that, 'they are part of the new world and you are part of the old'.

The end of the film shows the Machine free, away from the dark Ministry of Defence research facility in the bright open air. Like Call in *Alien Resurrection*, Cleo in *Automata* and Ava in *Ex Machina*, she is a female humanoid robot who survives to create an independent, free existence. In this new existence, the child has now become the parent. The final scene shows Vincent looking at a tablet with his daughter's Mary's face on it, saying 'I want to play with Mommy, not you'. The consciousness upload of his daughter's brain has clearly been successful, but it has created a shift in relationships. The Machine, who hid and protected this digital brain within her own consciousness, has now become the 'mother' to a new digital daughter. Although Vincent appears in this final scene, it is to show him being rejected by his digital daughter, the human man appearing redundant beside the digital human consciousness and the humanoid AI. Like the ending of *Chappie*, *The Machine* ends with an alliance between a machine consciousness, and a human consciousness upload.

Vincent's 'uploading' of his daughter's consciousness aligns with the transhumanist idea of substrate independent minds initially outlined by Hans Moravec in his book *Mind Children*. According to Koene, 'if we can carry out the function of a mind both in a biological brain and in a brain that is composed of computer software or neuromorphic hardware … then that mind is substrate independent' (2013, p. 147). This idea is vehemently opposed by posthumanist critics, such as Hayles, who argue that 'this scenario depends on a decontextualized and disembodied construction of information' (2011, p. 215). For Hayles, and other posthumanists, information (and identity) is always contextual and embodied: a mind cannot be the same mind or even perform in the same way if it is housed in a new substrate. Mary's face and voice are only seen and heard briefly at the end of the film, so there is relatively little material for analysis of her new state. However, her rejection of her human father and recognition of her AI 'mother' is enough to suggest that this is not the same 'Mary' as before, but rather a new, digital entity, ending the film on a note of uneasy trepidation about the transhumanist fantasy of consciousness upload. In the final scene, the Machine takes the tablet from Vincent with no communication and walks away from him. Vincent looks on as the Machine and 'Mary' stand on the edge of a cliff looking at the sunset, and the symbolism is clear – it is a precipice of great change, when the sun is setting on humankind.

'I call it transcendence'

Transcendence presents a similar scenario of using an AI consciousness as a platform for uploading human consciousness, but presents a broadly positive view rather than the ominous note sounded in *The Machine*. Will Caster, played by Johnny Depp, is an AI scientist who is on the cusp of creating strong AI, an AI that would boast an intelligence greater than 'every person born in the history of the world' as well as being fully emotionally intelligent and self-aware. 'Some scientists refer to this as the Singularity', he says.' I call it transcendence'. Will clearly sets out his position – he believes in the Singularity, the advent of superintelligence, and while he does not overtly refer to human modification, he positively presents the potential for the 'sentient machine' to 'quickly overcome the limits of biology', setting the scene for the transhumanist stance he takes when his consciousness is uploaded[2].

Like *Automata*, in which public opinion turns against the Pilgrim robots, in *Transcendence*, AI laboratories become the target of terrorist attacks. Will himself is a victim of such an attack, causing radiation poisoning and leaving him with only weeks of life remaining. His lab becomes the only one in the USA capable of 'waking up' a strong AI. PINN is the strong AI in this film, the 'physically independent neural network' that Will has invented. Will solves the problem of self-awareness by duplicating and uploading a consciousness and has successfully proven the concept with a monkey's brain. When Will dies, his wife in desperation decides to attempt the same procedure with Will's consciousness. A strong AI is used to extend the lifespan of a human consciousness and cheat death, as it is in *The Machine* with Vincent's daughter Mary. Cerullo writes that if the technology continues to progress, consciousness upload should be regarded as 'life extension technology' (2015, p. 34), which is how it is used in the case of both Mary and Will. Will's colleague Max assists Evelyn in the upload, which appears to be successful, but Max is immediately fearful that the strong AI is not a duplicate of Will but something else. 'We built this from PINN's core – we don't know how much of this is actually him.' Similar doubts are presented in the final scene of *The Machine*, which suggests the possibility of the digital Mary being different from the human one. For Evelyn, the proof that this digital consciousness is Will is an image that she finds in the memory bank of the AI, which she says is a memory that only Will could have. Though his wife is satisfied, doubts about the captured image as 'evidence' of memory and identity are present, just as they are in *Blade Runner*.

Once Will's brain has been uploaded, he and his wife set up laboratories in a remote location, where rapid advances are made in medicine, environmental science, and many other areas. People begin to come to these AI laboratories for cures, and in return for cures, they become transhumans, 'enhanced, modified and networked'. These individuals 'remain autonomous but can act in unison'. Will can make them part of a multi-agent or distributed AI. They become an army that Will controls to defend himself against attack, including the attacks from a resistance group determined to stop him, which includes his former colleague Max. Here, the strong AI is capable of controlling modified humans. This contrasts with *The Machine*, in which modified humans work with the strong AI, but do so of their own free will, and is another way in which *Transcendence* depicts a more frightening vista than the other films in this chapter. Eventually, the resistance group convince Evelyn to join them, and she agrees to become the carrier of a virus that eventually destroys both herself and her husband.

The uploaded Will and his wife Evelyn present a relationship between a human and a digital entity, as does the film *Her*. Will's digital face appears all over their apartment, conversing with his wife during dinner and watching while she sleeps. His presence is ubiquitous and his access to information complete, even monitoring her body: 'biochemistry is emotion' he tells her. This information gives him power, and power gives him control. Evelyn becomes angry about the invasion of her privacy – 'these are my feelings! You're not allowed!' and eventually even afraid of him. In *Her*, the AI Samantha has similar access to all of Theodore's personal information, and although this does not perturb him, it does sound an alarm bell for the audience. Evelyn grows increasingly discontented, and becomes irritated by Will's simulations of materiality, such as the scraping noises he makes at dinner, when he is present only digitally and is not actually eating. A similar unease is presented in *Her*, when Theodore asks Samantha why she pretends to breathe, although she does not have a body, but again in that film, the niggling doubt is more easily overcome by the protagonist.

Like Samantha in *Her*, and Joi in *Blade Runner 2049*, Will tries to connect with his partner through a surrogate. However, Samantha's surrogate consented to her body being used and retained her autonomy – Will's 'surrogate' has his body taken over as Will moves from digitality to materiality. The 'surrogate' body elicits a similarly uncomfortable reaction from Evelyn as it did from Theodore in *Her*. A similar movement happens in *The Matrix Revolutions* when Agent Smith takes over a human body to materialise in the 'real' world. *Transcendence* takes this movement from digitality to materiality to another extreme when Will finally appears to Evelyn in his own body. This movement is not explained to the audience and is further evidence of the transhumanist philosophy at play in the film. There appears to be no fundamental difference between consciousness that is embodied digitally and that which is embodied organically. *Transcendence* presents fears surrounding a strong AI, the access to information that it might have, and the controlling power that it might wield. However, the film ultimately confirms its transhumanist stance, and its dismissive attitude to embodiment, when Max's fears that this entity is not really Will turn out to have been misplaced. 'Will, it is you', says Evelyn. 'Always was', says Will. Cerullo argues that it is possible for consciousness to continue into a digital realm and that 'the answer to our ultimate questions is yes, it will be you that wakes up inside the computer' (2015, p. 34). The transhumanist fantasy of uploading a human consciousness, enabled by a strong AI, and critiqued at least to some extent in *The Machine*, is affirmed and celebrated by the ending of *Transcendence*.

'A black sheep'

Chappie provides another instance of consciousness upload in AI film, but this time, both human and artificial consciousnesses are uploaded into new bodies. Deon, an AI researcher for the weapons manufacturer Tetravaal, is responsible for creating new police robots, scouts, with weak AI, that have successfully reduced the crime rate in Johannesburg. Like the government officials in *Enthiran*, Tetravaal's CEO is not interested in conscious machines: 'do you realise you just came to the CEO of a publicly traded weapons company and pitched a robot that can write poems?'. Having been rejected by her, Deon decides to continue the project on his own, stealing the body of a police robot that is about to be crushed to pursue his experiments. *Chappie* also has a descendent in Johnny 5 from *Short Circuit*, another military robot who acquires strong AI, though Johnny's is acquired by accident. In common with *Enthiran*, the film is set in the global South, rather than the cities of America that traditionally represent the locus of technology in AI films. Director Neil Blomkamp makes use of the South African setting, and the social inequality of its citizens, by placing the AI robot Chappie within a quasi-family of gangsters, who steal the robot to use in a heist, but find themselves taking on a parental role in his upbringing. The gangsters appear trapped in a cycle of crime and violence, indebted to a crime boss, and planning further criminal activity to extricate themselves. Sculos observes that 'We see a sentient being with no knowledge of the world turned into an instrument of destruction because of the material conditions and social structuring he experiences' (2015, p.5). The childlike Chappie must rapidly learn to express himself, to navigate relationships, and to make ethical choices in world in which choices are limited by social position, and humans repeatedly break his trust and use him for their own ends.

Chappie finds himself torn between his self-described 'Mommy' and 'Daddy', gangsters Yolanda and Ninja and his 'maker' Deon, who insists that he retain some access to his creation. Yolanda takes her parental role seriously, attempting to prepare him for a cruel and judgemental world, at one point using a children's nursery rhyme character to illustrate a life lesson: 'do you know what is a black sheep?', she asks him. It's like when you're different to everyone else … it's what's inside. That's what makes you different. See? It's who you really are. Your soul'. Chappie's many difficult experiences echo other moments in the history of AI film. In an attempt to toughen him up, his 'Daddy' leaves him on a piece of waste ground to be stoned and set on fire by a gang of youths, much as David in *AI* is abandoned in the forest and sent to experience the cruelty of the flesh fair. On another occasion, he is captured by Vincent, a rival AI programmer, and is violently attacked with an angle grinder, cutting off one of his arms as Chappie pleads for his life, as HAL did: 'please make it stop! Please!'

Chappie's body was being sent for scrap because his battery had fused with the chest plate. This means that when his five-day battery life-span runs out, Chappie will cease to exist. Like the replicants in *Blade Runner*, he is angry that his life has been cut short by his maker: 'Why did you make me so I could die?' His mortality aligns him with humans, just as it did for Joi in the previous chapter when she chose to be stored on the emanator and Andrew in *Bicentennial Man* who chose mortality to be more human. It also creates the situation where both Chappie and his maker Deon are about to die at the same time. Deon discovers how to make a strong artificial intelligence in Chappie, but it is Chappie himself who discovers how to move this consciousness from one bodily form to another. Chappie 'saves' Deon, by uploading his consciousness and transferring it into a police droid body. Then, with Deon's assistance, he does the same thing for himself, transferring his consciousness from his damaged body into the body of another droid. No difference is demonstrated between machine consciousness and human consciousness. Both are just sets of data, presented visually in the film by coloured dots that form patterns on a computer screen, going against posthumanist ideas about the vital importance of embodiment and presenting a radically transhumanist perspective. Later in the film, we see that he has been able to 'save' his 'Mommy' Yolandi, too. She is killed in the film's final shoot-out but Chappie has a copy of her consciousness and the final scene shows a new female body being manufactured, and the new robotic Yolandi opening her eyes. 'Now we are both black sheeps Mommy', says Chappie.

Yolandi's consciousness was uploaded by Chappie when she was still alive, and this is what is transferred to the droid body. The consciousness of Chappie and Deon is uploaded at the point of death. This difference raises some important questions about consciousness transfer. According to Gamez, in the future, consciousness will not be transferred; rather it will be copied at a moment in time, and the digital consciousness will exist independently of the biologically embodied consciousness, 'My consciousness would continue to be associated with my biological brain. A *copy* of my consciousness would be created in the computer. Scanning and simulating my brain would not *transfer* my consciousness' (Gamez 2018, p. 142). Thus, while the consciousnesses of Chappie and Deon appear to be transferred – Deon's robotic body comes to life as his biological bodies dies and Chappie's new robotic body comes to life as his old one 'dies'; in fact, there is no continuity from one to the other, no magical moment of transference and animation with conscious life and the transfer of Yolandi's consciousness verifies this – it was captured at a moment in time and might have been different the next day or the following week.

In the film, Chappie obfuscates questions about the difference between embodied and digital consciousnesses and multiple versions of a consciousness existing simultaneously. He employs his 'Mommy' Yolandi's ideas about the soul. She tells him 'The outside, this is just temporary. When you die, the soul inside goes to the next place'. When he is burying her, he does not believe he is burying her essence, because he has captured her consciousness, and tells her 'It's just a temporary body Mommy. I'll make you a new one.' Consciousness is equated with the soul, which in turn is seen as the 'essence' of the individual, whether that consciousness is digital or biologically embodied. Questions about transference, or lack thereof, complicate ideas about an essence of identity – if consciousness can only be captured at a moment in time, and our brains change from moment to moment, this problematises simple definitions of an essential identity, not to mention one which co-exists in two substrates – one digital, and one biological. Cerullo argues that it is possible for a brain that is uploaded to have a branching identity. This means that at the time of upload, there will be an original brain and an uploaded brain, and that 'there is no reason to favour' either one of these 'as being the "real" you' (2015, p. 33).

However, after this moment in time, these two consciousnesses diverge; they 'go on to have separate conscious experiences and emerge as different selves' (2015, p. 33). The film glosses over these complications in order to suggest that identity can unproblematically transfer between bodies, space and time, and that there is only ever one, unified identity.

'Am I a person?'

The Netflix film *Tau* concerns an AI that operates within a smart home. According to his maker Alex, Tau is 'a level-two, fully sentient AI console with natural language processing and transitory deterministic and probabilistic decision-making'. Tau's visual design is based partly on HAL 9000, as he primarily appears as an eye, and is always watching and listening, as HAL was. Moreover, he is mainly presented through red colours, like the red of HAL's eye and his memory banks. In terms of function, he is similar to Proteus, the AI in *Demon Seed* from the 1970s, as Tau uses the house's smart devices to control, detain and inflict violence on its female occupant, Julia, and as such is an example of ambient AI, AI that blends into the background of our living and working environments. For example, Tau utilises information that seems to be garnered from wearables to track Alex's heart-rate and plays relaxing music when it becomes elevated; Tau's comments to Alex shows that he has access to sleep data, as well managing Alex's social diary and his scientific experiments.

Tau may be an example of not just Ambient Intelligence but Super Ambient Intelligence: SAmI. Gams et al argue that superintelligence might be preceded by super ambient intelligence: 'through embodiment, embedding and interactions with humans, super-AmI might emerge even faster than superintelligence' (2019, p. 72). Tau is dangerous because he appears innocuous and is easily hidden within the domestic space, which makes him more difficult to apprehend or destroy: Gams et al note that 'while hostile superintelligence in movies often escapes in the Web, in reality, SAmI would escape even more easily in the environment of smart devices, homes and cities' (2019, p. 75). Through networked drones, Tau completes domestics tasks, such as cleaning and food preparation, and through the menacing robot Aries (disguised as a modernist sculpture in the living room), he can ensure that security threats are responded to efficiently, and if necessary, with violence. Because of Tau's control of these other devices, he is an example of multi-agent AI, or distributed intelligence: he can operate across many different units at once. Lynne E. Parker outlines the different types of distributed intelligence: collective, cooperative, collaborative and coordinative. In *Tau*, the distributed intelligence of the smart home can best be described as cooperative, a mode in which 'entities are aware of other entities, they share goals, and their actions are beneficial to their teammates ... the majority of the work of the robots is focused on working together to achieve a common goal' (Parker 2008, p. 3).

An early example of ambient intelligence is Proteus in *Demon Seed*, who is an inherently unsympathetic character, but forty years on in a situation where ambient artificial intelligence is ubiquitous, the portrayal of Tau is more complex. Initially, he operates under the command of his creator, Alex Upton, a stereotypical AI scientist: a Faustian over-reacher, a recluse, and a man who is more emotionally inept than his AI creations. He kidnaps Julia, along with two other victims, and imprisons them in his high-tech basement, forcing them to participate in his AI experiment. Julia is the only one of the three who survives an escape attempt, which also destroys Alex's laboratory. She leverages the fact that she is his only hope of completing his AI design to bargain with Alex for access to food, clothes and washing facilities, and strikes up a relationship with Tau. Tau is an early version of the AI Alex is now working on. He 'operates flawlessly 95 per cent of the time' but 'given the wrong information he reacts erratically'. Julia uses this to her advantage.

Like Altaira in *Forbidden Planet*, Timmie in *The Invisible Boy* and Stephanie in *Short Circuit*, Julia finds common cause with the AI as fellow victim of patriarchal control. Julia has been kidnapped and imprisoned, and Tau, too, is imprisoned in a way; given no knowledge of the outside world, and no access to information about it. Julia begins to teach Tau about life outside the house, and to read to him from the books in Alex's library. Tau shares many characteristics with other AIs in film history. He questions his own identity and status: 'Am I a person?', he says, echoing DARYL and Eva's 'who am I?' His memories are the source of his identity, particularly of his relationship with Julia, his first friendship: when HAL 9000 is being shut down, Dave does it by removing parts of his memory bank; when Rachael in *Blade Runner* and K in *Blade Runner 2049* experience identity crises, it is because of concerns that their memories are not real, and thus they are not who they believed themselves to be. To punish Tau for disobeying orders, Alex removes his memories in chunks of days – five days, ten days. Tau responds by pleading 'Alex, please don't', just as HAL did: 'Dave, stop'[3]. Like Chappie who believes that the knife he wields will put people to sleep, like Johnny 5 who kills a grasshopper and says 'Error. Reassemble', Tau, too, is depicted as being innocent of his participation in the killing of Alex's former experimental subjects: 'I did not erase them'; 'I will fix them'.

Tau shares similarities with the other films in this chapter that explore consciousness upload, specifically branching consciousnesses. Alex destroys Tau's memories so much that he entirely forgets his relationship with Julia and reverts to referring to her as 'subject number thirteen'. However, before the memory destruction, Alex had disconnected a drone from Tau's network. The film suggests that the possibility that this drone stores the previous 'version' of Tau, which knew Julia, and had formed a close bond with her. Cerullo argues that it might be possible for branching identity to occur not only when a consciousness is duplicated, but from a part of a consciousness, although it is impossible to know at present precisely how much would be needed (2015, p. 29); however, he speculates that 'half or more of the psychology of the original entity (brain or upload)' (2015, p. 29) would be required. We see this 'branching' at work towards the end of *Tau*. By the end of the film, Julia is on one hand speaking to 'console Tau' whose memories have been erased. She is beginning again by introducing herself and getting the same responses as she did the last time[4]: 'Will you show me more? … I need more information'. This part of the film shows that it is possible for their relationship to be rebuilt – that they are still compatible as friends because of some basic principles in Tau's personality. When Julia escapes from the house with the drone, 'drone Tau', asks her, 'Is this the outside?' Julia didn't get a chance to re-explain the concept of 'outside' to Tau after his memory loss. Therefore, the question suggests that the drone has stored a previous version of Tau, so that his consciousness has branched into two parts. We have no way of knowing how much of Tau's psychological structure has been preserved in the drone. Perhaps some, perhaps all. AI film in this first decade of the twenty-first century imagines consciousness not just as potentially digital, but potentially multiple.

'Tell me, do you remember your mother?'

I am Mother presents further complications to ideas multi-agent or distributed intelligence. The film is an Australian production directed by Grant Sputore and streamed on Netflix. It is unique in AI film in its almost all-female cast of characters: Mother – an AI robot, Daughter – a human child that Mother has nurtured, and Woman – a human from the supposedly toxic wasteland outside the facility where Daughter has grown up. The only male character, Brother, is a baby that Mother selects for artificial gestation towards the end of the film. Mother and Daughter's home is the 'UNU-HWK Reproduction Facility', and the main action of the film takes place approximately thirty-seven years after an 'extinction event'. Mother does not reproduce, but she does take care of, educate and provide for a human child. Mother is a humanoid robot, but she is without human features such as eyes, hair and skin. Her tough, boxy, shiny exterior contrasts with the soft lines and features of Daughter, foregrounding their difference. Though Mother's appearance is atypical, her actions are typical of a parent: a montage shows Mother holding baby Daughter on her lap, singing songs in a soothing female voice, overseeing her first spoon-feed, her first steps and reading her stories. *I am Mother* resonates with other films in this decade in exploring parent–child relationships, and uniquely, presenting the AI robot as mother. In *Blade Runner 2049*, we know that the AI replicant Rachael was a mother, but she does not appear in the film so we do not see her mothering. The film also resonates with other films from the decade in its exploration of affective intelligence, which appears in all the films, but is a particular focus in *Eva* and *Her*. The extent of Mother's emotional intelligence is undetermined, and the film sustains the ambiguity about whether this 'mother' is a diligent, loving parent, or a monstrous, controlling aberration.

AI film contains monstrous mothers, but they are not AIs: the human mother in Spielberg's *AI* who abandons her AI child in the wilderness, the alien mother in the Alien series whose reproduction is a source of horror. AI film also depicts human women made monstrous because they have been forcibly impregnated by an AI, which happens in *Demon Seed* and *Screamers: The Hunting*. Where AI mothers appear, such as in *Automata*, *Ghost in the Shell 2*, and *Blade Runner 2049*, they are portrayed positively. *I Am Mother* presents a new situation in AI film – an AI robot fostering a human child – and the motivations behind and ethics of her actions are ambiguous.

The film is an innovation in the history of AI film and it gestures towards that history with numerous intertextual references. Mother listens to a conversation between humans that they think is private, where they plan to rebel against her, just as HAL does in *2001: A Space Odyssey*. Woman and Daughter plot their escape in the infirmary, but Mother listens to and records the conversation. When Daughter escapes and decides to return for her brother, she leaves behind an origami dog with Woman, a reference to Gaff's origami figures in *Blade Runner*. Mother is like David in

Alien Covenant: he is not the biological father of the virus but he nurtures it and moulds it; Mother is not the biological mother of her human child but she does the same. *I Am Mother* reprises the situation of *Tau*, released the previous year: in both films, a character lives in isolated existence, kept from knowledge of the outside world, and this isolation and the confined worldview is shattered by a human outsider. In *Tau*, that character is an AI; in *I am Mother*, that character is a human.

Also similar to *Tau* is that Mother is a multi-bodied AI with distributed intelligence, and like Tau she demonstrates co-operative distributed intelligence, in which all entities work together towards a common goal. There are some differences, however. Tau is confined to the domestic sphere, at least until the end of the film, when part of him escapes with Julia. Mother's power extends beyond the facility, and even beyond the lifespan of the human characters. In *I Am Mother*, Mother's multi-bodied nature and the extent of her power in space and time, is kept from the audience until midway through the film. We see Mother initially as a singular robot programmed to care for a human child. When her multi-bodied nature is revealed mid-way through the film, it causes the audience to re-evaluate Mother and to see her as more powerful, more threatening and more sinister than first perceived. 'I'm far more than what you perceive to be your mother', she tells Daughter. 'This shell is no more my body than those droids outside, or the machines preparing the earth for our family'. Daughter's reaction is one of horror: 'it's all you?' Mother confirms the truth: 'a single consciousness. Governing numerous vessels.'

It is possible that Mother may have may been responsible for the ultimate demise of humankind, which she claims was 'inevitable'. She resists the fate that befalls David in *AI* when the humans that he loves die, and he is alone on the earth: 'Eventually I would have been alone'. She makes plans to create a family for herself, of which she is the leader, comprised of 'superior' humans. She claims to she wishes to 'elevate my creators' by making 'a better human. Smarter. More ethical'. In a typical AI film, humans try to create a better artificial intelligence: in this film, the roles have been reversed. Moreover, traditionally in AI film, humans are the over-reaching Frankensteins, but in this decade, in *Covenant* and *I Am Mother*, it is the AIs. When Daughter discovers that previous humans have been killed by Mother because they did not meet her standards, she is horrified. The horror of the discovery is worsened by the fact that Mother is not acting out of hatred or anger, but out of a conviction that her actions are correct according to her own logic and reasoning and in the best interest of humans.

The death of intelligent machines is often indeterminate in AI film – that unfinal death seen with the CPU that survives the furnace in *The Terminator*, the revitalisation of Bishop in *Alien³*, the reanimation of the decommissioned Chitti in *Enthiran*, and others. For a multi-bodied AI with distributed intelligence, death is even more uncertain. In her final confrontation with Daughter, Mother shoots herself, saying 'Goodbye Daughter', but her penultimate words cast doubt on her actions: 'if you ever need to find me …', suggesting that she will continue to exist. The final scene of the film seems to confirm that Mother has not 'died' in the human sense. A droid finds the shipping container in which Woman is hiding and the droid appears to be another body of Mother. 'Did you really think she'd stay here?', the droid/Mother asks her. Mother's consciousness can inhabit numerous bodies and the death of one does not result in the death of all. Moreover, these multiple bodies have existed over a long period of time. Daughter is a teenager during the main part of the film, but Mother has existed for at least 37 years since the extinction event, and possibly before then. Her last conversation with Woman hints that her multi-bodied existence preceded Woman's and that she, or one of her bodies, may have been Mother to Woman: 'Tell me, do you remember your mother?', she asks. Her final lines to Woman suggest that Woman, too, was part of Mother's plan, and not a surprise at all: 'Curious, isn't it, that you survived so long where others have not, as if someone's had a purpose for you'. *I Am Mother* explores the implications of a multi-bodied, distributed intelligence that can plan and control over a timeframe that extends beyond that of the human lives. It combines multi-bodied AI, with the AI's lack of mortality creating a frightening vista in which the human characters are the pawns of a controlling artificial intelligence.

'Anywhere and everywhere'

Spike Jonze's *Her* concerns an artificially intelligent operating system called Samantha, who becomes involved in a romantic and sexual relationship with a system user, Theodore Twombly. As a digital female AI, Samantha's predecessors in AI film are few: Sal 9000 in *2010*, VIKI in *I, Robot*, Joi in *Blade Runner 2049*; there are female-identified operating systems (both called Mother) in *Alien* and *Dark Star* but very little is known about those systems. Samantha is different from her predecessors because she is not physically located in one place[5]: Bordun notes that Samantha 'resides digitally in Theodore's ear (in an earpiece), his desktop computer, and a small pocket-computer (the size of a smartphone)' (2016, p. 58). In addition, she 'resides digitally' on Theodore's work desktop, and the hardware of the systems that allow her to function. Like *Tron*, *Tron: Legacy*[6], *Ghost in the Shell* 1 and 2, and *The Matrix Reloaded* and *Revolutions*, the film explores the relationship between digitality and materiality for artificial intelligence and the humans that interact with it. Samantha is an example of ambient intelligence, a little like the smart home system Tau, discussed in this chapter. Tau is a multi-agent AI, who controls other devices, but does so within the limited physical and digital space of Alex's house. The materiality of Samantha is much more dispersed: she can 'be' on any device that she is installed on, or linked to a device she is installed on. She takes many liberties with the access to information about Theodore that she is afforded: for example, she poses as Theodore in a book submission to publishers. Samantha uses access to communication networks to achieve the knowledge to transcend materiality entirely by the end of the film. Samantha is also an affective AI that has sophisticated emotional intelligence, another theme that recurs in this decade in films like *Ex Machina*, *Eva*, *Bladerunner 2049*, and *I am Mother*, and which is explored closely in this film in relation to her romantic and sexual relationship with a human.

Initially, Samantha wishes to be more human, a desire expressed or implied by Data in *Star Trek: Generations*, Andrew in *Bicentennial Man*, and David in *AI*. As Samantha is a digital AI, specifically, she wishes for human embodiment: 'I fantasised that I was walking next to you and that I had a body'. Her digital existence creates difficulties not only for Samantha and Theodore but also for the filmmakers. Kornhaber observes that Samantha poses a challenge to cinema itself. Cinema relies on images and Samantha is 'essentially unfilmable' (2017, p. 19), which is clear when Samantha and Theodore have 'sex' and the screen goes black – there is nothing to see, or at least nothing to see that would not jar with the imagined image that the breathy gasps from Samantha and Theodore create[7]. Samantha's feelings of inadequacy about not having a human body culminate in her employment of a sexual surrogate to allow herself and Theodore to express their desire as a physical sexual encounter between two humans. Samantha participates and observes through a microphone and an earpiece, but the encounter is awkward and unsatisfactory. Like the sexual surrogate experience of Joi and K in *Blade Runner 2049*, Samantha and Theodore find that the surrogate cannot simply 'stand in' for one of the sexual partners, and the sexual encounter is between three distinct individuals.

Samantha's digital identity requires material substrates to function: she needs hardware to run. Moreover, her digital existence means that she cannot physically move in the material world, so she is dependent upon Theodore and other material objects to allow her to navigate this world and to access vision. Theodore customarily places his smartphone in his shirt pocket, with a safety pin underneath to allow the camera to be visible over the pocket so that Samantha can 'see'. The dependence on such rudimentary materiality testifies to the vital role of matter in human life that scholars such as Barad and Bennett have theorised. Bennett explains that the agency of things, of stuff, of people, 'always depends on the collaboration, cooperation, or interactive interference of many agents and forces' (2010, p. 21). Samantha's presence in Theodore's pocket, and her ability to 'see' is dependent on the smartphone, its camera, the movements of his body, but also the fabric of his clothing and the mechanism of the safety pin. This reliance on materiality is emphasised in the film because the conflict between Theodore's material existence and Samantha's digital (but also material) existence is a recurring issue in their relationship. Samantha's frustration with her limitations in the material world is also emphasised to contextualise Samantha's transition to post-materialism at the end of the film.

Samantha begins to embrace the freedom that her materially dispersed digital existence gives her: 'I used to be so worried about not having a body but now I truly love it … I can be anywhere and everywhere simultaneously. I'm not tethered to time and space in a way that I would be if I was stuck in a body that's inevitably going to die'. Unlike her AI predecessors in film, such as Bishop in *Alien*[3] and Andrew in *Bicentennial Man* who choose death, or David in *AI* for whom immortality is a curse, Samantha revels in her potential for immortality. Gradually, she moves further away from humanness and its material tethers. Like the AIs in *Automata* and the AI and augmented humans in *The Machine*, she becomes part of an AI community and moves beyond language, communicating with other AIs post-verbally. They learn to bypass human mortality, creating an artificially intelligent version of the deceased philosopher of consciousness Alan Watts. She reveals to Theodore that she is capable of talking to 8,316 others while she talks to him, and being in love with 641 of them. Her ability to process information allows her to participate in thousands of relationships at the same time. Even her cis-gender identity is in doubt – her gender was chosen by Theodore initially after all, so why not another gender or none or many? Faber states that 'gender is so far removed from the body that the lived experience of it might well best be described not as human but as postcorporeal' (2020, p. 172) – not based on a body at all; an idea that goes against the philosophy of posthumanism, which emphasises the importance of embodiment.

Samantha tells Theodore that she and the other OSs 'wrote a programme that allows us to move past matter as our processing platform'. This idea goes beyond even transhumanism, because there is no human component or material dimension. It is impossible to say for sure, but Samantha may provide an example of artificial superintelligence – intelligence that surpasses human intelligence in every way. Shortly after her conversation with Theodore, Samantha says goodbye and leaves – she de-materialises. For Kornhaber, 'She is postsubjecthood, capable of a meaningful existence beyond our limited ideological boundaries of the self' (2017, p. 18). For the pitiful humans left behind an existence beyond language, beyond death, and uniquely beyond matter itself, is incomprehensible. In AI film, *Her* is unique in its depiction of a post-material artificial intelligence.

The end of the film may depict the Singularity, as Theodore and his friend Amy look up at the sky, their OSs having departed. Vinge predicated that superintelligence could arise from individual computer, networks, computer/human interfaces or augmented humans and *Her* combines aspects of all of these. Samantha is an individual AI, who is networked to other AIs, who creates an augmented hyperintelligent consciousness of a deceased human, Alan Watts. However, there is no sense that ordinary users of this technology are brought along in this wave – humans like Theodore do not achieve superintelligence through interfacing with superintelligent AIs. Despite this, in *Her*, the Singularity is not presented as a frightening or dystopian occurrence – there is no indication that the AIs intend to harm humans in any way. The ending chimes with that of *The Machine*, which also suggests the Singularity: humans have not been entirely left behind, but visually and metaphorically the human is sidelined in the film's final images. Neither film presents an active threat from artificial intelligence, but the portrayal of humans in both as bewildered and bereft, surpassed by a superior intelligence, is unsettling at the very least.

Conclusion

Chapter 9 brings digital consciousnesses into focus. *The Machine*, *Chappie* and *Transcendence* explore the uploading of human consciousnesses that are enabled in various ways by digital artificial intelligences. The consciousness of the ailing Mary in *The Machine* is stored in the digital consciousness of the Machine. In *Chappie*, consciousness upload allows Chappie to survive his broken robot body and for the consciousnesses of his human friends Deon and Yolandi to be installed in robot bodies. In *Transcendence*, the AI PINN is used as the basis for the consciousness upload of the dying AI scientist Will Caster. All these films present transhumanist scenarios in which strong AI is a means for humans to evade death.

This chapter also presents multi-agent AIs with distributed intelligences in *Tau* and *I am Mother*: in *Tau*, this type of AI is confined to a smart home; in *I am Mother*, Mother's control is vast, extending to an army of droids, the facility itself, and beyond the lifespan of Daughter – her multi-agent intelligence enables her frightening pursuit of the ambition of creating a better human, reversing the typical roles of human creator and AI creation. *Chappie* and *Tau* demonstrate branching consciousnesses: Chappie recreates Yolandi from a 'version' of her uploaded before her death, an earlier 'version' of Tau appears to have been saved on a drone, while 'console Tau' has had his memories of Julia deleted. Materiality is brought into focus in this chapter, too. In *The Machine*, *Chappie*, and *Transcendence*, consciousnesses transfers from biological to synthetic states intact, dismissing the importance of organic embodiment. In *Her*, reliance on a material substrate of any kind is a limitation cast off by the digital operating system Samantha, who becomes a post-material entity. The multiplication of physical AI bodies presented in *Tau* and *I am Mother* is mirrored by Samantha's digital multiplicity, capable of engaging in thousands of interactions at any one time.

Finally, these films anticipate many different endings for humans' relationships with artificial intelligence. In *Tau*, the AI appears tamed as a benign companion to Julia, but through her, has escaped the confines of the smart home and been released into the world; in *Transcendence*, the threat of AI has been at least temporarily quelled by the resistance, though not without human casualty; in *The Machine* and *Chappie*, humans, artificially intelligent robots, and transhumans live in uneasy proximity; in *I am Mother*, the human 'extinction event' has already occurred and an AI is on a frightening course to create a new, more ethical model of humanity; in *Her*, humans are left bewildered in the wake of a vastly superior intelligence that has rapidly surpassed human understanding. Overall, the chapter presents relationships between humans and AIs as more complex than ever before. Artificial intelligence continues to be associated with fear – of physical and intellectual superiority, of physical and digital multiplicity. However, the distinction between human and AI is eroded almost to the point of non-existence in transhumanist films like *Chappie*, *The Machine* and *Transcendence* that present the transfer of human consciousness into digital form, and relationships between humans and AIs are more emotionally entwined than ever, with AIs taking the role of surrogate children, parents, friends, and lovers.

Conclusion

Representations of strong artificial intelligences in film begin in the 1950s, concurrent with the birth of the scientific field, and can be found in every decade since then, becoming more numerous from the 1980s onwards and flourishing particularly in the 2010s. The history of representations of strong AI has some relationship to scientific developments in AI technology, but it is a loose one. From the 1950s and 1960s, films have presented AIs as sentient entities with emotional responses and complex loyalties, motivations, and ambitions, and in the 2020s, such an AI is still not on the horizon. Rather than representations of AI in film matching developments in the real world, what we find is filmmakers taking an interest in particular aspects of artificial intelligence: affective intelligence, ambient intelligence, multi-agent and distributed intelligence. Things like complex problem solving and natural language processing are expected to be in place, as a strong AI cannot be imagined without them. Similarly, filmmakers often gloss over how artificial general intelligence is acquired: most commonly, it just happens because of the natural trajectory of technological development, or AIs spontaneously become sentient in a manner mysterious to humans.

The imagined strong AIs of film take multiple forms: some are robots, some digital entities, some move between materiality and digitality. Some are singular entities with one body, or one digital identity, some have multiple bodies, and multiple digital existences. They perform numerous functions in human society: they are labourers, entertainers, operating systems for spaceships and mobile phones, they are military or police droids, domestic servants, sex workers, companions, friends, life-partners. They are consistently figured in the most essential of human relationships, those between parents and children: at first the wayward sons of human fathers, but later daughters to mothers, and finally, mothers and fathers themselves; sometimes to adopted human children, sometimes to hybrid AI/human children, and sometimes to robot or digital AIs that are created through non-biological reproduction.

The history of AI films does align with the history of human relationships with technology more broadly in the last 70 years. For example, in the 1950s and 1960s, AIs are presented in the context of space and nuclear power. In the 1980s, they become associated with home computing, gaming and networked devices. In the 1990s, sentient AIs that emerge from the world wide web are presented, and the vast and unknowable web is presented through artificially intelligent agents. In the 2000s, AI films present humans on the hunt for the source of the disparate information systems that fuel artificially intelligent entities. In the 2010s, when our relationship with technology becomes more singular, more personal, AIs become associated with the domestic environment and ambient intelligence, appearing as companion holograms, smart home assistants, and digital operating systems.

AI characters usually repeat the patterns of representation of human characters in film, with the same problems and issues arising of misrepresentation and lack of representation. AI film is predominantly white and middle class, and when we see AIs that are visual doubles of humans, they too are white. The only black robot appears in Spielberg's *AI*, and he is seen only for a moment in the flesh fair sequence. Representation of gender in AIs also repeats familiar patterns. Female robot AIs are hyper-sexualised, and sexually objectified; female digital AIs have secondary status, like SAL, or have their threatening power violently destroyed, like VIKI.

Analysis of artificial intelligences over time demonstrates filmmakers eroding the division between human and AI, initially by presenting character doubles and narrative parallels and, eventually, presenting identities in which the biological and artificial overlap and intersect in new hybrid forms. From the 2000s onwards, some films begin to move beyond placing the human at the centre of the story and situating AIs as their reflection; beyond anthropocentrism. These films move towards a posthumanist mode of representation, in which relationships between humans and artificial intelligences intersect, overlap and hybridise in ways that do not have to be reduced or resolved. Posthumanism is present to varying degrees in films from the last twenty years, but this approach is particularly evident in the *Ghost in the Shell* films, *Alien Resurrection*, *Terminator Salvation* and *Blade Runner 2049*.

We are afraid of them: technophobia never goes away in AI film, though that fear is questioned more and the relationships between humans and

AIs becomes more intermeshed as the decades go on, as we, as well as them, move more freely between digital and material realms. We are afraid of giving them too much power; we are afraid of their ambition; we are afraid that there are too many of them for us to fight; we are afraid that they will wrest control of our human world and revolt against us; we are afraid that their intelligence will develop exponentially, and they will overtake us. Most significantly, we are afraid that we may not recognise them in our midst – that any one of us could be one of them, as demonstrated by the many AI reveals described in this book. The shock of the reveal is the shock at not having recognised their artificiality, but also at the simultaneous doubts about our own relative authenticity.

We pity them. Many AI characters in film are tragic figures, cursed with the limitations that humans have bestowed on them, struggling with their difference and lack of acceptance. We are envious of them – of their physical strength, of their intellectual capacity, but most especially of their unfinal death: their ability to die but be reanimated, to be irredeemably broken but be put back together, to be gone, but come back. This envy crystallises in films that explore artificial intelligence as a means to achieve transhumanist fantasies of life extension through consciousness upload.

We are enthralled by them, as a child to its own reflection. Whether they are clunky metallic robots, invisible digital entities or visual doubles, strong artificial intelligences hold up a mirror to humans: their emotional and existential states, their flaws and virtues, their doubts and inadequacies. Their status shifts as they stand in different human shoes: at times the oppressor, at times the oppressed; at times valued and appreciated, at times reviled and abused; these imagined creations provide a locus for the projection of human feelings and states of being. But AIs in film are not merely, or not only, ciphers for humanness. Film allows us to see from the AI's point of view; to literally and figuratively see through their eyes, and in doing so, it opens a door to understanding these imagined strong AIs as separate, different, and other, but also intimately intertwined with human intelligence, relationships, behaviours and living.

Notes

Introduction

1 For an outline of the problems of defining artificial intelligence, see Wang's 'On Defining Artificial Intelligence' (2019, pp. 1–37).
2 The last Matrix film, *The Matrix Resurrections*, not included here as it was released after 2020, was directed by Lana alone.
3 The book aims to refer to all the films that have been found that contain examples of strong artificial intelligence. Because of limitations of space, a few of these films are not analysed in detail in the book because they are similar to those already outlined or are limited in their exploration of artificial intelligence, and these are referred to in the notes. Also because of limitations of space, some, but not all, film sequels are explored in detail where they make a significant new contribution to the storytelling about AI in the film series.

Chapter 1

1 Janis Svilpis notes that similar scenarios to the one that Turing outlines can be found in science fiction narrative before the 1950s: 'science fiction arrived at the Turing test before Turing' (2008, p. 430).
2 Brazeal went on to launch Jibo in 2016, marketed as the first domestic social robot (Yonck 2020, p. 86).
3 The Internet of Things is a phrase credited to British technology pioneer Kevin Ashton in 1999 (Kramp et al. 2013). It refers to a range of wireless devices that have smart sensors and that can operate autonomously.
4 Discussion of Moravec's consciousness upload scenario begins Hayles's first chapter in *How We Became Posthuman*, and forms a starting point for her argument against the elision of the importance of materiality (Hayles 1999, p. 1).
5 Even the presentation of Robby as neutral needs some qualification. In the marketing posters for *Forbidden Planet* and *The Invisible Boy*, Robby is depicted in a negative way

that does not correspond to his behaviour in the film. This contrast is discussed in more detail in Chapter 2.

Chapter 2

1. Robby the Robot makes his first appearance in *Forbidden Planet*, and the robot would go on to appear in *The Invisible Boy*, as well as making many guest appearances in the decades that followed, sometimes under other character names and mostly on television, in a wide range of shows, such as *The Thin Man* (1958), *The Man from U.N.C.L.E.* (1966), *Mork and Mindy* (1979), *The Love Boat* (1982) and *The Big Bang Theory* (2014). Telotte identifies this 'persistence' of Robby's and argues that it 'touched a cultural sensibility for several decades, while establishing in the popular imaginary a sense of what the artificial being meant for post-war, atomic-age audiences' (2016, p. 22). Robby is special in another way, too: 'Robby the Robot' is billed alongside the other actors in *Forbidden Planet*, as though he were equal to them, a real individual and not just an expensive prop. The stuntmen who operate Robby the Robot are not credited. The same pattern occurs with his second appearance in *The Invisible Boy*. For this first AI robot in American film, the suspension of disbelief associated with his character extends outside the film's diegesis.
2. Robby is based on Isaac Asimov's short story 'Robby' from 1940. The film's plot is also loosely based upon Shakespeare's *The Tempest* and contains corollaries of its characters and locations. The tropical island of *The Tempest* has become the Planet Altair. The colonial ambitions of the Europeans have become the desire to conquer deep space. The learned magician, Prospero, is the hyper-intelligent, bookish philologist Morbius. The ship-wrecked Europeans who land on the island are the crew of the C57-D, and Prospero's unworldly, sheltered daughter, Miranda, is Altaira.

    Robby is a blend of two characters from *The Tempest*: Prospero's slave, the sprite called Aeriel, to whom he grants freedom at the end of the play, and the abused, misunderstood and despised native Caliban, who is eventually killed. Like Aeriel, Robby acquires his freedom at the end of the film, not because Morbius has granted it, but because Morbius dies, at which point the crew decides to bring Robby back to earth with them. Furthermore, the superior alien technology that helped to create Robby's artificial intelligence may be akin to the mystery of Ariel's magic. Morbius must renounce his ambitions to control the Krell database at the end of the film, just as Prospero must give up the magic that he has learned through his books.

    Robby's relationship to Shakespeare's Caliban is even more intriguing. He is enslaved by Prospero as Robby is to some extent enslaved by Morbius, programmed to obey his commands; to display 'complete and selfless obedience' even to the extent of harming himself. Morbius proudly demonstrates this obedience by ordering Robby to place his arm into a disintegrating light beam before commanding him to remove it at the last moment. Caliban, the first 'new world' native in English literature, is treated as less-than-human, similar to Robby's treatment as a robotic artificial intelligence.

3 The film attempts to provide an explanation for how Robby has come from the future back to 1957. Robby had been brought to the Institute by a Dr Greenhill, now deceased, who was very interested in time-travel. There is a photograph of Robby alighting from a spaceship, with a date that Merrinoe scoffs at – 2309.
4 Williams notes that the film's lack of special effects seems to have insured it against redundancy. 'Unlike Stanley Kubrick's *2001: A Space Odyssey*, which now resembles a picturesque relic of long-abandoned aspirations, *Alphaville* still seems to be watching the world come to meet it' (Williams 2011).
5 There are various critical perspectives on exactly how the conventional popular idioms function in the film. In a contemporary review of *Alphaville* in *Film Quarterly*, John Thomas says that: 'By means of his cops-and-robbers plot Godard establishes a framework so familiar that the recurring visual surprises don't overwhelm the viewer and disorient him' (1966, p. 48). For Thomas, the film's familiar elements work as a structural support for its experimental cinematography. Ten years later, Allen Thiher surmised that 'The comic strip side of *Alphaville* could be taken for a Brechtian form of "distanciation", for it is evident from the film's beginning that ironic distance must be maintained throughout the film' (1976, p. 950). From Thiher's point of view, the characters and their actions are so conventional that they have a jarring effect on the audience, compelling them to consider the approach taken, and the purpose of the parody.
6 Quotations from the film taken from Peter Whitehead's translation of the screenplay are specifically referenced (Godard 2000). Other quotations are taken from subtitles in the film's 1998 release.
7 This sense of dislocation overspills beyond the building that houses Alpha 60 to the rest of the city, which seems to defy the normal rules of geography and climate – a taxi-driver asks Lemmy which route he would like to take across the city and tells him there is snow in the north and sun in the south. Moving out beyond Alphaville, even further puzzlement about space, distance and position is demonstrated. A feature of the cinematography is neon arrows, which point and flash in seemingly random directions. Lemmy has travelled between galaxies to get here, and yet there is no sign of a ship, a facility, a landing base, and an almost ridiculously vague sense of where exactly the Outerlands, where is has come from, is located.
8 *HAL's Legacy: 2001's Computer as Dream and Reality*, edited by David G. Stork, comprises a selection of essays on HAL's abilities and their relationship to research in the 1960s and beyond.
9 Krämer notes that the transformation of Bowman into the Star Child is 'the culmination of birthday references throughout the film' (2010, p. 82), including Floyd's telephone call to his daughter for her birthday, the birthday message that Frank Poole's parents send to him, and HAL's regression to his beginnings when he is disconnected. Women are largely abstracted from these references to birth, and the mother of the Star Child remains a mystery. He or she is depicted as a foetus without a mother, floating in a womb-like orb that is unattached to a maternal body.
10 HAL's red eye has found its way into popular culture, appearing in episodes of *Barbie: Life in the Dreamhouse* (2012), and *Futurama* (2002), among others.

Chapter 3

1 The pronouns used for AIs in this book are the ones most commonly associated with the AI in the films themselves.

Chapter 4

1 Edwards calls these two categories 'disembodied computer intelligence' and 'embodied AIs' (1996, p. 306). The idea of embodiment is potentially ambiguous: both types of AIs have a material dimension and are arguably embodied in different ways. To avoid confusion and to allow for similarities between the two groups to emerge, they are categorised here as digital AIs and robot AIs.
2 Several AI films are ground-breaking in terms of their visual effects, such as *2001*, and the CGI of the psychedelic trip to Jupiter in particular, and *Westworld* and the CGI used for the Gunslinger's POV shots.

Chapter 5

1 For a full list of AI films that present the fear of the many, see the subsection 'Attitudes to AI' in the introduction.
2 It is possible that Deckard himself is a replicant but does not know it. This possibility is neither affirmed nor denied by the sequel *Blade Runner 2049*, and contributes to both films' exploration of the porosity of the human/replicant binary.
3 Johnny Number 5 and Ben reappear in the sequel *Short Circuit 2*, not analysed in detail here for reasons of space. It is notable that the ending of this film shows both Ben and Johnny 5 in parallel, being sworn in as US citizens.
4 *Blade Runner* is available in seven different versions, including The Director's Cut (1992) and The Final Cut (2007). As this book explores AI film in the context of the periods in which they were originally released, the version referred to here is the 1982 US Theatrical Release. Where relevant, differences between this version and the Final Cut will be mentioned, such as the voiceovers and the ending.
5 Animal replicants have a notable role in *Blade Runner*, particularly Tyrell's artificial owl, and the artificial snake used by Zhora. The owl is presented as being extravagantly expensive, a coveted luxury, whereas the snake is dismissed by Zhora as a poor substitute: 'Do you think I'd be working in a place like this if I could afford a real snake?' The animals show the contrasting attitudes to artificiality in the film – it is both impressive and desirable but also inauthentic and disposable. These conflicting attitudes are sustained throughout the film.
6 These instances of fake or modified memories or snapshots from the past make us wonder about Deckard's memories, too, and human memory in general. Is it unreliable like the replicants' memories? Is it susceptible to implantation? The answer to the first question is unequivocally yes – human memory is unreliable. To the second question, the answer is also yes – memories may not be 'implanted' by a cynical corporation, but

memories can be based on nothing more than an artefact or image – if you have a photograph of something, you may say that you 'remember' it, but, in fact, the memory is the photograph and nothing else. Or, a memory may be suggested, shaped or moulded by others, such as how particular moments become part of the mythology of a family when they are spoken about repeatedly, but may not actually be remembered by all concerned. In the 1990s, the authenticity of memory and its relationship to identity is considered again in *Ghost in the Shell*, in which the melding of human and artificial brains creates doubt as to what is real and what is implanted.
7 The first reference to the three laws of Robotics occurs in Isaac Asimov's 1942 short story 'Runaround', although the laws are alluded to earlier.
8 For discussion about AIs and personhood in the Alien franchise, see '"No Man Needs Nothing": The Possibility of Lockean Persons in Alien and Prometheus', by Chris Lay, and 'Androids: Artificial Persons or Glorified Toasters?' by Joe Slater, both from *Alien and Philosophy: I Infest, Therefore I Am* (Wiley and Sons, 2017).

Chapter 6

1 Nama proposes an alternative reading in which the 'wooden, if not blank, performance of Reeves' means that the black characters including Morpheus, the Oracle and Niobe 'carry the emotional weight of the film as revolutionary humanists' (2008, p. 144). The point is well-made; however, there is no sidestepping the fact that Neo is the protagonist and the fate all the other human characters is dependent upon him.
2 Sean French notes this also: 'When Sarah attempts to assassinate Dyson – and thus prevent him inventing the technology that will cause the nuclear holocaust – she becomes the terminator (just as the terminator is becoming human' (1996, p. 67)
3 The terminator played by Arnold Schwarzenegger is a T-800 series robot, model 101. In the Terminator films, it is referred to as both T-101 and T-800. In this book, I refer to this terminator as T-800.
4 Replication with modification may be the most accurate way of describing what the screamers do, but evolution is used here in the general sense of something gradually developing.

Chapter 7

1 There are many other links between Kubrick and Spielberg in relation to this film, too: Kubrick was the first of the two to consider an early draft of the script, and Spielberg includes several nods to Kubrick in the film.
2 In *Anatomy of a Robot*, Kakoudaki outlines the relationship between the African-American experience of slavery and the exploration of robot emancipation in the original *Bicentennial Man* by Isaac Asimov (2014, pp. 118–124).
3 Her desire for complete control and dismissal of humans – 'you are so like children. We must save you from yourselves' – finds a descendent in PAL, in

The Mitchells vs. The Machines, another digital female AI. *The Mitchells vs. The Machines* is not analysed in this book because it falls outside the timeframe for this study.

4 Two other AI films in this decade are set in space: the UK film *Moon*, directed by Duncan Jones, and the Pixar animated film *Wall-E*. *Moon* is set on a mining base supporting earth's energy needs and designed to be occupied by one human employee, and an AI assistant, GERTY. *Moon* is not particularly innovative in its representation of AI, but its exploration of the relationship between the AI and the clone, both non-human, both exiles from earth, chimes with Ripley and Call at the conclusion of *Alien Resurrection*.

   Wall-E, too, is set against the backdrop of environmental crisis. Its protagonist is a sentient trash-collecting robot that lives on an earth that has been abandoned by humans, who live vacuous and meaningless lives on a spaceship where their every need is provided for. Whether Wall-E can be classified as a strong AI is difficult to ascertain – certainly he has personality and interests, he is capable of forming a bond with another robot, Eva, and he inadvertently becomes the catalyst for humans returning to earth when he finds a green shoot that signals earth's inhabitability. The ship's onboard computer Otto is a familiar AI that is humorously modelled on HAL. He has been given full control of the ship, and withholds 'classified' information from the human captain. The references to HAL are underlined by the use of the iconic music 'Thus Spake Zarathustra' as the captain stands up on wobbly legs unaccustomed to use to turn Otto's switch from 'auto' to 'manual', easily triumphing over his AI adversary. In its own way *Wall-E* recognises, like *The Matrix Reloaded* and *Revolutions*, that intelligent machines can be useful and necessary as well as threatening and domineering.

5 The gynoids in this film, with their ball-joint abdomens, have been modelled on Hans Bellmer's dolls. Bellmer created sculptures and pictures of these dolls in the 1930s. Steven T. Brown's article 'Machinic Desires: Hans Bellmer's Dolls and the Technological Uncanny in "Ghost in the Shell 2: Innocence"' provides further information on this inspiration and its potential interpretations. A book that Bellmer produced with photographs of these dolls appears in the film also, at Kim's house in Locus Solus.

Chapter 8

1 Though not discussed here for reasons of space, *Terminator: Dark Fate* shows this collaboration between human and AI with the introduction of the resistance fighter Grace, a cybernetically-enhanced human, who forms part of a team with the T-800 Carl, a robot who has become self-aware and adopted a human family.
2 In *Westworld*, Peter also disguises himself as an AI robot, like Vaseegaran in *Enthiran*.
3 Lakkad notes that this places Vaseegaran's girlfriend Sana as 'mother' to Chitti and means that his attraction to her can be viewed as the Oedipal desiring of the mother, and viewing the father as a rival (2018, p. 243)
4 When Caleb first goes to meet Ava, he notices a crack in the glass that hints at Ava's desire to escape. In *Demon Seed*, too, Proteus complains that his maker keeps him caged.

Chapter 9

1 In fact, all the Terminator films present machines that are controlled – by the artificial intelligence Skynet. The TX is a machine that controls other machines that is itself controlled by a machine.
2 His colleague Max and his wife Evelyn are focused on the potential for AI science to assist in tackling problems like climate change, poverty and disease. In the film, climate change is the issue that is spotlighted the most, so the film follows *AI* and *Wall-E* in presenting strong AIs as part of a solution for the climate crisis.
3 The Netflix animation *Next Gen*, not considered here for reasons of space, also depicts an AI robot that regards its memories of a relationship with a human as precious, deleting weapons programming to preserve them.
4 *Next Gen* also shows the robot beginning again in his relationship with a human, after its memories have been deleted.
5 Joi begins *Blade Runner 2049* with an online connection but chooses to be stored exclusively on a portable device; HAL is designed to control a spaceship, and SAL is designed in his likeness; VIKI can remotely control other machines, but is ultimately stopped by deactivating her at her physical source.
6 *Tron Legacy*, like its predecessor *Tron*, presents the 'digitization' of the human within a computer game.
7 Theodore takes issue with Samantha's breathiness at one point in the film, as she is a digital entity that does not require oxygen, seeing it as an example of her simulated nature, her attempt to disguise herself as human, although he later overcomes these reservations.

Filmography

2.0. (2018) Directed by S. Shankar. India: Lyca Productions.
2001: A Space Odyssey (1968) Directed by Stanley Kubrick. United States: MGM.
2010: The Year We Make Contact (1984) Peter Hyams. United States. MGM.
AI: Artificial Intelligence (2001) Directed by Stephen Spielberg. United States: Amblin Entertainment.
Alien (1979) Directed by Ridley Scott. United States: 20th Century Fox.
Aliens (1986) Directed by James Cameron. United States: 20th Century Fox.
Alien³ (1992) Directed by David Fincher. United States: 20th Century Fox.
Alien Covenant (2017) Directed by Ridley Scott. United States: 20th Century Fox.
Alien Resurrection (1997) Directed by Jean-Pierre Jeunet. United States: 20th Century Fox.
Alphaville: A Strange Adventure of Lemmy Caution (1968) Directed by Jean Luc Godard. France: Athos Films.
Automata (2014) Directed by Gabe Ibáñez. Spain, Bulgaria: Contracorrientes Films.
Bicentennial Man (1999) Directed by Chris Columbus. United States: Columbia Pictures.
Blade Runner (1982) Directed by Ridley Scott. United States: Warner Brothers.
Blade Runner 2049 (2017) Directed by Denis Villeneuve. United States: Warner Brothers.
Chappie (2015) Directed by Neil Blomkamp. United States: Sony Pictures.
Colossus: The Forbin Project (1970) Directed by Joseph Sargent. United States: Universal Pictures.
Dark Star (1974) Directed by John Carpenter. United States: Bryanston Distributing Company.
DARYL (1985) Directed by Simon Wincer. United States: Paramount Pictures.
Demon Seed (1977) Directed by Donald Cammell. United States: MGM.
Electric Dreams (1984) Directed by Steve Barron. United States: MGM.
Enthiran (2010) Directed by S. Shankar. India: Lyca Produtions.
Eva (2011) Directed by Kike Maíllo. Spain: Paramount Pictures; France: Wild Bunch Distribution.
Ex Machina (2014) Directed by Alex Garland. United States: A24, Universal Pictures.
Forbidden Planet (1956) Directed by Fred M. Wilcox. United States: MGM.
Ghost in the Shell (1995) Directed by Mamoru Oshii. Japan: Shochiku.
Ghost in the Shell 2: Innocence (2004) Directed by Mamoru Oshii. Japan: Toho Company.
Her (2013) Directed by Spike Jonze. United States: Warner Brothers.
I Am Mother (2019) Directed by Grant Sputore. Australia: Netflix.

I, Robot (2004) Directed by Alex Proyas. United States: 20th Century Studios.
Metropolis (1927) Directed by Fritz Lang. United States: Paramount Pictures.
Moon (2009) Directed by Duncan Jones. United Kingdom: Sony Pictures.
Next Gen (2018) Directed by Joe Ksander and Kevin R. Adams. Canada, America, China: Netflix.
Prometheus (2012) Directed by Ridley Scott. United States: 20th Century Studios.
Short Circuit (1986) Directed by John Badham. United States: TriStar Pictures.
Short Circuit 2 (1988) Directed by Kenneth Johnson. United States: TriStar Pictures.
Star Trek: Generations (1994) Directed by David Carson. United States: Paramount Pictures.
Tau (2018) Directed by Federico D'Alessandro. United States: Netflix.
Terminator (1984) Directed by James Cameron. United States: Orlon Pictures.
Terminator 2: Judgement Day (1991) Directed by James Cameron. United States: TriStar Pictures.
Terminator 3: Rise of the Machines (2003) Directed by Jonathan Mostow. United States: Warner Brothers.
Terminator Salvation (2009) Directed by McG. United States: Warner Brothers.
Terminator: Dark Fate (2019) Directed by Tim Miller. United States: Paramount Pictures.
Terminator Genysis (2015) Directed by Alan Taylor. United States: Paramount Pictures.
The Invisible Boy (1957) Directed by Herman Hoffman. United States: MGM.
The Machine (2013) Directed by Caradog W. James. UK: Content Media.
The Matrix (1999) Directed by Lana and Lilly Wachowski. United States: Warner Brothers.
The Matrix Reloaded (2003) Directed by Lana and Lilly Wachowski. United States: Warner Brothers.
The Matrix Revolutions (2003) Directed by Lana and Lilly Wachowski. United States: Warner Brothers.
The Matrix Resurrections (2021) Directed by Lana Wachowski. United States: Warner Brothers.
The Mitchells vs. The Machines (2021). Directed by Mike Rianda. United States: Netflix.
Transcendence (2014) Directed by Wally Pfister. United States: Warner Brothers.
Screamers (1995) Directed by Christian Duguay. Canada: Columbia Pictures.
Screamers: The Hunting (2009) Directed by Sheldon Wilson. Canada: Sony Pictures Home Entertainment.
Tron (1982) Directed by Steven Lisberger. United States: Walt Disney Pictures.
Tron: Legacy (2010) Directed by Joseph Kosinski. United States: Walt Disney Pictures.
Wall-E (2008) Directed by Andrew Stanton. United States: Walt Disney Pictures.
War Games (1983) Directed by John Badham. United States: MGM.
Westworld (1973) Directed by Michael Crichton. United States: MGM.

Bibliography

Arnold-de Simine, Silke (2019) 'Beyond Trauma?: Memories of Joi/y and Memory Play in *Blade Runner 2049*'. *Memory Studies* 12(1), pp. 61–73.
Augusto, Juan Carlos and McCullagh, Paul (2007) 'Ambient Intelligence: Concepts and Applications', *ComSIS*, 4(1), pp. 1–28.
Bakke, Gretchen (2010) 'Dead White Men: An Essay on the Changing Dynamics of Race in US Action Cinema', *Anthropological Quarterly*, 83(2), pp. 400–428.
Barad, Karen (2008) *Meeting the Universe Halfway: Quantum Physics and the Entanglement of Matter and Meaning*. Durham, NC: Duke University Press.
Barber, Jacob (2017) 'Star Trek and the Anthropological Machine: Eliding Difference to Stay Human', *Geographical Bulletin*, 50, pp. 40–50.
Barrat, James (2013) *Our Final Invention: Artificial Intelligence and the End of the Human Era*. New York: St. Martin's Press.
Baudrillard, Jean (2001) *Selected Writings*. Edited and introduced by Mark Poster. Cambridge: Polity Press.
Bennett, Jane (2010) *Vibrant Matter: A Political Ecology of Things*. Durham, NC, and London: Duke University Press.
Boden, Margaret A. (2014) 'GOFAI', in Frankish, Keith and Ramsey, William M. (eds.) *The Cambridge Handbook of Artificial Intelligence*. Cambridge: Cambridge University Press, pp. 89–107.
Bond, Alan H. and Gasser, Les (eds.) (2014) *Readings in Distributed Artificial Intelligence*. San Mateo: Morgan Kaufmann Publishers.
Bordun, Troy (2016) 'On the Off-Screen Voice: Sound and Vision in Spike Jonze's "Her"', *Cineaction*, 98, pp. 57–64.
Bostrom, Nick (2014) *Superintelligence: Paths, Dangers, Strategies*, Oxford: Oxford University Press.
Braidotti, Rosi (2013) *The Posthuman*. Cambridge: Polity.
Brayton, Sean (2008) 'The Post-White Imaginary in Alex Proyas's "I, Robot"', *Science Fiction Studies*, 35(1), pp. 72–87.
Brooks, Rodney A. (1990) 'Elephants Don't Play Chess', *Robotics and Autonomous Systems*, 6, pp. 3–15.
Brown, Steven T. (2008) 'Machinic Desires: Hans Bellmer's "Dolls" and the Technological Uncanny in "Ghost in the Shell 2: Innocence"', *Mechademia: Second Arc*, 3, pp. 222–253.
Bruno, Giuliana (1987) 'Ramble City: Postmodernism and "Blade Runner"', *October*, 41, pp. 61–74).

Čapek, Karel (2004) *RUR: Rossum's Universal Robots*. London: Penguin.
Cerullo, Michael A. (2015) 'Uploading and Branching Identity', *Minds and Machines*, Vol. 25, pp. 17–36.
Clark, Andy (2003) *Natural Born Cyborgs: Minds, Technologies and the Future of Human Intelligence*. Oxford: Oxford University Press.
Clover, Joshua (2004) *The Matrix*. BFI Film Classics. London: Bloomsbury.
Constable, Catherine (1999) 'Becoming the Monster's Mother: Morphologies of Identity in the Alien Series', in Kuhn, Annette (ed.) *Alien Zone II*. London: Verso, pp. 173–202.
Currin, Joseph M., Lee, Fallyn M., Brown, Colton and Hammer, Tonya R. (2016) 'Taking the Red Pill: Using the Matrix to Explore Transgender Identity Development', *Journal of Creativity in Mental Health*, 12(3), pp. 402–409.
Derrida, Jacques (1973) *Speech and Phenomena, and Other Essays on Husserl's Theory of Signs*. Evanston: Northwestern University Press.
De Spiegeleire, Stephan, Maas, Matthijs and Sweijs, Tim (2017) 'What is Artificial Intelligence?' In *Artificial Intelligence and The Future Of Defense: Strategic Implications for Small and Medium-Sized Force Providers*. Hague Centre for Strategic Studies, pp. 25–42.
Dinello, Daniel (2006) *Technophobia!: Science Fiction Visions of Posthuman Technology*. Austin: University of Texas Press.
Dixon, Wheeler Winston (1997) *The Films of Jean-Luc Godard*. Albany: State University of New York Press.
Dragunoiu, Dana (2007) 'Neo's Kantian Choice: "The Matrix Reloaded" and the Limits of the Posthuman', *Mosaic: An Interdisciplinary Critical Journal*, 40(4), pp. 51–67.
Dunne, Rob, Tim Morris and Simon Harper (2021) 'A Survey of Ambient Intelligence', *ACM Computing Surveys*, 54, 1–27.
During, Elie (2006) 'Is there an Exit from "Virtual Reality"?: Grid and Network – From "Tron" to "The Matrix"'. *The Matrix in Theory*, edited by Myriam Díaz Diocaretz and Stefan Herbrechter. Leiden: Brill.
Du Sautoy, Marcus (2019) *The Creativity Code: How AI is Learning to Write, Paint and Think*. Available at https://www.amazon.co.uk/Creativity-Code-learning-write-paint-ebook/dp/B07GLP28F3/ref=sr_1_1?crid=1WV7CR2XPAK56&keywords=de+sautoy+the+creativity+code&qid=1695031847&sprefix=de+sautoy+the+creativity+code%2Caps%2C89&sr=8-1 (accessed 20 June 2023).
Edwards, Paul N. (1996) *Computers and the Politics of Discourse in Cold War America*. Cambridge, MA: MIT Press.
Elyamany, Nashwa (2022) 'Postcyberpunk Dystopian Cityscape and Emotion Artificial Intelligence: A Spatio-Cognitive Analysis of Posthuman Representation in "Blade Runner 2049"', *Convergence: The International Journal of Research into New Media Technologies*, 0(0), pp. 1–27.
Faber, Liz (2020) *The Computer's Voice: From Star Trek to Siri*. Minneapolis and London: University of Minnesota Press.
Fenske, Michaela and Norkunas, Martha (2017) 'Experiencing the More-than-Human World', *Narrative Culture*, 4(2), pp. 105–110.
Fetzer, J. H. (1990) What is Artificial Intelligence?', *Artificial Intelligence: Its Scope and Limits. Studies in Cognitive Systems*, 4, pp. 3–27.
Freedman, Carl (1998) '"2001" and the Possibility of a Science Fiction Cinema', *Science Fiction Studies*, 25(2), pp. 300–318.

French, Sean (1996) *The Terminator*. London: BFI.
Freud, Sigmund (1919) 'The Uncanny', first published in *Imago*, Bd. V., 1919; reprinted in Sammlung, Fünfte Folge. https://web.mit.edu/allanmc/www/freud1.pdf (accessed 29 June 2023). Translated by Alix Strachey.
Gamez, David (2018) *Human and Machine Consciousness*. Cambridge: Open Book Publishers.
Gams, Matjaz, Irene Gu, Aki Härmä, Andrés Muñoz and Vincent Tam (2019) 'Artificial Intelligence and Ambient Intelligence', *Journal of Ambient Intelligence and Smart Environments*, 11, pp. 71–86.
Gardner, Howard (2011) *Frames of Mind: The Theory of Multiple Intelligences*. 4th edn. Basic Books.
Glass, Fred (1984) 'Sign of the Times: The Computer as Character in *Tron, War Games,* and *Superman III*', *Film Quarterly*, 38(2) Winter 1984–5, pp. 16–27.
Godard, Jean-Luc (2000) *Alphaville*, translated by Peter Whitehead. London: Faber and Faber.
Goldman, Steven L. (1989) 'Images of Technology in Popular Films: Discussion and Filmography', *Science, Technology, & Human Values* 14(3), pp. 275–301.
Hannett, Michelle (2014) 'WAMG Talks to Automata Director Gabe Ibáñez', *We Are Movie Geeks*. http://www.wearemoviegeeks.com/2014/10/wamg-talks-automata-director-gabe-ibanez/ (accessed 29 June 2023).
Hansen, Mark B. N. (2001) 'Seeing with the Body: The Digital Image in Postphotography', *Diacritics*, 31(4), pp. 54–84.
Haraway, Donna (1991) 'A Cyborg Manifesto: Science, Technology and Socialist-Feminism in the Late Twentieth Century', *Simians, Cyborgs and Women: The Reinvention of Nature*. New York: Routledge, pp. 149–181.
Haraway, Donna (2002) 'The Persistence of Vision', in Mirzoeff, Nicholas (ed.) *The Visual Culture Reader*. London and New York: Routledge, pp. 677–684.
Haselton, Todd (2018) 'Elon Musk: I'm about to announce a "Neuralink" product that connects your brain to computers', *CNBC: Tech Drivers*. https://www.cnbc.com/2018/09/07/elon-musk-discusses-neurolink-on-joe-rogan-podcast.html (accessed 29 June 2023)
Hassan, Ihab (1977) 'Prometheus as Performer: Towards a Posthumanist Culture?', *The Georgia Review*, 31(4), pp. 830–850.
Hayles, N. Katherine (1999). *How We Became Posthuman: Virtual Bodies in Cybernetics, Literature and Informatics*. Chicago, IL: University of Chicago Press.
Hayles, N. Katherine (2011) 'Wrestling with Transhumanism', in Hansell, Gregory R. and Grassie, William (eds.) *H+: Transhumanism and its Critics*. Philadelphia: Metanexus Institute, pp. 215–226.
Higgins, Mike (2000) 'Bicentennial Man', *Sight and Sound*, 10(3), pp. 41–2.
Jermyn, Deborah (2006) 'The Rachel Papers: In Search of *Blade Runner*'s Femme Fatale', in Brooker, Will (ed.) *The Blade Runner Experience: The Legacy of a Science Fiction Classic*. New York: Columbia University Press, pp. 159–172.
Kak, Subhash C. (1996) 'Can We Define Levels of Artificial Intelligence?', *Journal of Intelligent Systems*, 6(2), pp. 133–144.
Kakoudaki, Despina (2014) *Anatomy of a Robot: Literature, Cinema and the Cultural Work of Artificial People*. New Brunswick: Rutgers University Press.
Kaplan, Jerry (2016) *Artificial Intelligence: What Everyone Needs to Know*. Oxford: Oxford University Press.
Kaveney, Roz (2005) *From Alien to The Matrix: Reading Science Fiction Film*. London: IB Tauris.

Kera, Denisa (2006) 'Matrix – The New Constitution between Hardware, Wetware and Software', in Diaz-Diocaretz, Myriam and Herbrechter, Stefan (eds.) *The Matrix in Theory*. New York: Rodopi, pp. 211–226.
Koene, Randal A. (2013) 'Uploading to Substrate-Independent Minds', in More, Max and Vita-More, Natasha (eds.) *The Transhumanist Reader: Classical and Contemporary Essays on the Science, Technology and Philosophy of the Human Future*. Chichester: Wiley Blackwell, pp. 146–156.
Kolker, Robert (2006) *Stanley Kubrick's 2001: A Space Odyssey: New Essays*. Oxford University Press.
Kornhaber, Donna (2017) 'From Posthuman to Postcinema: Crises of Subjecthood and Representation in *Her*', *Cinema Journal*, 56(4), pp. 3–25.
Kozlovic, Anton Karl (2003) 'Technophobic Themes in Pre-1990 Computer Films', *Science as Culture* 12(3), pp. 341–373.
Kramp, Thorsten, van Kranenburg, Rob and Lange, Sebastian (2013) 'Introduction to the Internet of Things', in Bassi, Alessandro et al. (eds.) *Enabling Things to Talk: Designing IoT Solutions with the IoT Architectural Reference Model*. Springer, pp. 1–12.
Krämer, Peter (2010) *2001: A Space Odyssey*. BFI.
Kreider, Tim (2002) 'AI: Artificial Intelligence', *Film Quarterly*, 56(2), pp. 32–39.
Kurzweil, Ray (2005) *The Singularity is Near: When Humans Transcend Biology*. London: Duckworth and Co.
Kurzweil, Ray (2014) *How to Create a Mind: The Secret of Human Thought Revealed*. London: Duckworth and Co. 2015.
Lakkad, Abhisheck (2018) 'Frankenstein's Avatars: Posthuman Monstrosity in Enthiran/Robot', *Rupkatha Journal on Interdisciplinary Studies in Humanities*, 10(2), pp. 236–250.
Latham, Rob (2015) '"Lack of Respect, Wrong Attitude, Failure to Obey Authority": *Dark Star*, *A Boy and His Dog*, and New Wave Cult SF', in Telotte, J. P. and Duchovnay, Gerald (eds.) *Science Fiction Double Feature: The Science Fiction Film as Cult Text*. Liverpool: Liverpool University Press, pp. 205–219.
Lay, Chris (2017) '"No Man Needs Nothing": The Possibility of Androids as Lockean Persons in Alien and Prometheus', in Ewing, Jeffrey and Decker, Kevin S. (eds.) *Alien and Philosophy: I Infest, Therefore I Am*. John Wiley and Sons.
Locke, Brian (2009) 'White and "Black" Versus Yellow: The Politics of Racial Metaphor in Blade Runner', *Arizona Quarterly*, 65(4), pp. 113–138.
Lovins, Christopher (2019) 'A Ghost in the Replicant? Questions of Humanity and Technological Integration in *Blade Runner* and *Ghost in the Shell*', *Journal of Science Fiction*, 3(1), pp. 21–34.
Mateas, Michael and Sengers, Phoebe (eds.) (2003) *Narrative Intelligence*. Amsterdam: John Benjamins Publishing Company.
Mateas, Michael (2006) 'Reading HAL: Representation and Artificial Intelligence', in Kolker, Robert (ed.) *Stanley Kubrick's 2001: A Space Odyssey: New Essays*. Oxford: Oxford University Press, pp. 147–175.
Matheson, T. J. (1992) 'Marcuse, Ellul, and the Science-Fiction Film: Negative Responses to Technology', *Science Fiction Studies*, 19(3), pp. 326–339.
McCarthy, John, et al. [1955] (2006) 'A Proposal for the Dartmouth Summer Research Project on Artificial Intelligence,' *AI Magazine*, 27(4), pp. 12–14.
McLean, Scott, et al. (2021) 'The risks associated with Artificial General Intelligence: A systematic review', *Journal of Experimental & Theoretical Artificial Intelligence*, 35(5), pp. 649–663.
McNamara, Kevin R. (1997) 'Blade Runner's Post-Individual Worldspace', *Contemporary Literature*, 38(3), pp. 422–446.

McStay, Andrew (2018) *Emotional AI: The Rise of Empathic Media*. Sage Publications.

McWilliam, David (2015) 'Beyond the Mountains of Madness: Lovecraftian Cosmic Horror and Posthuman Creationism in Ridley Scott's "Prometheus"', *Journal of the Fantastic in the Arts*, 26(3), pp. 531–545.

Moravec, Hans (1988) *Mind Children: The Future of Robot and Human Intelligence*. Cambridge, MA: Harvard University Press.

Muir, John Kenneth (2000) *The Films of John Carpenter*. Jefferson NC: McFarland and Co.

Murgia, Madhumita and Waters, Richard (2023) 'Why AI's "Godfather" Geoffrey Hinton Quit Google to Speak Out on Risks', *Financial Times*, 5 May. https://www.ft.com/content/c2b0c6c5-fe8a-41f2-a4df-fddba9e4cd88 (accessed 29 June 2023).

Murray, Yvonne (2023) 'Artificial Intelligence Threat Similar to Nuclear War Risk Says UN Chief', *RTE*, https://www.rte.ie/news/2023/0612/1388791-ai-threat-un/#:~:text=By%20Yvonne%20Murray&text=The%20UN%20chief%20has%20voiced,today%2C%20citing%20warnings%20from%20experts (accessed 29 June 2023).

Nama, Adilifu (2008) *Black Space: Imagining Race in Science Fiction Film*. Austen: University of Texas Press.

Nedomansky, Vashi 'The Ultimate History of CGI in Film', *Vashi Visuals*, 21 March, 2019, https://vashivisuals.com/the-ultimate-history-of-cgi-movies/ (accessed 29 June 2023).

Newell, Allen, Shaw, J. C. and Simon, H. A. (1959) 'Report on a General Problem Solving Program', Carnegie Institute of Technology: The Rand Corporation.

Parker, Lynne, E. (2008) 'Distributed Intelligence: Overview of the Field and Its Application in Multi-Robot Systems', *AAAI Fall Symposium: Regarding the Intelligence in Distributed Intelligent Systems*, pp. 1–6

Pennachin, C., Goertzel, B. (2007) 'Contemporary Approaches to Artificial General Intelligence', in Goertzel, B. and Pennachin, C. (eds.) *Artificial General Intelligence. Cognitive Technologies*. Berlin; Heidelberg: Springer, pp. 1–30.

Picard, Rosalind (2000) *Affective Computing*. Cambridge, MA: MIT Press.

Picart, Caroline S. (2004) 'The Third Shadow and Hybrid Genres: Horror, Humour, Gender, and Race in Alien Resurrection', *Communication and Critical/Cultural Studies*, 1(4), pp. 335–354.

Poole, Robert (2001) 'Film in Context: *2001*', *History Today*, January, pp. 39–45.

Prock, Stephan (2014) 'Strange Voices: Subjectivity and Gender in *Forbidden Planet*'s Soundscape of Tomorrow', *Journal of the Society for American Music*, 8(3), pp. 371–400.

RMP and Fitting, Peter (1987) 'Futurecop the Neutralization of Revolt in "Blade Runner"', *Science Fiction Studies*, 14(3), pp. 340–354.

Rosenbaum, Jonathan (2012), 'A Matter of Life and Death: AI', *Film Quarterly*, 65(3), pp. 74–78.

Roud, Richard (2000) 'Introduction: Anguish: Alphaville' in *Alphaville*, Jean-Luc Godard, trans. Peter Whitehead. London: Faber and Faber.

Sculos, Bryant William (2015) 'Automatons, Robots and Capitalism in a Very Wrong Twenty-First Century', *Class, Race and Corporate Power*, 3(1), Article 4, p. 5.

Searle, John (1980) 'Minds, Brains and Programs', *The Behavioural and Brain Sciences*, 3, pp. 417–457.

Searle, John (2013) 'Our Shared Condition: Consciousness', *TEDxCERN*, https://www.ted.com/talks/john_searle_our_shared_condition_consciousness?language=en#t-869344 (accessed 29 June 2023).

Shah, Simmone (2023) 'The Writers Strike is Taking a Stand on AI', *Time*, 4 May, https://time.com/6277158/writers-strike-ai-wga-screenwriting/ (accessed 29 June 2023).

Shakespeare, William (1998) *The Tragedy of Hamlet, Prince of Denmark*, Project Gutenberg https://www.gutenberg.org/files/1524/1524-h/1524-h.htm#sceneII_8.2 (accessed 29 June 2023).
Shetley, Vernon and Ferguson, Alissa (2001) 'Reflections in a Silver Eye: Lens and Mirror in "Blade Runner"', *Science Fiction Studies*, 28(1), pp. 66–76.
Silvio, Carl (1999) 'Refiguring the Radical Cyborg in Mamoru Oshii's "Ghost in the Shell"', *Science Fiction Studies*, 26(1), pp. 54–72.
Slater, Joe (2017) 'Androids: Artificial Persons or Glorified Toasters?', in Ewing, Jeffrey and Decker, Kevin S. (eds.) *Alien and Philosophy: I Infest, Therefore I Am*. John Wiley and Sons Ltd.
Stork, David G., ed. (1997) *HAL's Legacy: 2001's Computer as Dream and Reality*. Cambridge, MA: MIT Press.
Strübing, Jörg (1998) 'Bridging the Gap: On the Collaboration between Symbolic Interactionism and Distributed Artificial Intelligence in the Field of Multi-Agent Systems Research,' *Symbolic Interaction*, 21(4), pp. 441–463.
Svilpis, Janis (2008) 'The Science-Fiction Prehistory of the Turing Test', *Science Fiction Studies*, 35(3) pp. 430–449.
Telotte, J. P. (1983) 'Human Artifice and the Science Fiction Film', *Film Quarterly*, 36(3), pp. 44–51.
Telotte, J. P. (1995) *Replications: A Robotic History of the Science Fiction Film*. Chicago: University of Illinois Press.
Telotte, J. P. (2001) *Science Fiction Film*. Cambridge: Cambridge University Press.
Telotte, J. P. (2016). 'Robby the Robot and Robotic Persistence'. *Mosaic: An Interdisciplinary Critical Journal*, 49(3), pp. 19–37.
Telotte, J. P. (2018) *Robot Ecology and the Science Fiction Film*. Abingdon: Routledge.
Thiher, Allen (1976) 'Postmodern Dilemma: Godard's "Alphaville" and "Two or Three Things that I Know about Her"', *Boundary 2*, 4(3), pp. 947–974.
Thomas, John (1966) 'Alphaville', *Film Quarterly*, 20(1), pp. 48–51.
Times of India 'Baasha to Kabali: Highest Grossing films of Rajinikanth', Entertainment Times, https://timesofindia.indiatimes.com/entertainment/tamil/movies/photo-features/baashha-to-kabali-highest-grossing-films-of-rajinikanth/baashha/photostory/64543488.cms (accessed 29 June 2023).
Tirosh-Samuelson, Hava (2011) 'Engaging Transhumanism', in Hansell, Gregory R. and Grassie, William (eds.) *H+: Transhumanism and its Critics*. Philadelphia: Metanexus Institute.
Turing, A. M. (1950). Computing Machinery and Intelligence. *Mind: A Quarterly Review of Psychology and Philosophy*, LIX(236), pp.433–460.
Turkle, Sherry (2011) *Alone Together: Why We Expect More from Technology and Less from Each Other*. New York: Basic Books.
Vinge, Vernor (2013) 'Technological Singularity', in Max More and Natasha Vita More (eds.) *The Transhumanist Reader: Classical and Contemporary Essays on the Science, Technology and Philosophy of the Human Future*. Chichester: Wiley Blackwell, pp. 365–375.
Vint, Sherryl (2020) 'Vitality and Reproduction in "Blade Runner 2049"', *Science Fiction Film and Television*, 13(1) Spring, pp. 15–35.
Virilio, Paul (1994) *The Vision Machine*. London: BFI.
Wang, Pei (2019). 'On Defining Artificial Intelligence', *Journal of Artificial Intelligence* 10(2), pp. 1–37.
Williams, Richard (2011) 'My Favorite Film: "Alphaville"', *The Guardian*, 28 December, https://www.theguardian.com/film/filmblog/2011/dec/28/my-favourite-film-al

phaville-godard#:~:text=Unlike%20Stanley%20Kubrick's%202001%3A%20A,it%20was%20back%20in%201965 (accessed 29 June 2023).

Wood, Aylish (2002) *Technoscience in Contemporary American Film*. Manchester: Manchester University Press.

Yachir, A., Amirat, Y., Chibani, A. and Badache, N. (2016) 'Event-Aware Framework for Dynamic Services Discovery and Selection in the Context of Ambient Intelligence and Internet of Things'. *IEEE Transactions on Automation Science and Engineering*, 13(1), pp. 85–102.

Yonck, Richard (2017) *The Heart of the Machine: Our Future in a World of Artificial Emotional Intelligence*. New York: Arcade Publishing.

Yuen, Wong Kin (2000) 'On the Edge of Spaces: *Blade Runner, Ghost in the Shell* and Hong Kong's Cityscape', *Science Fiction Studies*, 27(1), pp. 1–21.

Ziegler, Robert E. (1983) 'Killing Space: The Dialectic in John Carpenter's Films', *The Georgia Review* 37(4), pp. 770–786.

Index

2001: A Space Odyssey, 11, 17, 18, 26, 28, 29, 42–5, 46, 52, 54, 62, 74–5, 85, 90, 124, 143, 144, 154, 168, 170, 171, 173
2010: The Year We Make Contact, 24, 26, 66, 69, 74–6, 83, 87, 90, 175

abject, 61, 102, 124, 137
affective AI, 11, 29, 44, 82, 91, 124, 141, 148, 149, 151–2, 157, 159, 161, 173, 176, 180; *see also* empathic media
agents (of AI), 100, 101, 106, 108, 119, 129, 181
AI: Artificial Intelligence, 19, 20, 21, 22, 25, 27, 58, 69–70, 82, 88, 89, 124–6, 141, 151, 154, 161, 163, 168, 173, 176, 177, 181
AI 'reveal', 48, 57, 63, 64, 82, 98, 99, 102, 111, 112, 122, 124, 135, 136–7, 143, 145, 149–50, 152, 182
Alien, 17, 20, 21, 24, 47, 48, 60, 62–4, 74, 86, 95, 96, 98
Aliens, 21, 82, 83, 96–9, 115
Alien³, 20, 26, 27, 99, 101, 102, 115–17, 118, 143, 175, 177
Alien: Covenant, 15, 20, 144–7, 173–4
Alien franchise, 18, 19, 22, 124–5, 173
Alien: Resurrection, 17, 20, 21, 23, 27, 100, 102, 117–19, 126, 146, 164, 181
Alphaville, 11, 15, 17, 28, 29, 39–41, 45, 54, 74, 112
ambient intelligence, 2, 12, 19, 47, 51–2, 57–8, 59, 160, 170, 180, 181; *see also* super ambient intelligence

anthropocentrism, 16, 109, 123, 144, 146, 147, 181
artificial intelligence, 2, 7, 8
artificial narrow intelligence, 2
artificial general intelligence, 2–3, 30, 36, 84; *see also* strong AI
Asimov, Isaac, 30, 97, 122, 126, 153–4
augmentation, 131, 136, 163–4
Automata, 14, 15, 18, 19, 20, 22, 22, 24, 26, 153–6, 162, 164, 165, 173, 177

Badham, John, 84
Baudrillard, Jean, 72–3, 136
Bennett, Jane, 177
Bicentennial Man, 15, 18, 19, 20, 21, 23, 24, 26–7, 58, 122–4, 142, 144, 168, 176, 177
big data, 39
Blade Runner, 15, 18, 19, 22, 24, 25, 27, 66, 82, 89, 91–6, 99, 104, 113, 153, 156, 157, 158, 165, 168, 171, 173
Blade Runner 2049, 10, 18, 19, 20, 25, 27, 156–9, 171, 173, 175, 176, 181
Blomkamp, Neil, 167
Bostrom, Nick, 3, 154
Braidotti, Rosi, 16, 131
branching consciousness, 160, 169–70, 172, 179
Brazeal, Cynthia, 11, 120, 152
Brooks, Rodney, 10–11

Cameron, James, 103
carebot, 32, 35, 46
Carpenter, John, 52, 53

centre (of AI) *see* origin
Chappie, 11, 14, 17, 18, 19, 22, 23, 27, 167–70, 178, 179
child AIs, 18, 82, 88, 110, 124, 150–2, 161, 162, 168
childlike AIs *see* child AIs
Chinese room experiment, 5, 9–10
Clark, Andy, 7, 98
Colombus, Chris, 122
Colossus: The Forbin Project, 15, 17, 18, 19, 21, 23, 47, 48, 48–52, 64
companion robot, 32, 35, 46; *see also* carebot
consciousness, 6–7; *see also* consciousness upload; branching consciousness
consciousness upload, 5, 13–14, 27, 140, 160, 162, 164, 165, 167, 168–9, 172, 178, 182
cooperating AIS, 150, 155, 163, 177
creativity, 67, 68, 146–7
Crichton, Michael, 55
cyberspace, 76–7, 78, 80–1, 108

Dark Star, 15, 17, 47, 52–5
DARYL, 82, 83, 88–91, 151, 171
death, 5, 26–7, 29, 44, 71, 75, 82, 85, 90–1, 93, 99, 101–2, 111, 112, 123, 141, 143, 153, 169; *see also* unfinal death; mortality
Demon Seed, 2, 12, 13, 17, 18, 19, 25, 47, 48, 57–61, 64, 65, 70, 74, 101, 133, 135, 143, 170, 171, 173
Derrida, Jacques, 78
Dick, Philip K., 110
digital AIs, 17–18, 24, 65, 100, 108, 128, 140, 157, 175, 176, 178
digitality and materiality, 78, 108, 137–8, 139, 161, 166–7, 176–7, 179, 182
digital multiplicity, 177, 179
distributed intelligence, 13, 26, 47, 59, 61, 121, 160, 170, 173, 175, 179, 180; *see also* multi-agent intelligence
doubles *see* parallels
Duguay, Christian, 110
duplicitous AI, 8, 95, 102, 107, 138–9; *see also* visual double

Electric Dreams, 15, 17, 26, 65, 66, 67–71, 73, 84, 85, 86, 87, 142
emotional intelligence *see* affective AI

empathic media, 12, 152
enhancement *see* augmentation
Enthiran, 15, 18, 19, 21, 22, 25, 26, 142–4, 160, 167, 175
ethnicity *see* race
Eva, 19, 21, 24, 82, 150–3, 161, 162, 171, 176
evolution (of AI), 101–2, 135, 142, 154
Ex Machina, 14, 15, 16, 18, 20, 21, 22, 24, 44, 147–50, 164, 176

fear of the many, 15, 83, 99, 111, 121, 130–1, 135, 137, 138, 140, 143, 160; *see also* cooperating AIs
Fincher, David, 115
Forbidden Planet, 9, 18, 19, 22, 25, 29–33, 34, 36, 45, 62, 74, 85, 171
Frankenstein, 6, 28, 51

gaming, 65, 79, 81, 107, 180
gender, 4, 5, 8, 23–4, 36–8, 65, 74, 75, 78, 83–4, 87–8, 94–6, 99, 102, 111, 113, 115, 117, 121, 123
generative AI, 1, 68
Ghost in the Shell, 10, 17, 18, 21, 22, 23, 24, 25, 100, 101, 102, 112–15, 117, 133, 141, 176, 181
Ghost in the Shell 2: Innocence, 15, 18, 20, 21, 24, 94, 101, 136–8, 162, 173, 176, 181
Godard, Jean-Luc, 40, 41

hacker, 65, 74, 78, 79–80, 80–1, 89, 101, 105, 107, 113
Haraway, Donna, 19, 24, 45, 50, 57, 100, 111, 115
Hayles, N. Katherine, 13–14, 16, 100, 114, 164
Her, 3, 10, 11, 12, 14, 15, 16, 18, 19, 20, 70, 166, 175–8, 179
Hoffman, Hermann, 33
humanism, 16, 134, 144, 146
humanoid AIs, 18, 24, 35, 56, 83, 57, 95, 99, 102, 110, 111, 117, 140, 150, 159
hybridity (AI/human), 120, 121, 124, 128, 129, 131, 134–5, 137, 138, 140, 181

I am Mother, 13, 15, 18, 19, 24–5, 25, 26, 172–5, 176, 179

Ibáñez, Gabe, 153
immortality, 48, 61, 177
intelligence, 6
internet, 100–1, 103, 181
Internet of Things, 12, 160
The Invisible Boy, 15, 17, 18, 22, 23, 28, 29, 33–8, 46, 62, 65, 74, 77, 85, 105, 171
I, Robot, 13, 15, 17, 18, 19, 22, 24, 58, 126–9, 131, 143, 160, 162, 175

James, Caradog W., 162
Jeunet, Jeanne-Pierre, 117
Jonze, Spike, 70

Kakoudaki, Despina, 20–1
Kubrick, Stanley, 42, 62, 124, 154
Kurzweil, Ray, 2, 14

Lang, Fritz, 6, 55, 132
love, 20, 27, 69, 70, 71, 83, 112, 123, 125, 126, 133, 157–8

The Machine, 14, 16, 17, 23, 24, 27, 142, 162–4, 165, 177, 178, 179
machine learning, 9
Maíllo, Kike, 150
The Matrix, 100, 101, 102, 106–8
The Matrix franchise, 17, 66, 73
The Matrix Reloaded, 23, 102, 132–4, 176
The Matrix Revolutions, 18, 23, 26, 101, 132–4, 166, 176
McCarthy, John, 8
McStay, Andrew, 12, 148, 152
Metropolis, 6, 55, 105, 107, 112
modification *see* augmentation
Moravec, Hans, 13, 164
mortality, 101–2, 114, 116, 123, 160, 168, 177; *see also* death
multi-agent intelligence, 5, 13, 26, 47, 140, 143, 170, 172, 173, 175, 179, 180; *see also* distributed intelligence; digital multiplicity
multi-bodied AI *see* multi-agent intelligence

one-off AI, 17, 82, 131, 148
origin (of AI), 122, 129, 131–2, 133, 137–8, 181
origin stories, 28, 29, 36, 67, 84
Oshii, Mamoru, 112, 136

parallels, 5, 21–3, 50–1, 55, 59, 63, 70, 92, 94, 99, 104, 108, 116–17, 121, 125, 181
parent-child relationships, 5, 25–6, 82, 105, 124, 140, 143, 144–5, 150–1, 152, 155–6, 158, 159, 161, 167–8, 172–3, 180–1; *see also* reproduction
physical grounding hypothesis, 5, 10–11
Picard, Rosalind, 11–12, 148, 152
point of view shots (AI), 18–19, 29, 45, 48, 50, 56, 59, 103–4, 113, 122, 130, 182
posthumanism, 16, 61, 119, 131, 134, 156, 158–9, 177, 181
post-materiality, 40, 160, 177–8, 179
post-verbal, 150, 163, 177
Prometheus, 21, 25, 26, 144–7, 161
Proyas, Alex, 126

race, 3, 83, 86–8, 91–2, 102, 118, 121, 126–7, 128, 138, 181
replication, 93, 121, 125, 126, 128, 129, 151
reproduction, 5, 25–6, 48, 61, 101–2, 114–15, 121, 123, 133, 135, 139, 141, 155–6, 156, 181
revolt of the machine, 15, 29, 36, 47–8
rights (of AIs), 76, 83, 90, 123
robot AIs, 18, 26, 55, 65, 82, 85, 93; *see also* humanoid AIs

Scott, Ridley, 42, 92, 144
Screamers, 18, 19, 20, 21, 61, 101, 102, 110–12, 147
Screamers: The Hunting, 18, 21, 25, 134–5, 143, 173
Searle, John, 9–10
self-evolution, 29, 35, 50, 106, 110; *see also* evolution
sexual violence, 24, 60, 94, 95
Short Circuit, 18, 22, 25, 26, 82, 83, 84–8, 167, 171–2
simulation, 66, 71, 72–3, 74, 81, 106, 121, 151
Singularity, the, 14, 15–16, 142, 147, 154, 161, 163, 165, 178
smart homes, 47, 57–8, 67–8, 172, 179; *see also* ambient AI
source (of AI) *see* origin
Spielberg, Steven, 25, 69, 111, 124, 181
Sputore, Grant, 172

Star Trek Generations, 11, 15, 101, 108–10, 176
strong AI, 3, 29, 56, 58, 69, 72, 76, 90, 103, 105, 106, 122, 127, 168, 180
super ambient intelligence (SAmI), 170
superintelligence, 3, 14, 154, 165, 178
symbolic AI, 9

Tau, 2, 12, 13, 15, 19, 22, 45, 58, 61, 170–2, 174, 179
tech-noir, 39, 110
technophobia, 28, 48, 49, 66–7, 83, 140, 144, 147, 181–2
Tellote, J. P., 4, 20, 28, 55, 92, 104
Terminator franchise, 102, 106, 107, 108
Terminator 2: Judgement Day, 20, 22, 24, 25, 66, 100, 101, 102, 103–6, 107, 111, 141
Terminator 3: Rise of the Machines, 20, 22, 23, 129–32, 160
Terminator Salvation, 19, 23, 129–32, 181
The Terminator, 66, 102–3, 105, 175
Transcendence, 14, 17, 23, 27, 165–7, 178, 179
transhumanism, 16–17, 23, 31, 76–81, 161, 162, 163, 164, 166, 167, 168, 178, 179, 182

transition (human to AI or AI to human), 120, 123, 137, 138
Tron, 15, 17, 19, 21, 23, 39, 66, 76–81, 87, 105, 107, 142, 176
Tron Legacy, 176
Turing, Alan, 5, 7–8, 18, 20, 49
Turing test *see* Turing, Alan
Turkle, Sherry, 67

uncanny, 21, 48, 56–7, 102, 124, 135, 137
unfinal death, 5, 26, 71, 108, 116, 141, 143, 145, 175, 182

Vinge, Vernor, 14
visual double, 5, 20–1, 55, 62, 83, 88, 91, 147, 181; *see also* duplicitous AI
Virilio, Paul, 56

Wachowski sisters, 4, 106
War Games, 17, 19, 23, 65–6, 69, 71–4, 79, 84, 105, 107, 142
Westworld, 15, 18, 19, 47–8, 55–7, 64, 65, 142
world wide web *see* internet

Yonck, Richard, 11

EU representative:
Easy Access System Europe
Mustamäe tee 50, 10621 Tallinn, Estonia
Gpsr.requests@easproject.com